TEACHER OF THE YEAR

TEACHER OF THE YEAR
The Mystery and Legacy
of Edwin Barlow

LAWRENCE MEYERS

H.H. & Sons

Copyright © 2008 by Lawrence Meyers

Published by H.H. & Sons
1005 Riverwood Place
Franklin, TN 37069

ISBN: 978-0-9820183-1-6

Library of Congress Control Number: 2008936563

Cover & Layout Design by Amy Ngwaba
www.madmuse.com

Cover Photograph by David Highbloom

Please Visit

WWW.MISTERBARLOW.COM

For all my teachers

Contents

◆

Part 3
The Mister Barlow Nobody Knew

Part 4
Understanding Mister Barlow ...

Epilogue   295

Appendix

INTRODUCTION

"NOW, what I want is, Facts. Teach these boys and girls nothing but Facts. Facts alone are wanted in life. . .You can only form the minds of reasoning animals upon Facts: nothing else will ever be of any service to them. This is the principle on which I bring up my own children, and this is the principle on which I bring up these children. Stick to Facts, sir!"

- Charles Dickens, "Hard Times"

Edwin David Barlow is dead. This is a fact. There are other facts, too. One fact is that he died on December 17, 1990. Another fact is that he taught at Horace Greeley High School for over thirty-six years. Yet another fact is that he was the first recipient of the Teacher of the Year award in 1984.

There are a few other facts, though not nearly as many as would be known if you or I had died. Mister Barlow taught basic algebra, geometry, physics, and Advanced Placement Calculus. His only known address was Horace Greeley High School, 70 Roaring Brook Road, Chappaqua, New York. When his true abode was found, there were no sheets on the bed. There was exactly one book in the one-room domicile. Despite this apparent destitution, the fact is that Mister Barlow willed the bulk of his estate to the charitable Horace Greeley Education Fund. The amount of this gift was exactly $478,346.30.

Despite the thousands of students who had passed through his classes over thirty-six years, only two people were present at his interment at Arlington National Cemetery. The Honor Guard present for the ceremony fired exactly twenty-one shots.

1

The last important fact is that I was his student in the mid-1980's for Advanced Placement Calculus. And the fact is that he is the best instructor I have ever had, before and after high school, during his life and beyond his death.

But this is where the list of facts comes to an end. Upon his death, there were no libraries to reveal his taste in literature, neither wife nor relatives to mourn at his funeral, no closet of clothes to be disposed of, no records to be combed through, no diplomas on the walls to indicate his educational background, no photographs of other people in his life, and no one to claim his body at Northern Westchester Hospital.

There were no more facts available about Edwin Barlow when he died.

But there were many to discover.

* * *

There is one question that I had to repeatedly ask myself while researching Mister Barlow's life and writing this book.

Why?

The research phase took almost two years. The writing took considerably longer. I spent more time on this project than anything else I had ever done. Why on earth did I exert such effort? Why, out of all the teachers I'd had, did this one instructor have such an effect on me? Why, out of all the projects I could undertake, did I choose to try and chronicle a life as shrouded in mystery as his? Why choose him?

I knew he was important to me. His classroom style had a rigidity and attention to detail that provided a template from which I would borrow the rest of my life. Within a mathematics class, he found ways to deliver important life lessons. Both during and after high school, he provided assistance with my studies and my search for the right occupation.

But there was more to it than that. He was important to many Greeley students. I'd assumed that it was because he had a positive impact on so many of them. Of course, it turned out that a heck of a lot of people found him to be destructive and cruel. Others just saw him as a source for humorous speculation. Still, even those students could not deny that he had an impact on them, and therefore he had importance to my quest. I also knew that whatever lessons one could glean from his life would eventually fade if I didn't somehow preserve them.

So I had discovered this controversial teacher and felt I had to share my experiences. I knew he was unique and that students and teachers alike, from elementary school through doctoral programs, would learn something from his profound and risky classroom style. Yes, I suppose every high school has their eccentric teacher, their brilliant but odd instructor, their Man of Mystery. But I doubt any of them—and I do mean any—put on the show Mister Barlow did, or had as astonishing a life as I would discover he had.

But there was still another level of intrigue about Mister Barlow. He made specific efforts to ensure his privacy. He went to great lengths to erase his past. It was almost like he wanted his own personal history to vanish even as it unfolded. Why did he do this?

All of these disparate reasons added up to the feeling that there was something grand to be learned from his life. And there was. I discovered that he spent much of his life searching for the same thing everyone does, although it is known by many different names.

Learning specific facts about him proved to be a challenge. I had almost nothing tangible with which to begin my hunt. Most people could form a complete picture of me by walking into my house and spending a few hours rifling through my personal belongings, peeking at my computer and Email, watching what I had recorded on TiVO, and speaking to my friends and relatives.

Mister Barlow, however, had no possessions. He had few conversations with anyone. There was barely any paper trail or official documentation of his life. Much of his public persona was very likely an ongoing piece of performance art, a grand prank that ran to sold-out audiences for 36 years. Learning about him was like trying to track footprints at high tide.

My research required some five hundred alumni and faculty interviews, the hunting down his surviving family, obtaining tax and medical records from New York State, reading several pieces of classic literature, parsing my way through complex theological and philosophical texts, researching educational theory, trying to separate the well-worn legends about him from the reality, scouring the country to find someone (anyone) who knew him, and unearthing the scattered fragments of a piece of ignored American history and sewing them back together.

Without intending it, I became a unique biographer of his life. I became the solitary expert on this man's life. Nobody else knew what I knew. I, and I alone, had the keys to Mister Barlow's life vault. I was humbled by the responsibility and have taken great care to form supportable conclusions. His life has been filled with enough rumor and innuendo.

In one sense, nothing that happened to Mister Barlow was all that unusual. He did not land on the moon. He did not walk on the ocean floor. He did not discover the Lost Ark of the Covenant. Instead, the adventures that confronted Mister Barlow were profound because they were so universal, so absolutely relatable, and thus all the more devastating. The true drama of his life made his outrageous classroom antics and fiery persona look like a dime sideshow.

Ultimately, his story was about how he transcended great tragedy and loss, and from the ashes built and led a life with a specific philosophy. Moralists and ethicists will examine the structure of his life for years to come and wonder how anyone could have the sheer will and determination to set upon a path in life and never stray from it.

And so, I opened my investigation into the life of Edwin Barlow, beginning with a recollection of my brief relationship with him.

Part I

The Mister Barlow I Knew

CHAPTER ONE

Abandon All Hope Ye Who Enter Here

"What is <u>that</u>?"

Mister Barlow's voice shatters the customary silence of his classroom with the violence of a boulder plummeting into a serene algae-covered pond. His booming voice, perfectly modulated in frequency and volume, rifles from the back of the classroom, through the musty air. Every muscle in every student's body seizes. Collective breaths are held. Only the second hand of the clock above the door defiantly presses on, each successive "tick" raising the level of suspense.

A grotesque tableaux stands before us.

The student at the blackboard is bent at the waist, chalk firmly in hand, just completing the end of a diagonal line separating two numbers (presumably a fraction). His eyes are glued to the board. His feet are locked in place. His lips are pressed tightly together. The only movement I can ascertain is a vein pulsing in his neck, as blood pulses through it at an increasingly rapid pace.

The clock powers on relentlessly.

Tick, tick, tick.

Snap!

The force of student's tensed muscle cleaves the chalk at its center, sending a cloud of microparticles floating past the board.

Finally, he replies.

"It's a fraction?" the student says. He's certain that he's correct, yet his voice rises at the end of the sentence, betraying a lack of confidence.

I, too, am certain that a fraction has been written on the blackboard. The mystery that crops up in all of our minds is not whether Mister Barlow is going to yell at this unfortunate soul—we're certain he will—but what he could possibly consider wrong about two numbers separated by a diagonal line.

"That is not a fraction, Mr. Jones! Do you know why it is not a fraction"?

The student replies that, "it is one number over another and that makes a fraction."

There is the briefest of hesitations before Mister Barlow speaks from behind his desk, one no different from our own except for its placement at the back of the classroom. We haven't yet witnessed the legendary nuclear explosions that spew forth from our instructor, but the Enola Gay has at last arrived.

Mister Barlow's rubbery face contorts with genuine anger. The edges of his mouth tighten and the bellowing commences, growing increasingly louder, the tirade slicing across the room, with certain words especially enunciated to have the maximum effect.

"No, it isn't, you vegetable! A fraction consists of a numerator separated from a denominator by a horizontal line whose length does not exceed the width of either number written! What you've written could be mistaken for any number of things!"

The detonation seems to last an eternity. The words spew forth in one long wave, a mushroom cloud elegantly rising over Ground Zero. The student is fiercely lectured about his lack of knowledge of classical mathematics presentation and how mathematicians would never make such a careless mistake. Once the mushroom cloud disperses, Mister Barlow punctuates his oration with a firm quotation, jabbing his finger at the student from the back of class, emphasizing <u>every</u> <u>single</u> <u>word</u>. . .

*   *   *

I have seen Mister Barlow many times during my three previous years at Greeley. It is hard not to notice him. He is a short, oddly built man with a round torso. His disproportionately short limbs give his head a more imposing appearance, characterized by an unusually broad forehead framed by a long, brushed-back silver mane—such that the midpoint of his face is at the eyebrow line. He carries intense eyes, low-mounted ears, and distinctively sculpted lips that rarely lift into a smile (in the classroom anyway).

Most intriguing is his gait. I find I am able to define every teacher's personality by how they ambulate through campus. My six-foot-five geometry teacher, Mr. Frauenthal, saunters from one building to the next. In him I see a teacher of great confidence. His strides are enormous, his back slightly hunched, as he often must lean down to hear his students or to avoid slamming his brow on a doorframe. I note the firm, heavy impressions of "Stormin'" Norman Peterson, his relentless pace no doubt driven by his role as Vice-Principal and disciplinarian. The popular English teacher, Mister Boyle, strolls leisurely, reflecting his congenial relationship with the students.

Mister Barlow, however, shuffles through campus. He limps slightly, his somnambulistic stare fixed straight ahead. One never knows if he is looking at you, through you, past you, or into some other dimension. He always wears ancient, thin trousers and a navy-blue parka. His long straggly hair never seems to grow, nor does it ever seem to be cut. A piece of one ear is missing.

No matter how much a student is roughhousing or running or dancing, they always cut a wide swath for Mister Barlow. He never alters his pace and the students never, ever, bump into him. Unlike other teachers who are both openly and secretly subject to ridicule, Mister Barlow is untouchable—literally and figuratively.

The myths and legends about Mister Barlow could be the stuff of a Grimm fairy tale. Everyone purports to know the truth about him. They say he was in World War II and part of his ear was shot off. They say he was in World War II and the back of his head was blown off and replaced with a steel plate. They say he was in World War I. They say he was in Korea and had his balls blown off. They say he'd been in World War I, World War II, and Korea and had had the back of his head and part of his ear _and_ his balls blown off. They say he receives a one hundred percent disability paycheck from the government each month.

They say he'd lost his wife and children in a terrible car crash. Others say his family was lost in a terrible house fire. Others say they'd been murdered. They say he lives at the school, that he showers in the locker room, that he sleeps above the rafters in the auditorium or in the nurse's office or in his car. They say he sleeps at his classroom desk. They say he doesn't sleep, ever. They say he lives in Mount Kisco, in Katonah, in Bedford Hills, in Chappaqua, in White Plains, in Connecticut, in Boston, in Portugal. They say students have tried to follow him home, only to be led on wild goose chases. They say he has been followed home, but then changed his address. They say he is a vampire. They say he rises every night along with the Headless Horseman in nearby Sleepy Hollow cemetery. They say he is Horace Greeley himself, that he is Methuselah, that he is Elvis.

11

All I know is that some or all or none of these things may be true or false or half-truths. Nobody knows for certain. Mister Barlow exerts great effort, it is said, to protect his privacy. Nobody, however, knows why.

Prior to AP Calculus, my only experience with him is as the monitor for my study hall sophomore year. The study halls are universally despised among students and faculty. They are just an excuse to keep students from roaming campus, the unfortunate by-product of a progressive system where students created their own schedules. Greeley went very far in promoting student freedoms, but they drew the line at "free time," except for seniors.

Some teachers let the students socialize in study hall. Others suggest the kids try to get a modicum of homework done. However, all instructors would prefer to be in the coffee lounge.

Mister Barlow, however, sits at the head of the room while the students fiddle at their desks. He never actually establishes any rules. Everyone remains steadfastly silent and does homework, simply because it is Mister Barlow's study hall. What else could one do? What else would anyone <u>dare</u> to do?

One day, after never having uttered a single word all term, he asks a student in the front row, "Mister Jameson, I heard a student in the hall yesterday say they were apathetic about politics. Can you tell me what he meant by that?"

I expect this is some kind of trap. From what I hear, Mister Barlow likes to yell at his students. Even though we aren't his students, he does hold sway over the room, so theoretically nobody is safe.

Bobby Jameson rouses from a half-slumber, shrugs and replies, "I think he means that he doesn't care."

"Would you please go over to the Common Area and look up the word 'apathy' in the dictionary, and then return here?"

Bobby leaves the room while the rest of us wait in confusion. What the hell is going on? I am still convinced it's some kind of trick. Yet, Bobby returns and reports that that "apathy means being objective or having clear judgment."

"Thank you, Mister Jameson. Did the dictionary educate you about the origin of the word?"

Bobby nods his head.

"Its origins are in Stoic Philosophy, which teaches that one's life may be free of suffering through *apatheia*, from the Greek, meaning—Mister Jameson?"

"Having clear judgment," Bobby replies.

"So, if anyone knows how we are to free ourselves from the suffering of these wretched study halls via apatheia, please inform the group."

Mister Barlow sits down, picks up his book and doesn't speak another word. We all exchange puzzled glances. Such was my introduction to Stoic Philosophy.

He delivers one other lesson in study hall, and this one comes directly to me. Late in the term, I had heard that one might escape study hall by telling Mr. Barlow you had work to do in the library. Naturally, this is just an excuse to roam freely through campus with the seniors.

I finally get up the courage one November morning to attempt this ruse. My legs quake as I approach him, a rattling Tin Man to his Oz. Mister Barlow's nose is buried in a hardcover version of <u>Alice in Wonderland</u>. I make my request in a quiet, meek voice. He fixes me with his penetrating gaze. It is hard to look Mister Barlow in the eye. He doesn't ever seem to blink. His eyes seem to probe me to my very core, like the paintings whose eyes seem to follow me in the art galleries.

"You have research to do in the library?" he asks in a deep gravelly voice that reminds me of the intonation Satan always had in the movies.

"Yes," comes my weak reply.

"What's your name?" he asks sternly.

Oh, shit. This had never happened to anyone else. Why me? I am always singled out, always the one with the worst luck, always Charlie Brown to everyone else's Snoopy.

"Meyers. Larry Meyers." Now I am really done for.

"Well, Mister Meyers, your word is good enough for me. Run along."

I scuttle out. The encounter leaves me unnerved. He knows my name. What if he checks with the library? How would the library even know I was there? It doesn't matter. He took me at my word. Nobody ever does that. What idiot takes the word of a teenager? The worst part is that I have been stupid enough to actually give my word, and because I am one of those "good" kids, the kind that always follows rules and never cuts a class, I must follow through on my word or the guilt will haunt me for weeks.

And now I have given my word. This means I must go the library, which I do. And yet, I actually feel empowered by Mister Barlow in this moment. This silly old-fashioned concept of trust actually has a kind of perverse value to me. With this remarkably powerful expression, Mister Barlow has boosted my confidence.

My word is good enough to take.

But why does Mister Barlow's confidence in me somehow carry more value than that of my parents? How can it be that this man with whom I have no tangible relationship holds greater sway over me by simply placing his trust in me?

"Your word is good enough for me." So simple. So timeless. So unfashionable.

14

This is the last time I ever ask Mister Barlow to go to the library in study hall. I feel I cannot breach his trust. It is to be my only encounter with him until AP Calculus.

*   *   *

"Mister Barlow doesn't teach class so much as call on students to do problems on the blackboard. Now, listen carefully. Don't look out the window, or he'll yell at you. Don't talk back to him, or he'll yell at you. Don't be late, or he won't let you in, and the next class he'll yell at you. Don't leave the class until you are dismissed, or he'll yell at you. When you have a test, you'll get those little blue books to do the problems in. On the front of those books, there's a space where it says "Teacher," and then a line to fill in his name. <u>Do not ever</u> write "Barlow" only. Write "Mister Barlow," or he'll yell at you. Be prepared with paper and pen every class, because if he catches you without them, he'll yell at you. And if you get called to the blackboard, and you can't do the problem," my older brother pauses, "He'll—"

"He'll yell at me," I reply.

"He'll yell at you," Jon says. "He'll call you "stupid" or "vegetable boy." He'll call you all kinds of names you've never been called before. It'll be awful. He yelled at me once. I nearly wet my pants. Just pray you aren't one of the 'Who's Who' that always get called."

I'd heard of the "Who's Who." It is the term Mister Barlow bestows upon the seven best students in the class. This presents a conundrum. As it happens, I am a pretty good student and have always done well in mathematics. How am I to get an "A," be the good student I have always been, and somehow avoid being in "Who's Who"?

Jon finishes his briefing on Mister Barlow. It was no different that what I had heard from other sources. Jon had survived the class and was now at the University of Pennsylvania. If he could do it, why couldn't I?

I spend the next week obsessively rifling through a mental Rolodex of my peers, convincing myself that there are at least seven better students than I in the class. Of course there are. There must be. Greeley is loaded with exceptional students. Many graduates go on to the Ivy League or other highly respected institutions. Greeley had once been on some major periodical's list of the fifty best high schools in the nation, due in no small part to the excellent quality of instruction there and the fact that it is located in the wealthy New York City suburb of Chappaqua.

Yes, there will be plenty of smarts in my class. I will still be able to excel, sitting quietly and never being called upon, earning a good grade for my college application, and never be in "Who's Who." Maybe I can just be a "Who." A "Who" is fine with me.

My aspiration has always been to be a "B+" student. A "B+" is just fine, as it allows for respectable achievement while still leaving open the possibility of unexpected success. Since I am a pessimist in the worst way, I am comfortable with reduced expectations of my own work, and so the occasional premium grade always comes as a pleasant surprise. In mathematics, however, I routinely exceed my own expectations. Unfortunately, this could put me on Mister Barlow's radar screen. If I am a good enough student, he will find me. It is only a matter of time.

Jon did provide one glimmer of hope. "If you can make it through the first six weeks, and not be called on, you're safe for the whole year. He makes up the "Who's Who" list in the first six weeks." Six weeks. I pull out a calendar and mark the day. October 17. I dub it "Safe Day" in my mind.

"Oh, and he'll give you a quiz in the last ten minutes of each class. If you don't turn it in at the end of class, it becomes your homework. It's just one problem and it doesn't really count in your grade."

Okay, that is another way to avoid "Who's Who." I make another mental note to always turn the quiz in the next morning. That should keep me firmly ensconced in the "Who" camp. Just a Who. Nothing more, nothing less. Respectable, but not notable. Who.

I ask if it is true that one's grade for the AP Calculus class is decided by one math problem Mister Barlow gives in the year's final class. Jon nods decisively.

This single grade-determining problem is of much consternation. What if I choke? I have a tendency to do that in academics, and always in any kind of sporting event. I remind myself that how one's grade is determined is just a rumor. The truth is that nobody knows anything about Mister Barlow, much less how he decides on grades.

I am already regretting my decision to try and excel beyond my own expectations and earn college credit for the AP class. How could I have been so stupid? Why not just languish in mediocrity?

*   *   *

The first day of school may be the most universally dreaded annual moment in human history. It is certainly true in my case. It isn't that I am a misanthrope so much as I vastly prefer to have control of my time. The summer provided me that time, but now that time was in the hands of a publicly funded, taxpayer supported institution.

I pull my beat-up tan Dodge Dart into the Greeley parking lot this first day of senior year, doomed to the purgatory of "Friendly Ed" Barlow's

AP Calc class. I suck it up and march onto campus with sunken eyes that stare only at the floor, or to sneak a glance at a pretty girl. I wend my way through the expansive campus, consisting of some dozen brick buildings connected by covered walkways. Students buzz everywhere, most still wearing summer fashions, enjoying the last vestiges of the warm weather.

As I slog through campus towards Mister Barlow's room, I must remind myself of school mores. The summer allows me to drop all façades because my time is singularly devoted to my group of friends. We are the so-called "freaks" of Greeley, roaming about Westchester County engaging in one of the few uninspiring activities suburban teens can enjoy.

The Freaks are Greeley's non-conformists, rebelling against the values of the more conservative and wealthy Greeley population. We do not dress in anything remotely fashionable, although my wardrobe falls in a nebulous range between Preppie and just plain thoughtless (jeans and mismatched turtleneck). We enjoy British humor, Rocky Horror, playing Frisbee, and more than half of us smoke various forms cigarettes and/or cannabis as the occasion warrants—except me, of course. That would've have elevated me to an intolerable level of cool.

Now, however, I am back at school and am reminded that the relationships between students exist on many different planes. An alien might suspect high school students suffer from multiple personality disorder based upon their behavior when keeping different company. We have the requisite cliques: The Partiers, the Preppies, the Jocks, the Theatre People, The Intellectuals, The Remedials, the Nerds, and the Freaks. There is also a large degree of clique-crossover. Most kids pass freely from one clique to another, building friendships and rivalries, being included or ostracized depending on whatever insult occurs that week. So there I am—a Freak during free time and over the summer, an Intellectual during school hours, and by all accounts, a Nerd twenty-four seven.

The upperclassmen enjoy numerous electives, so those with similar interests create yet another societal subset. Between classes, we each gravitate towards the clique we each associate with on a regular basis outside of school. Yet when not in proximity of one's pack, individual encounters take on entirely different dynamics. A jock traveling with his fellow jackals may slam me into the nearest wall as they pass. Yet that same jock, encountered individually, may strike up a conversation about our history teacher. As much as I may hate that jock, it's an unspoken rule that one must behave according to the rules of the pack when in their presence. Since we have a mutual respect for each other's intelligence, the social enmity is placed in stasis as we discuss the French Revolution. For example, after giving a presentation on the German hyperinflation of the 1920's in history class, a boy who had always been aggressively unpleasant towards me was so impressed, that he complimented me and left me alone from that day forward.

But, hell, that's high school. Those issues paled in comparison to the matter at hand: make it to Safe Day without being noticed by Mister Barlow.

I enter L-Building, and shuffle for room 111. I scope out the students milling outside Mister Barlow's classroom, desperately seeking an obvious population for Who's Who, and finding instant relief in the faces of the Intellectuals I see. Confident that my peers will distinguish themselves to a far greater degree than I will, I enter Mister Barlow's dungeon five minutes before the 7:40 AM bell.

The floor is covered with orange industrial carpet. A large window fills one wall on the far side of the room from the entrance. This window looks across a grassy hillside sloping down towards the Metro-North commuter train tracks, the Saw Mill River Parkway beyond it, and the rocky, forested hills beyond. A blackboard stretches across the entire wall to the left. Six columns of five seats populate the room. To the right, in the back of the classroom, Mister Barlow sits behind a plain student's desk.

Seating is of paramount importance towards reaching Safe Day. So, following a carefully designed strategic plan, I have already decided exactly where to sit. A seat in the front row is akin to painting a bull's eye on my head, while the back row has the universal reputation of housing the poorest students, which does not fit with my desired profile of being a "Who", so I eliminate these choices.

That leaves the three center rows. I fear my eye might stray, so I don't want to sit by the window. I don't want to sit too close to Mister Barlow, though, lest he see me and call me to the board. This leaves the middle row, in the center of the room, surrounded and lost in the crowd of other students. If I am lucky, a tall student will sit behind me and to my left, obscuring me from Mister Barlow's gaze entirely.

Unfortunately, other students have already figured this out as well, and all of my choices are gone before I am even through the door.

I panic and avert my gaze from Mister Barlow. Without time to reassess, and fearful of attracting attention by gawking at the remaining seats, I grab one in the second row, closest to the door. It is not ideal, but tomorrow is another day, and I make a mental note to arrive earlier.

I construct my workspace. Clean, crisp new notebook. Plenty of pens to avoid running out of ink at an inopportune moment. Ruler, protractor, calculator, and last year's calculus notebook. I sit, hands folded on my desk, awaiting the start of class and wishing invisibility would become a scientific reality.

Mister Barlow sits in the back of the room to my left, engrossed in Alice in Wonderland, his eyes never straying from the page. I wonder why he's chosen to re-read the same book he read in our study hall two years ago. I also wonder why he's reading it at all. It's a children's book. Why on earth is a math teacher reading a holdover from elementary school?

The rest of the students file in and I delight in noticing the Intellectuals select seats within easy sight of Mister Barlow. The tension is palpable. The clock above the door slides backwards a half-inch, as it always does, before snapping forward to the next minute with an audible THUMP three seconds later, presenting us with the appointed hour for the beginning of AP Calc. Mister Barlow rises, closes the door and returns to his desk in the rear of the classroom, behind me and to my left.

And he speaks.

"Mister Kim, would you approach the blackboard?" James Kim is a junior this year, and is well known as a quite and humble prodigy, much as his older sister Stacy. James is directed to write a problem on the board. I diligently copy everything that is written on the board in the neatest penmanship I have ever, or would ever, produce during my life. It isn't just because this is Mister Barlow's class, but because this is *Advanced Placement* Calculus.

As the lesson progresses, I pay increasing attention to the material and less to my nerves, and soon find myself intensely absorbed in the material. For English or Social Studies I can, and often do, zone out when the material is uninteresting. Math and science, however, demand strict attention. To miss out on even one concept means severing a causal and logical link in the topic at hand. That usually means having to ask for help from another student or, in this case, Mister Barlow. It also means potential humiliation at his hands, so I take this class more seriously than anything I ever have before, or will ever have again.

The forty-five minute period seems to pass with unprecedented speed. I have never been in a class in which I did not glance at the clock. School is school, and to me that has always meant wanting to leave as quickly as possible. But here I am, engrossed, and with a few minutes left Mister Barlow rises from his desk and shuffles to the front. There he makes a final point regarding the material of the day, linking together each of the problems various Intellectuals have written on the blackboard into one coherent concept. Then he announces, "Now take out a piece of paper for today's quiz."

Not so bad, I think. The material has been clearly presented. It has been easy to follow. Quiz as expected. Best of all, I have been ignored. Making it to Safe Day seems easier now. Mister Barlow writes the quiz question on the board, sets the chalk down, and tells us to bring him the answer when we finish.

A few students approach his desk with their solutions. I hear scribbling as he writes something on each paper, then each student quietly exits class, gingerly closing the door. As it happens, I finish a minute or so before the end of class and debate whether or not I should turn in the paper. The desire to proudly present a correct solution to this fiercest of instructors is surprisingly strong. I do, deep inside, want to excel and be recognized for it.

This runs counter to my usual feelings when around fearful entities—such as the bullies who stride down school hallways. When I see them, I make myself as small and inconspicuous as possible, literally attempting to blend into the wallpaper, as an obsessive interior voice chants, "Don't notice me. Don't notice me. Don't notice me." The voice is often punctuated by the sound of said bullies bodyslamming me further into the wall. My books splay to the ground and I must peel myself from the plaster, hoping the pain in my solar plexus is not the result of a crushed pancreas.

Anyway, Mister Barlow definitely qualifies as a fearful entity. As such, his mere presence overwhelms any courage I have to stand up and be recognized. So I stay firmly seated.

Moments later, we hear the piercing loudspeaker tone that announces the end of class. Mister Barlow growls to the remaining students, "This problem is now your homework."

And that is it. Class over. Nobody is yelled at. Nobody is humiliated, decapitated, or burned at the stake. I leave class feeling foolish for believing all that I've been told.

Over the next three weeks, a pattern develops before class that will last the entire year. I arrive at school around 7:20 AM. If I have successfully completed Mister Barlow's homework, then I hang around with some friends. If I have failed to figure out Mister Barlow's puzzle, or just plain forgot (a rare instance), I solicit the help of ever-patient James Kim along with the other flummoxed students.

I hand the completed problem to Mister Barlow at the beginning of each class. My plan is simple. Hand it to him, turn around, and get back to my seat as quickly as possible.

Class commences. A concept is presented, the method of problem solving is laid out for us, and Mister Barlow calls a student to write on the board. Two or three examples are provided and solved by those called upon. Mister Barlow requires a concept to be explained "twice, for the 'B' students and then a third time so the 'C' students can grasp it." The student at the blackboard must work out the problem step by step, with Mister Barlow commenting on what the student is doing after each step.

After a few days of this method, I decide that I am in the hands of an exceptional instructor, or at least one whose methods work for me, although I find it difficult to articulate why I feel this way. It doesn't matter that he isn't at the board much himself. To me, it is the presentation of the material that matters. Mathematics requires a rigorous and logical approach in order to be taught well. Calculus itself requires one to recall much of what has been learned in other areas of math, and to directly apply it. There is little memorization that is either required, or of much use.

Thus, an instructor must emphasize every single step in any derivation or calculation in order to adequately guide a student through a concept, lest future lessons cause confusion. Examples must be chosen carefully, so as to demonstrate the concept precisely. Mister Barlow has such mastery of his subject and has taught it for so long, that he is confident in his approach. I, in turn, quickly gain confidence in my own work.

Perhaps this is yet another reason some think so highly of him. If school is, as some say, more about instilling confidence in students than actually educating them, then Mister Barlow has won the day. At least, that's how I feel at the moment. Mister Barlow's subsequent tirades give me, and others, reason to doubt if confidence is what he truly imparts to his students.

There are more subtle criteria for determining the worth of a teacher, and Mister Barlow illustrates them in a more circumspect manner. After a day of working through some difficult material, Mister Barlow asks a student if he felt his time has been well spent in class. The student agrees, and Mister Barlow adds, "Good. Because to be wholly devoted to some intellectual exercise is to have succeeded in life. And if the man who wrote Treasure Island believes this, it must be true. Now take out a piece of paper for today's quiz, and let's hope you all succeed in life."

Each time I depart Mister Barlow's class, I indeed feel that I have succeeded in something that day. I leave understanding the material and feeling confident about that comprehension. There is also the occasional bonus when Mister Barlow sprinkles subtle life lessons in with the mathematics. It's as if he knows teenagers are least apt to listen to their parents, so he throws in a little wisdom to make up for it.

It takes until the seventh class before Mister Barlow finally lives up to his reputation. It is, in many ways, a relief to us all. The entire class has been on pins and needles waiting for the cobra to strike, and with each passing day, the tension has only increased.

The transgression is minor in my eyes. The unfortunate student has written a fraction on the board using a diagonal line instead of a horizontal one. Many of us have been raised in the same school district and have been taught that a diagonal line is perfectly acceptable when presenting a fractional value. Mister Barlow disagrees, and expresses himself in no uncertain terms.

As Mister Barlow's tirade spews forth, I note some curious behavior from the other students. They do not look at the board or the offending student, but at their own desks. For all the cruelty that teenagers inflict on one another, for all the rivalries, teasing, mocking, and competitiveness that pervades high school culture, there exists in Mister Barlow's class a startling sense of decorum. It is a sociological phenomenon the likes of which I've never seen.

The unfortunate student is being given his privacy.

I expect everyone to stare and maybe even snicker when Mister Barlow rips into someone. Instead, the class shows sympathy by looking away from the young man during Mister Barlow's reprimand. Once the shouting is complete, the student starts back towards his seat. Mister Barlow does not let him off so easily.

"Where are you going? Get rid of that abomination and let's get it right!"

The student returns to the board and dutifully draws a horizontal line, making certain it is no longer than the width of the numbers written above and below, and completes the rest of the problem. The class holds its collective breath, willing the poor fellow to finish without another error. He does, and returns to his seat. Mister Barlow makes a firm point to us all, jabbing his finger at us to emphasize every word, his unblinking eyes burning into each and every one of us.

"Mathematics may be compared to a mill of exquisite workmanship, and what you get out depends on what you put in; and as the grandest mill in the world will not extract wheat flour from peascods, so diagonal lines written as a fractional expression will not yield a "5" on the AP exam—with apologies to Thomas Huxley!"

I have no idea who Thomas Huxley is, but I assume he is important enough to have been read by Mister Barlow. I also assume he is important enough to have been quoted, so I scribble down this excerpt. "What you get out depends on what you put in." I'd heard this pithy saying before. Maybe it imprints because, on this occasion, it is delivered with such gusto. I certainly want my intellectual mill, such as it is, to yield the best product. Mister Barlow is clearly demanding that I feed it only the finest wheat.

I credit that particular day's class for teaching me the value of devoting oneself to the matter at hand. Within a mere seven hours at his hands, and one browbeating to his credit, Mister Barlow has seared this lesson into my brain. This concept holds far greater weight than any mathematics he actually teaches me in the class. Whereas I struggle today to recall how perform an integral, devoting myself to my work remains an enduring hallmark of my life.

I can also state with some authority, that for the rest of the year, nobody in our class ever drew a diagonal line on any blackboard or sheet of paper within fifty feet of Mister Barlow's classroom.

CHAPTER TWO

A Shot Across My Bow

When people ask if a comparison can be made between Mister Barlow and anyone else, I am at a loss. Mister Barlow is unique. The closest approximation to his methods and demeanor is John Houseman's portrayal of Professor Kingsfield in the television series <u>The Paper Chase</u>. Professor Kingsfield is erudite, imperious, and demanding like Mister Barlow. He expects his students to be prepared, exacting, analytical, and to think. He and Mister Barlow share a common approach, encapsulated in a line from the show. "You teach yourselves the law (mathematics). I train your minds. You come in here with a skull full of mush, and if you survive, you'll leave thinking like a lawyer (mathematician)."

The other comparison is more obscure, but also more accurate of the tone of our classes. In an episode of Steven Spielberg's television anthology series <u>Amazing Stories</u>, entitled <u>Go to the Head of the Class</u>, Christopher Lloyd portrays the terrifying high school English teacher, Bo Beans. With his straggly shoulder-length hair, a booming voice laced with sarcasm, and iron grip on his classroom, he bears an uncanny resemblance to Mister Barlow. This remains true despite the fact that he happens to have his head magically removed from his body on Halloween night, and chases a terrified student through town. No doubt many of Mister Barlow's students have had similar nightmares.

Much like Bo Beans, a lot of people despise Mister Barlow's methods. They are daring. They are controversial. They are uncompromising. I believe his rigorous approach stems from his desire to see us excel in his class and beyond. If he is hard on us now, we may not be so intimidated when we get to college.

As for why he strikes fear into the hearts of high schoolers, I believe that, for those who are uninterested in math, they are likely to remain that way no matter what any instructor does. Mister Barlow, however, must motivate these students, and his style accomplishes that. It is also possible that some of these students may become inspired by his technique. Those who are already motivated are more likely to remain so than be put off by him. In the end, he is really just playing the odds. At this point, he's been doing it for thirty years, so he must have seen progress.

Of course, nobody is forced to stay in his class. In the case of his algebra class, students may transfer to another teacher. In the case of AP Calc, everyone has chosen to take the course out of interest and/or a desire for college credit.

*　*　*

October blows into Westchester County with a pleasantly chilly blast of air. By mid-month, each class has settled into a routine. Although taking advanced classes in European History and Chemistry, I fill out my schedule with what "gut" classes I can, allowing my free time to be truly free. I spend the requisite time studying for the SAT's, filling out college applications, and counting the number of classes before Safe Day.

Meanwhile, every other morning belongs to Mister Barlow, and these mornings require me to think. I cannot rely on memorization in this class. Mister Barlow demands that we use our minds. If someone experiences a brain fart, he hollers at them, "Use your head, you vegetable!" or "Bang your head on the blackboard, urchin boy, and maybe the answer will come to you!"

These reprimands are always delivered in the same terrifying voice. They always seem to have the desired effect.

Sometimes he lightens the attack. A student who is stymied at the board is asked if he knows of Rene Descartes' statement, "I think therefore, I am!" and promptly adds, "If you stop thinking, you'll vanish! And then I'll have to call your mother and explain that the reason you've disappeared is because you were being stupid!"

In short, Mister Barlow's classroom philosophy boils down to the Arthur Miller line from <u>Death of a Salesman,</u> "Attention must be paid!"

I have a brush with Mister Barlow four weeks into the year, though it does not involve mathematics. My fashion sense is of dubious value (some would say it still is), and I make the ignorant choice of wearing an ugly lime-green down jacket to school during cold weather. When I button the jacket, I bear a distinct resemblance to a discolored Michelin Man. Had I kept more chic company, this idiosyncratic fashion statement might have been corrected before doing me irreparable social harm. However, as most Freaks revel in their individualism, this ounce of prevention never occurs to either them or me.

So one day before class, Mister Barlow politely asks a young lady to hand out some mimeographs. It is too much work for one person, so Mister Barlow growls, "Well, don't do it all yourself. Give some to that green creature over there." I dutifully join in the distribution, vowing to burn my jacket that very night, cursing myself for so blithely wearing such a colorful target garment. AUGH! So much for Safe Day. This will surely be a blow to my plan.

Then again, I have been struggling with my plot of avoidance. Despite my better judgment, and knowing the associated risk, I have gained enough confidence in my work to turn in one of every three quizzes in class now. I have decided this is still not enough to be a "Who's Who," but just enough to demonstrate a bit of aptitude, perfectly suited to my desired profile. The green jacket, however, has put me on Mister Barlow's radar, and I must play my cards carefully to avoid further attention.

Fortunately, Safe Day is within reach, and I still elude Mister Barlow's interest during class. The "Who's Who" now seems established, and I arrange to turn in only one of every three quizzes the same day. Mister Barlow continues to castigate several students, both "Who's Who" and otherwise, for various transgressions. But he also reins in his renowned ire, often poking genial fun at someone with a droll quip. These comments are delivered without his usual force, and anyone owning an ounce of humor knows Mister Barlow is gently chiding them.

One student, caught scratching his chest, elicits a comment of "Stop scratching your chest, Mr. White, you aren't a gorilla." A Metro-North commuter train passes outside as it always does at 8:10 AM, and Mark Green commits the mistake of looking at it.

"Yes, Mr. Green, it's a choo-choo."

Should a student equivocate when giving an answer, such as, "Yes. I mean, no," then he is greeted by a bark of "Well, which is it? We haven't got all day." Mister Barlow is pressing us to think, to make a firm decision, and to pay attention. They seem like minimal requirements for a high school classroom, yet they take on a far greater weight with this instructor running the show.

Safe Day arrives. The names of the Who's Who are chiseled into stone. I let out a deep sigh of relief. Freedom from persecution, right?

Unfortunately, universal rules do not apply when I am involved.

There are three significant distractions plaguing me the day Mister Barlow first calls on me. The first is seasonal in nature. October ushers in a beloved three-month period that commences with the first coloring of the trees and ends on New Year's Day. The cooling temperatures, explosions of color, the little chill that accompanies me home each day—they all wrap my soul in a sweet melancholia in which I gladly revel. It is the one period of the year when my base-level mood is in tranquil synchronicity with the climate. If I had been typed by Amway guidelines, I'd certainly qualify as an "autumn person."

Indeed, autumn always infuses me with a vague and undefined sadness, which delicately seeps in through every wall of my home, along every stroll through campus, and while touring Chappaqua's winding country roads. But rather than engender a disconsolate mood, these mystical days brew a strange nostalgia within me, a longing for that which I have not yet discovered, and cause a palpable desire to escape from the pervasive loneliness I experience in every waking moment. The season expands my susceptibility to flights of fancy, resulting in a potentially fatal lack of classroom attentiveness.

The second distraction has vexed my spirit for two years. It infects most teenagers and, once infected, the unfortunate victim can fall prey to it without warning. I speak of a romantic infatuation, of course. A crush. Not just any crush, mind you, but The Crush of all crushes.

I first notice her in Health class, some two weeks into our sophomore year. The class sits at desks that form the perimeter of a large square. She wears a navy blue jacket with a thick white stripe that runs across her chest. She wears her brown hair the same way the entire time she is in high school: shoulder-length, straight, with bangs. She has the slightest overbite, not enough to make her look dopey, but just enough to add a dash of sex appeal.

And she is smiling. Not at me, but at a friend who sits beside her as he cracks a joke. Cupid empties a quiver full of javelins into me. In less time that it takes for my heart to skip that single beat, this young woman becomes the standard-bearer for love at first sight in my lonely and pathetic teenage existence. From then on, seeing her always brightens my day. I marvel at the long hair flowing onto her back, and the sleeves of her denim jacket dangling just beyond her wrists as she walks through campus. All she needed was red hair and Charlie Brown would've had nothing on me.

The third distraction is a jagged pebble lodged in my shoe, which I fail to notice until after class has begun. Removing my shoe in the middle of Mister Barlow's class is inconceivable.

So the combination of a seasonal susceptibility to daydreams, laced with the tartness of a longing heart, and the pang of an igneous rock digging into my heel, all form a witches' brew that poisons my intellectual capacity at the worst possible moment. I may as well have been blindly stumbling through the feline-infested Serengeti, drenched in gazelle blood with antlers tied around my head.

The problem on the board is a very simple integral. When the words "Mister Meyers" slash across the room, I rise and mechanically walk to the blackboard, the stone jabbing me repeatedly in my heel as I walk, my imaginary romantic interlude with The Crush swept from my consciousness with each footstep. The classroom remains in customary silence.

I look at the integral. I manage to write "=" under it, preparing to transform the equation into its intermediary form before solving it.

I freeze.

All higher brain function ceases. Only vital organs operate. I function on minimal life support for what seems like an eternity. I don't even hear the clock tick. I must have entered some new universe, because how else could thoughts be running through my head at the same time that the rest of my brain had shut down?

How is it, I wonder, that I could have been so completely absorbed in a daydream and forget everything else? How could both my conscious and unconscious minds be completely captivated by something unrelated to Mister Barlow's class while actually <u>in</u> Mister Barlow's class? How could I put myself in this vulnerable, and possibly fatal, position?

A kindly student in the front row hisses at me.

"X-squared," she whispers. "X-squared."

This jump-starts my brain. Reality slams into me. The answer mercifully snaps into my mind and at literally that instant, I hear the angry sigh from the back of the room. Mister Barlow's patience has run out.

I don't register all the words that spew forth. "Stupid," "vegetable boy," and/or "simpleton" are somewhere in his invective, his tone bordering between anger and rage. A moment later—I have no idea how long I am at the front of the class because I have long since dissociated from the situation—I realize I have put my hands behind my back and just stare patiently at the ceiling, waiting for the blistering artillery to quiet. Mister Barlow boils over at my behavior, becoming increasingly annoyed, assaulting my "arrogance" and "for standing up there like you're God's gift to mathematics!"

He has no idea that neither of his accusations is true. I simply expected to eventually be on the receiving end of Mister Barlow's bashing, and that I should take it like a man.

Unfortunately, this makes it appear that I don't care what he is saying to me. I think that made it worse. Eventually the words, "Now sit down!" fling at me and I return to my seat. Another student finishes the problem and, realizing how simple the problem is, I shake my head in great disappointment with myself.

Upon exiting class, I wonder if Mister Barlow will call on me again. What happened to the six-week rule? It was well past Safe Day, a full seven weeks into the term.

On the one hand, I feel awful at this drubbing. It does not, however, undermine my confidence or work ethic. If anything, I try harder, hoping to be called on again to redeem myself. It occurs to me that Mister Barlow may be employing psychological brinkmanship. If he plays the stern father figure, the one whose approval his students constantly seek, perhaps this will serve as motivation. He may also be teaching us how not to be rattled by criticism.

To make certain this incident doesn't repeat, I sweep away the autumn leaves from my mind, and banish the Crush to my subconscious while in Mister Barlow's class. I also empty both shoes anytime I enter his classroom, usually earning odd glances from my peers.

Mister Barlow speaks nary a word to me over the next three weeks. Class proceeds per the norm, until one day in November, my name is uttered once again. On this occasion, I am paying careful attention in. The problem on the board is simple. I gingerly write the next step in the problem, expecting the worst from Mister Barlow.

"Mister Meyers has elected to divide the integral into two parts which is certainly a reasonable approach and nothing to be ashamed of."

It is a gift. The phrase "nothing to be ashamed of" is his way of building confidence. He knows I do good work, as judged by the endless parade of correct quizzes and homework assignments I turn in. I complete the problem and return to my seat. There is apparent wisdom in his method, at least for me. I do feel more confident. I imagine that he sees me as a bright and capable student, but one who prefers to do his work quietly at his desk, rather than being put on the spot in front of the class. The best teachers are able to identify not just which students are motivated to excel, but <u>how</u> they are best able to excel. Mister Barlow gets another "A" in my internal grading system.

I also think I inadvertently defanged him with my apparent devil-may-care attitude when he chewed me out several weeks ago. Perhaps he realizes that I expect, and am even inured to, his invective. This might undermine the fear he tries to strike into the other students, so perhaps this is another reason he leaves me alone.

I discover that Mister Barlow's approach works for me. His tirade serves to motivate me, to prove to him I am more capable than my one flawed performance demonstrated. Earning his approval becomes important. Somehow, his ability to command respect differs from that of many parents, including mine. Maybe it's because I know that my parents love me, so that I don't feel a need to earn that love. Perhaps I still yearn to encounter someone who is capable of transforming me.

At the same time, however, I understand how Mister Barlow's scheme can have devastating consequences on another type of student. Rather than respond to Mister Barlow's throwing of the gauntlet, another type of student might shut down altogether. To them, he is not a mentor but an antagonist.

In retrospect, Mister Barlow's approach toughened me up. When I enter the real world, I discover that a lot of people like to buttress their own ego by trying to dress others down. The difference is that Mister Barlow gave me every reason to respect him, while these megalomaniacs have not. Whereas Mister Barlow impressed upon me that the only thing that matters is to use your mind, these mental defectives seem to think that shouting and using profanities will make me respect them or work harder or God know what. But what they don't realize is that my work ethic, as formed primarily by Mister Barlow, developed into something very simple: It is only the work that matters. Attention must be paid.

As for Mister Barlow, our latest encounter permits our relationship to expand ever so slightly as the year progresses. On my end, I am no longer terrified of him, though an undercurrent of fear still exists. I suppose we understand each other, and that seems adequate for both of us.

CHAPTER THREE

Familiarity Breeds Curiosity

In November, Mister Barlow hands out our yearlong assignment known as "The 128 Integrals." These problems span the bulk of the curriculum for the entire year and our deadline is the last day of school. Diligent students check in on this list every two weeks to see if the next batch of problems is ready to be tackled with new tools learned in class. Like all work in Mister Barlow's class, it is to be done in pen, with one line drawn through mistakes. James Kim is given the entire answer key and we are told we can refer to it at any convenient time for him. I decide I want to solve all of these integrals on my own and earn Mister Barlow's respect for the work done. Avoidance is silly. Why not try and stand out a bit?

While I readily absorb the class material, I find Mister Barlow's mid-term exam challenging. This concerns me. I've paid such careful attention all semester long and feel confident in my knowledge, yet the "Who's Who" boasts about the simplicity of the exam. I require every second of the period and barely finish, earning a "4". I chalk it up to a bad day and nerves, and hope the AP exam will not be so difficult.

I certainly have it easier than a "Who's Who" member named Dennis Andrews, as Mister Barlow addresses him the day we receive our corrected exams.

"Mister Andrews, would you tell the class the grade written on your examination book?"

"There's a '5', then it's crossed out and replaced by a '4', and then that's crossed out and a '5' is written next to it," Dennis replies.

"And do you know why I initially downgraded you to a '4', Mister Andrews?'

Dennis resignedly says he doesn't, and we all wait for the proverbial other shoe to crash down on his skull.

"Because of what you wrote next to the word 'Instructor'. What did you write there, Mister Andrews?"

"Barlow," Dennis said, unaware of where he is being led.

And the Nagasaki bomb detonates.

"That should read *Mister* Barlow! It took me thirty-five years to earn that title, Mister Andrews, and no clod is going to deprive me of it! If I have the courtesy and respect to refer to you by the title 'Mister', you damn well better do the same for me! Do you have any idea why I insist on being addressed in this manner? Do you?"

A crimson-faced Dennis musters a "no," Mister Barlow's voice leaps in volume and his tone changes from anger to rage-tinted indignation.

"Because familiarity breeds contempt, Mister Andrews! And I'll be damned if I permit you or anyone in this class to demonstrate contempt for me! The only reason you got a '5' instead of a '4' was because I decided to grade you on the basis of your work, not on the basis of your provincial manners!"

I silent thank my brother, and can state with some authority that nobody in our class ever wrote the word "Barlow" without the appropriate title in Calc AP for the rest of the year.

But what of this antiquated saying, "Familiarity breeds contempt"? My previous math teacher, John Lee, allowed us to use his first name and I wasn't contemptuous of him. Yet Mister Barlow's maxims always contain more substance than meets the eye. I assume this proverb must hold a deeper meaning, there for any industrious soul to root out.

Sure enough, the phrase has its origins in one of Aesop's fables, <u>The Fox and the Lion</u>, which teaches that the fear or fascination with something is reduced when one gets to know it better. Even the New Testament has a version of it, in Matthew 13:57, when Jesus said that "a prophet is not without honor, save in his own house".

I suspect Mister Barlow's primary lesson is to remind us to be respectful of others. Yet the subtler lesson is that he will not tolerate collegiality (in the classroom, anyway) because it will diminish students' fear of him. Since some of his strategy is based on fear, to lose that advantage means losing the students.

While I doubt Mister Barlow has some grand plan or overarching wisdom that he is doling out to us, I am now certain that there is more going on in his class than mathematics.

* * *

As sad as I am to see my cherished autumn season wither away, the last of its brown leaves gathering on our perpetually overgrown front lawn, I am equally relieved to bid farewell to the college admissions process. The topic of every senior discussion is where people are applying. I defer my responses, lest I fail to be accepted at my more prestigious choices. I am derided for my non-disclosure policy, but I feel I can't compete with many of the Intellectual's Ivy League choices. It seems wise to remain coy in order to avoid later humiliation.

Although I am apparently an attractive candidate for many universities, I sell myself short by only applying to two Ivy League schools, and five other programs I am sure to be accepted at. I apply for either chemistry or chemical engineering programs, although my choice of major is more a selection by default than out of any real passion for the subjects. I am good with numbers, generally enjoy science, and find chemistry easier to understand than physics. I am, however, not confident enough in my performance in Mister Barlow's class to ask him for a recommendation.

I choose the sciences despite the fact that my real passion was making Super 8 films, which I'd been doing since age 14. They are the only creative endeavors I take pride in, because I utterly lack in artistic talent. I have no talent for drawing. My sense of perspective is unintentionally akin to German Expressionist films. My three-dimensional conceptualization is, two-dimensional. I have no interest in painting, sculpture, or silly little craft projects that we all must suffer through at summer camp. My clay pots in 6th grade art class are lopsided. My 4th grade clay sculpture is, in my own mind, of a man on an island with a hut carved from a tree, and stones littering the island. It still sits in my parent's living room, and is generally regarded as an abstract curiosity or a misplaced paperweight. When given a choice as to what to sculpt in 7th grade, I choose dice. Yes, I mold two clay dice. I scoot out from this same art class under the pretense of going to the bathroom, only to instead wander the halls for extended periods of time to escape the boredom. Eventually, my teacher becomes concerned that I have a bladder problem, informs my parents, and a week of parental anxiety ensues over a non-existent bladder infection.

Meanwhile, I have friends construct my plastic napkin holders and metal boxes in Industrial Arts. Pipe cleaners, cellophane, and stained glass are my nemeses. There is no single greater waste of my time or school resources than any class with the word "art" in it.

But when it comes to telling stories or pulling the trigger on a movie camera, I am in heaven. The works are crude, but in my teenage mind they are masterpieces. The actual making of the movie holds fascination for me because it is something tangible that I am able to create. Metal boxes with gaping holes wide enough for melted solder to drool out of them do not provide me with a sense of accomplishment. A movie is real. I can hold it in my hand, I can entertain people with it, and it will last forever. The storytelling itself doesn't yet hold the significance it will in the future, but the vehicle by which it is delivered does. It will make me immortal, if only in some small way.

The best thing about making these little movies is that when I am right in the midst of it, when the film is running through the camera and the action is unfolding, everything else drops away. I am in that moment of creativity. All else is lost.

My parents, however, are wise and practical people with practical jobs, and Chappaqua is a practical community that places emphasis on securing a high-paying job after college. Having a passion for a topic is not a realistic criterion for a choice of occupation. While I know my parents will support whatever choice I make, there is no encouragement to explore filmmaking as a college degree.

Meanwhile, Mister Barlow somehow knows which students are applying where, and whenever one of the "Who's Who" makes a blackboard error, he reminds them, "that kind of stupidity won't fly at Harvard, Mr. Handel."

He also modulates his vitriol as we approach Christmas. He still calls students "stupid" after a mental error, but is quick to add that the word stupid "is not a derogatory term. Rather, it means 'intellectually lazy', and isn't a permanent state of mind. At least, let us hope not, for your sake."

On one occasion, he reads aloud from Alice in Wonderland and asks us to perform a calculation to determine the speed at which poor Alice strikes the bottom of the rabbit hole. Her velocity is such that she ends up a

42

shattered mess, thus proving that "Lewis Carroll was a softie. She should've ended up dead."

Quizzes are handed back without having been reviewed because "I can't read this penmanship. It looks like a chicken dipped its legs in ink and ran across the page. Do it again!"

Mister Barlow garnishes his lessons with frequent literary references, most of which are a mystery to me. On one occasion he asks the class for ideas on how to solve a particular integral, and the class is silent in response. He declares that we'd not yet been given the tools to solve the problem, and is simply inquiring for suggestions. He adds that we shouldn't fear him losing his temper at our guesses, because in the words of Yeats, "One should not lose one's temper unless one is certain of getting more and more angry to the end, and such a situation does not exist here."

When a student is caught glancing out the window at some snow flurries, she is rewarded with, "Miss Wilkinson, the north wind doth blow, and we shall have snow, and what will poor robin do then, poor thing?" The student is speechless and he answers, "He'll sit in a barn, and keep himself warm, and hide his head under his wing, poor thing." From there, he continues the lesson without missing a beat, no doubt enjoying the laughter of the class.

It is these occasional references to nursery rhymes and pop culture that keep him engaged with the students on a slightly more personal level, demonstrating that even he has things in common with them.

I decide that I like Mister Barlow, because these moments of levity show his dark sense of humor, which is akin to my own. I suspect his verbal blastings are just an act, a constant reminder to pay attention.

Meanwhile, although Mister Barlow has recognized my desire for anonymity, he makes certain that I do not become complacent. At this point,

I think Mister Barlow understands me well enough that I try to finish each day's quiz while still in class. I am having an unreasonably difficult time with one day's quiz and, as I sit deep in thought, he snarls, "Come on, Mister Meyers, you're dogging it!" Suddenly, the curtains are thrust aside and the answer appears before me. I finish the problem and present it.

"What took you so long?" he gasps.

"I was being stupid," is the best I could manage.

Mister Barlow raises his eyebrows in resigned agreement, as he corrects my paper. I enjoy his facial expressions. His countenance has a wonderful elastic quality. My favorite expression is his wide-eyed disbelief at something. His eyes grow as large as billiard balls, he asks for clarification on the astonishing matter, than follows with a wry comment. On one occasion, a "C" student is the first to hand him a completed quiz. His eyes expand, his shoulders straighten up and we all wait for the misguided youth to discover the multiple errors he made.

But instead, the student has solved it correctly, earning a backhanded compliment of, "Let this be a lesson to you all. Mr. Jackson has demonstrated that Providence works in mysterious ways." Even the student cracks a smile at that one.

As I drive home past the bare branches and scattering of dead leaves on Chappaqua's roads, two thoughts come to mind. How is it that I segued from not turning in any quizzes to going for the daily home run? I think Mister Barlow not only worked wonders for my confidence level, but also cleverly put us all under a daily deadline to finish the quiz. The lesson is how to work under pressure, and I am beginning to get the hang of it.

I also wonder what will become of Mister Barlow this Christmas. I think we all expected a "Bah, Humbug!" out of him, but he failed to oblige. So, is there a prize turkey to be had at his table? If so, is there anyone to share it with him? Is there a Tiny Tim somewhere to be rescued by his generosity or a Little Suzy Who to steal gingerbread cookies from? Does he have a Christmas tree? Are there presents underneath it, or merely coal in a stocking hung above a musty fireplace? Does he even own a stocking?

More importantly, why does an instructor consume my thoughts just prior to a school vacation?

* * *

The puzzle that is Mister Barlow's past, and trivial queries as to where he actually lives and with whom he socializes arise frequently in conversation. There are persistent rumors that he lives at Greeley, that he showers in the locker rooms early in the morning, and that he sleeps on campus during the week.

Being a James Bond fanatic, I toy with the idea of following him after school, to see if he actually leaves campus. I went so far as to price out walkie-talkies so that an accomplice and I could tail him from a discreet distance, switching off the pursuit lest he become suspicious. I abandon this stunt after deciding my grade might be at risk.

I ponder his mangled ear and the war rumors. It is difficult to get a direct look at his ear because that would require one to stare, and more than one student has been admonished in his class for staring, to wit, "Stop staring at the floor, Miss Rose, or your eyeballs will fall out of their sockets."

He is just so different from any other teacher, such a stark incongruity among a relatively normal faculty. Doesn't he have friends? A family? Does he see movies? Does he like his eggs over-easy or scrambled? After spending far too much time considering solutions to these mysteries, I always arrive at the same conclusion: He isn't a vampire and he isn't Elvis.

I decide I want to solve one mystery about him. I will do whatever it takes, but I want to find out something about him that nobody else knows. I have no idea why I am driven to do this. I assume it comes from a desire to get to know this mysterious person more, to find out why his approval holds import for me, beyond just being a teacher.

A week later, I arrive at Greeley at five A.M. to seek out Mister Barlow's coffin, his batcave, his Holiest of Holies, or wherever he hangs his hat if he in fact hangs said hat at Greeley. The campus is gloomily silent. The air is damp and chilly. A mist has settled over campus. A bullfrog emanates the occasional burp. I tread lightly from building to building, fearful that the slightest sound might awaken whatever ghouls skulk in the shadows at this Godforsaken hour.

Half the buildings are unlocked, allowing me the rare privilege of exploring the bowels of Greeley that I normally never see. The boys' locker room is empty, and there are no signs of a shower having been taken there recently. I reluctantly, but gallantly, exclude the girl's locker room from my investigation. I poke and prod through the deepest crevasses of campus, the rafters of the auditorium, and the faculty lounges. I partly expect to find Mister Barlow asleep in some hovel and partly expect to accidentally release a mummified Horace Greeley from a sacred entombment.

I save L-building for last, as it is Mister Barlow's most likely resting place, and want to eliminate all other possibilities first. Like a sudden shock in a horror movie, I round a corner and run right into him.

I didn't consider that should I seek out Mister Barlow that I might actually <u>find</u> him. Now that I have done so, I realize there is no good reason for being at Greeley this early, except to look for him, and he is certain to know that.

"Good morning, Mister Meyers," he says, nonchalantly.

There's a very long pause before I answer. My reply needs to be perfect, beyond question, without giving any indication of why I am here. My brain obliges, rifling through its store of data. I had heard that Mister Barlow went to great lengths to help students, even visiting a seriously injured student in the hospital. Rather than have the kid miss out on six weeks of lessons and have to repeat the class, Mister Barlow allegedly went there every day to teach the day's lesson.

Okay, that works.

"Uh. . .glad that I found you. I'm having trouble with, well not trouble so much as, well, yes trouble with three integrals from our year-long assignment."

The best part about this excuse is that it has the added benefit of being true. Mister Barlow doesn't even blink. He invites me to the classroom to work them out, and I realize that one rumor about Mister Barlow has just been proven true. It may not have been the one I sought the answer to, but I did solve one mystery.

I follow him down the hall to his classroom, automatically stopping at the doorway to empty my shoes of rocks. Having halfway removed one shoe, I suddenly think better of it, wondering what he'll think of this odd ritual. I try to slip my shoe back on whilst hopping on one foot, lose my balance, and hit the ground in a heap. I replace my shoe, leap to my feet and scuttle after Mister Barlow, who failed to notice my bizarre behavior.

We sit face to face across two desks in his room and he guides me through the problems over the next ninety minutes. It is here that I learn of Mister Barlow's true love of teaching, and his total dedication to students. It is five-thirty in the morning. He set aside his correcting of papers to help me.

His instruction is even better than in class. He asks a lot of questions. First, look at the integral. What is it asking? How will I proceed?

Can the integral be manipulated or simplified? What methods are available to solve the problem? To solve each step in the problem? When I'm unsure about which method to use, he encourages me to try something. When it doesn't work, he reminds me about certain elements to watch for which will help identify that choice as being inappropriate in future situations.

As we proceed, I feel like I am a member of an orchestra. Mister Barlow is the conductor. The equations on the page are the music.

It was really just complex problem solving. The solutions required eight 11" x 14" pieces of paper, multiple transformations of equations, and multiple integrations within the body of the initial integration itself. Mister Barlow is patient throughout the lesson, never scoffs, never shouts, and provides me with a couple of tools we have not yet learned in class.

I thank him when we finish, he says, "you're welcome," and I depart. There is never any mention of my suspicious appearance at school so early, nor any other discussion about any other topic, nor are any other mysteries solved. As for my initial mission objective, I knew he was at Greeley when I arrived, but at what time he exactly arrived, and whether or not he had ever left, are known only to him and to God.

*   *   *

Springtime arrives, bringing college acceptance letters with it. A whole new round of interrogations begins amongst the Seniors as to people's intended enrollments. I am grateful to have the high-class problem of having to choose between Tufts and Cornell, but self-doubt undermines any clear thought. I wonder if I have the chops for Cornell. Everyone encourages me to go there, but I can't seem to pull the trigger on this decision. I don't want to find myself blown out of the water by superior competition. I prefer, as always, to be the big fish in a small pond. I prefer to aim a bit lower and succeed then swing for the Ivy League fences. What to do?

I drop by Mister Barlow's classroom after school and put the question to him. His eyes transform into billiard balls and I have my answer.

"Do you mean to tell me that you would choose any other institution over the Ivy League?"

"That's what everyone else says, too."

"Tufts is a first-class university. But when you apply to graduate school or for a job, do you think you'd have a chance against an Ivy League graduate?"

"I guess not," I say.

"Besides, you'd be bored at a university that caters to those below your intellectual capacity, Mister Meyers."

He knows I aim lower than I should. For all his apparent gruffness, he cares. He cares deeply. I wonder about the depths of his disappointment when a student who should have done well on the Advanced Placement Exam does terribly.

I end up being an example of this student.

On the day of the AP exam, I open the test booklet and stare at the problems facing me. Immediately, I am in trouble. Normally, when faced with a mathematics problem at this level, there is a clear point of attack. The question must first be translated so that an equation can be created to solve. In advanced calculus, the questions focus on figuring the area between curves. Once translated into an equation, such as an integral, one must choose how to solve it using all the tools that have been taught during the year.

I have trouble translating the questions into equations. Even after doing that, their solutions evade me. I try every method I learned under

Mister Barlow, yet I struggle through the entire exam and leave the room feeling miserable. An entire year of Calculus with Mister Barlow down the drain! I would need at least a score of three to earn any college credit, and at least a four to feel I had done Mister Barlow justice. Even worse, when I compare notes with other students, I hear them describe the exam as having been easy. Even the non-"Who's Who" expresses this sentiment. I have, once again, choked under pressure. I push the entire matter from my mind. It's too disappointing to me, and I feel as though I let Mister Barlow down.

One thing cheers me up. All year I have felt the need to earn Mister Barlow's respect, however tacitly. Towards the last day of school, Mister Barlow offhandedly announces the "excellent classical presentation of the 128 integrals by Mister Meyers."

This compliment, coming from such a stern force, carries more weight than any other teacher's. I think it's because of the infrequency with which he sings someone's praises. The compliment has truly been earned, and thus carries more value. It also comes at the right time. I felt I had failed him on the AP Exam, so this is a consolation prize.

Many years later, while a graduate student, I would take a directing class with Hollywood legend Nina Foch. She turns out to be the female reincarnation of Mister Barlow, using almost all the same tactics. She would tell us that we would never hear a compliment in her class, because we wouldn't get many of them while working in Hollywood, either. "I have no notes" would be her equivalent of the earned compliment and, when she said those words, I knew I'd done something pretty great.

The yearbook is published around this time. Mister Barlow never submits his actual photo. Instead, a picture of some awful gargoyle or monster appears with his name. It is a running joke as to what would appear in the book each year, and it is the first picture people flip to after seeing one's own. This year, he provides a gothic print of a skeleton standing on a stage, with candles lit at either end. The caption below it reads, "Don't just stand there! Tap dance!"

Now, why of all things does Mister Barlow choose these odd photos to put in the yearbook? Furthermore, why does this year's photo have a caption attached instead of his name? He must know that the yearbook is a touchstone for students, that they'll likely pick it up in the many years to come, find his entry and...what? They'll laugh? They'll shake their heads in wonder at the eccentric teacher they had for math? Maybe. I think it's because he knew that this is the way they'll remember him. For a man who apparently had no other social life, maybe he was choosing the yearbook as his own epitaph. Or maybe I read too much into it. Maybe it is just his way of being funny.

The last day of school begins with Mister Barlow's legendary final exam. As promised by my brother, it consists of one single problem based solely upon what we'd learned following the AP exam. As usual, I choke and am unable to finish the problem during class. I spend the rest of the day suffering through yet another failure. By the time I saunter to my final class, I am at wit's end with the problem, and can only imagine how disappointed Mister Barlow must be with me. I catch up to Dennis Andrews and he helps me past the one obstacle that had been vexing me. The rest of the problem is easy, I quickly finish and as the final hideous tone sounds for the last time during my stint at Greeley, I dash to Mister Barlow's classroom.

I hesitate outside, start to remove my shoes, realize that time is of the essence, abandon the ritual, and stride in.

He sits, as always, behind the desk as his last class departs. I set the problem down in front of him, hoping he will treat it as any other quiz or homework assignment. He looks it over, and then looks me sternly in the eye.

"Mister Meyers, did anyone help you with this?"

He doesn't know it, but we have come full circle from that first day in study hall. I know if I say that I haven't received help, he would reply, "Then your word is good enough for me." I can't do that to myself or to him. It isn't fair, it isn't right, and I'd never be able to live with it.

"Mister Andrews helped me a little," I say quietly.

He writes a "5" on the paper and hands it back.

"Mister Meyers, you won't get any second chances at Cornell and you probably won't get many in life, either. Don't try to please anyone but yourself."

"I will. Thanks, Mister Barlow. Have a good summer."

"And you."

Without realizing it, I extend my hand. Mister Barlow grasps it with his small, calloused palm and shakes it. I feel our relationship suddenly change. There is a human connection that goes beyond teacher and student. It's as if he now regards me as an adult—quite a change from sitting in his class that first day in abject fear of him.

As I leave, he offers one final piece of advice.

"Mister Meyers, you may want to have both shoes on your feet when you get to Cornell."

I look to my feet, then the doorway. One sneaker lies on its side. I smile sheepishly, snatch up the shoe, and leave Mister Barlow's classroom for the last time. . .as an official student.

But I will remain his unofficial pupil for some time to come.

CHAPTER FOUR

Failing College

The Cornell acceptance letter arrives. Rather than leap for joy, I am restless and disoriented throughout the summer. The idea of leaving home weighs heavily on my mind. I have never spent time away from the nest. I hated summer camp, so the prospect of a sleep-away was anathema. Most of the counselors at the day camps I actually did attend spent most of their time wondering about the strange little boy who never wanted to participate in any of the games. I wanted to create my own worlds, landscapes of the imagination where I directed the action, playing with my toys in my house under my own supervision. The real world did not appeal to me.

I am deeply troubled about going to college, afraid of the unknown, and worried about the level of scholastic ability other students will demonstrate. I may have been in the top ten percent at my high school class, but everyone at Cornell will have the same distinction. My concerns are not mitigated when my AP exam scores come through. I manage a "3" in the Calculus exam, enough to place out of one semester of calculus, but the score is below my own goals and I know Mister Barlow will be disappointed.

I consider visiting him prior to my departure for Cornell, for a pep talk or sage words to give me a confidence boost, but I am too ashamed to do so. This man had given his all for an entire year, and I'd even gone to him for extra help. How can a teacher not take some kind of pride in seeing his students do well? It seems like his students are his whole world, that perhaps this reclusive man doesn't have anything else to judge his life upon besides the success of his students. If a student does poorly on the AP exam, does a tiny fireball within consume a little bit of him?

53

Unable to face him, I focus on the future. I have been provided with a great education, and Mister Barlow's rigorous approach to mathematics will serve me well. I just need to attack each class at Cornell as I had Mister Barlow's, and everything will be fine—absolutely fine.

* * *

"Hello, Mister Meyers. How is Cornell treating you?" Mr. Barlow asks, removing his glasses and looking up from a book. He is at his customary location, behind a desk at the rear of the classroom. The only difference is that this classroom is in a different building from where I studied with him. Classes have let out for the day. It is just he and I, and I have not checked my shoes before entering his classroom.

"Not so great," I reply sadly.

I expect voiced disappointment at my score on the AP exam, but he makes no mention of it. I want to dispense with the topic, so I bring it up.

"I seem to have followed up by disappointing performance on the AP exam with mediocre grades in math and physics, among other things."

He suppresses a knowing smile under the fist resting on his mouth. I suppose that in all his years teaching, I am not the first to choke on the AP exam. I suspect Mister Barlow isn't one to focus on spilt milk. I think he instead looks to future potential, instead of at past mistakes.

"You wouldn't be the first to have a rude awakening at university. You're up against the best and brightest."

"And they've been taking me out to the woodshed for a solid beating."

He roars with laughter at my unintentional joke. He isn't being nasty. He just appreciates my dark sense of humor at the moment. He offers me a seat.

Failing College

"How is life in the Ivy League?"

"Well, Cornell is beautiful. It has these plantations, apple orchards, and farms. Two gorges cut through campus, water rushing through them all year long, and they have these hundred-foot long icicles during winter. They also have the false reputation of being the most popular method of suicide on the campus, though if one must fling oneself off a bridge, I can't imagine a better view on the way down.

He laughs again. I know he wants to enquire after my studies, but I'm not ready to discuss them yet.

"The food is good. I stuffed myself on the dining hall food after some pranksters on my dorm floor taped a Q-tip with a smiley face on my door, and labeled it "The Larry Doll". Then there's my roommate, an innocuous Chinese engineering student named Erik. He fancies himself an audiophile and has decked out our room with expensive stereo equipment. This excludes, however, anything resembling a compact disc. Having amassed a significant vinyl collection, he refuses to give in to progress. (To this day he is known for the apocryphal statement, "The compact disc will never last").

Mister Barlow stares blankly. "Compact disc?" he asks.

It hits me that he has no idea what I am talking about. Either that, or he's playing a joke. Yet his face shows complete sincerity. Suddenly, I am in the unique position of being a teacher to Mister Barlow. It takes me a moment to figure out exactly what I'm supposed to do. Then I realize that he probably appreciates learning as much as teaching, so I launch into a description of the compact disc, while cautioning him that I don't really understand the technology behind it. He seems utterly fascinated, nods and processes this information, then asks about my studies.

"I've done better, Mister Barlow. The chemical engineering major requires me to take five classes per semester. I've got Chemistry Honors,

Physics, 2nd semester Calculus, Introduction to Chemical Engineering, and the required Freshman Writing Seminar. On top of this, all freshmen are required to take two semesters of physical education".

"Ah, I see. You seem a likely candidate for baseball."

"No, I chose *Fundamentals of Flying Disc Sports.*"

He stares blankly at me.

"Uh, Frisbee. I play it a lot during the summer."

"You said you had five classes?"

"It's too much. I am in a lecture or discussion group for twenty hours a week. Another four hours is spent in chemistry lab breathing the same toxic chemicals I had inhaled at Greeley, two more hours is spent suffering in a chemical engineering lab, and I must drag myself to Frisbee class for two hours a week. The instruction in all of the classes, save "Writing About Film" and Physics, is uninspiring at best and boring at worst. "

His eyes transform into billiard balls. "At *Cornell?*"

"Mister Barlow, teachers here at Greeley are passionate about their subjects and pass it on to us. But my professors are more interested in research than teaching. Most of the textbooks are inadequate. Chemistry is a hazy blur, and I have to rely on my high school notes to get me through. And don't get me started about the math professor!

Mister Barlow fixes a stern gaze on me. "What about him?"

"He's…he's a fossil, is the only way I can describe him. He shuffles, I mean, he literally scrapes his feet along the floor, bent over, barely able to raise his arm to write on the blackboard."

Mister Barlow shakes his head. He seems almost angry.

"Writing About Film is the one respite I have. We watch great films, from <u>Top Hat</u> to <u>Psycho</u> to <u>All About Eve</u>. I love this class."

"The worst part of it all, though, is after an exhausting and frustrating day in lectures and chem lab, I wander up to the co-ed dormitory floor. I peek into the room of this beautiful Swedish student where she, in her perky voice, says, 'Hi, Larry! Look what I made today in 'Food Chemistry'! She opens her refrigerator door with a flourish and presents me with a cake."

"She baked a cake?"

"This is her tremendous accomplishment of the day. She made a cake in her Food Chemistry class".

Mister Barlow's jaw drops.

"To be fair, that's life in the School of Hotel Administration. It's a top-notch school for its field, or so I hear."

"I certainly hope they teach them more than baking!" he replies.

"You know how difficult this is for me? To see them have it so easy? Look, the hotel school is tops in the nation and graduates move on to terrific jobs. But this is after the most ridiculous classes of—I don't know, 'Design Your Own Hotel!' and 'How to Greet People with a Smile.' A hotelie's big final exam is running the campus hotel's restaurant for an evening. Mister Barlow, their worst case academic scenario is a burnt pot roast, while mine is spilling any number of lethal acids down my pants."

"To every man his own," he says.

"I suppose. They just remind me of decadent French monarchs, prancing about in their powdered faces and hoop skirts, daintily sampling the day's confections while we, the Proletariat, suffer through an honest day's labor. They'll get paid better, too."

"Enough about them. You said you were having trouble in your classes?"

'Yes, as those brainless twits play with Easy-Bake ovens, I struggle with Chemical engineering, the single most perplexing subject I have ever failed"

"Failed? You mean, literally?"

"Mister Barlow, you know that I have always been a good student. I have a good mind, and am facile with numbers, equations and calculations. Math and science come easier to me than most. Only in very rare instances do I find myself truly clueless about a situation—whether it is in academia or everyday life. Reading the Dead Sea Scrolls in the original Aramaic would be easier than understanding anything about chemical engineering! I comprehend <u>nothing</u>. I cannot even take the first step in solving any of the problem sets.

"It's as if every other student in the class somehow has knowledge that I have never learned, or access to some mystery text. I feel I have been left out of some joke."

"Can you figure out why that is, Mister Meyers?"

"I just don't understand what's going on. My first exam, I got a whopping nine points. Nine. Out of one hundred. I have never scored that low on anything in my life. Nine. Out of one hundred! My first exam at college."

Mister Barlow listens, but has no comment.

"My only consolation is that the professor does not fail freshman. It is a lost cause and my efforts are better directed to more salvageable situations. So along those lines, I'm wondering if you can help me out with some math and physics next weekend."

"Of course, Mister Meyers. Anytime you like, for as long as it takes to get the material clear. Would next Saturday work?"

"It would. Thanks, Mister Barlow."

58

"You're welcome, Mister Meyers."

I turn to leave, then stop and look back at him.

"Uh, here?"

"Where else, Mister Meyers?"

I sneak out of Cornell the next Friday night, feeling like a low-rent Steve McQueen hustling out of a German POW camp, evading the search lights that are the prying eyes of my dorm-mates. I escape, sans motorcycle, with nary a cry of, "*Achtung*! He is going for extra help!"

I meet Mister Barlow early the next morning, textbooks in hand, and we dive into triple integrals, and the mysteries of mechanics and forces acting on imaginary blocks of wood sliding down frictionless inclined planes. Mister Barlow patiently leads me through each topic and refuses to move on without being certain I understand it. It is a highly intensive day of studying, and by the end, I feel more confident.

I offer something in exchange for his assistance but he flatly refuses to accept anything. I ask if I can return for more help, and he says that all I have to do is call the school office and have them put a note in his box. I shake his hand and thank him again.

"On your next exam, Mister Meyers, remember you can't do anything about anyone else's score, only your own."

He is right, of course. I need not worry about all the other brilliant students I am up against. They will always score well. I cannot compete with them, and will have to use all of my intelligence just to survive.

After my private tutoring session, I am struck by Mister Barlow's tremendous generosity. It did not matter that I am no longer his official student. He helped me with such grace and without hesitation that I realized he must have done this before.

Back at Cornell, I succeed to a certain degree. Mister Barlow's tutoring, which becomes a bi-weekly affair, does me a world of good. Each session with him leaves me feeling increasingly confident, each time he refuses compensation, and each time he makes certain to drop a kind word about not being too hard on myself. It is never a direct statement, but an offhand comment such as, "You know, Mister Meyers, that the questions on an exam are really no different than the ones we see here in your textbook. Only the circumstances involving those questions are different."

I concede in the Chem Engineering class, content to receive a "D," which damages my pride for a few days. I defer any decision about my Chem Engineering major until the end of freshman year when I can evaluate my options.

The fall term draws to a close. Christmas lights twinkle all over campus and the incessant rain gives way to snow. My time with Mister Barlow pays off. I manage a "B" in Math and "B-" in Physics.

Now, if I can only survive the next seven semesters of increasingly difficult subject matter, everything will be fine—absolutely fine.

CHAPTER FIVE

Dinners and the Categorical Imperative

The term "Spring Semester" is a misnomer at Cornell. The truth is that students return in late January and suffer through the winter, which stretches into mid-April. I struggle through five more courses, including another semester of calculus, which requires two visits to Mister Barlow. His help is invaluable and I improve my grade to a "B." The rest of my science-based studies are a predictable disaster.

A week before Greeley lets out for summer, I stop by Mister Barlow's classroom and invite him to dinner. Actually, to be more accurate, I first spend a week thinking about asking Mister Barlow to dinner, weighing the wisdom of making the request, repeatedly equivocating over whether it would be prudent, and then decided to do so at the last possible moment.

Much to my surprise, he accepts and allows me to choose the restaurant. I select a place well out of Chappaqua to protect his privacy. It isn't a formal restaurant, but the cuisine is well regarded. I do not expect to learn any personal details about him. It just strikes me as a gesture I should make as thanks for his help, that it would be something he would appreciate, and because I genuinely like him. Behind the gruff persona, I really enjoy his sense of humor.

I arrive first. He seems to appreciate good manners, and I decide that sitting down before his arrival would be in poor taste. He arrives, greets me with a handshake and we sit down. I expect the evening to be awkward, with not the slightest idea of what we will discuss. But Mister Barlow keeps the evening interesting simply because he always has something to say.

He orders a roast chicken. I offer to select a bottle of wine, despite being so ignorant about them that I believe a cabernet sauvignon refers to a live porn show in New Orleans' red-light district. Fortunately, he declines the offer and orders ginger ale instead. Interestingly, he asks what label I would've chosen. Suddenly put on the spot, I recall one of the damnable hotel students rave about a certain vineyard once and name that.

Mister Barlow shows immediate interest and concern for my studies, asking if I've "beaten back the intellectual ruffians from the woodshed." I tell him that, thanks to him, the woodshed is under siege but they have not yet stormed the walls. He roars with laughter, which trails into a slight coughing fit before he recovers.

He probes me with intriguing questions about whether or not I enjoy my classes, questions that nobody has ever asked me, except for my parents. I constantly reassure them that all is well, lest they worry. But with Mister Barlow, I feel compelled to tell the truth. How else can I garner truly useful advice? I tell him I don't find the topics terribly interesting. I enjoy being in the laboratory, despite my exposure to hazardous materials, because I derive some kind of pleasure from synthesizing things.

"A science career seems unlikely when I can barely manage an average score. The only job I will ever get in chemistry will be in hazardous waste management."

"Do you have any more fossils for instructors, Mister Meyers?"

"No, but my chem professor must think he's funny because of the offhanded comments he made before each exam. He surveyed each question, noting typos and the like, and then said, 'But that doesn't matter because none of you will answer this correctly anyway'. His exams stump even the most brilliant students. I can't understand why he designs his exams this way. All it does is demoralize the entire class."

Mister Barlow nods. "He may have been trying to weed out the weaker students."

"Maybe," I say. "But this professor didn't seem to care about the students."

"How do you mean?" Mister Barlow fixes me with his gaze.

"You always made yourself available. But most students can't get near the professors."

Mister Barlow lets out a disapproving grunt. "The drawback of a big university, Mister Meyers. If one is going to teach, they should teach. If they want to do research, then that's what they should do. Never the twain shall meet."

Somehow we end up discussing the practical application of mathematics and physics to understanding how nature and the universe operate. I tell him that I am keenly aware of the mathematical structures that exist in nature. The crystalline structure of snowflakes has always fascinated me. I love astronomy, and wax rhapsodic about physics, of all things, and the study of planetary bodies holds some interest for me. Is it a coincidence that the planets orbit the sun in circular and elliptical planes? How can it be that things like black holes can exist, a place where gravity is so strong that light can't escape? What would it be like to enter a black hole? How can light exhibit both wave-like and particle-like qualities and did this have anything to do with what my Christian friend called "The Duality of Man"?

"Mister Meyers, I do believe you're a romantic!"

"Is that bad? Does means I am not cut out for the sciences?"

"Hardly. Einstein was a romantic, too. Do you think that was an obstacle to his genius? I think I may have been wrong about you."

"How so?"

"A person's intellect doesn't always determine his vocation. Some of history's first-class thinkers were philosophers, not scientists."

"You mean I shouldn't be a chemical engineer?"

"You're no dunce, Mister Meyers. You're can handle whatever the Ivy League throws at you. But that doesn't mean you'd be happy doing it."

I nod absently, absorbing his words, but not yet comprehending them. The conversation veers away from science to science fiction and, of all things, the classic television series Lost in Space. I still watch re-runs when I stumble across them. Mister Barlow claims to be a fan of the show. I assume he is joking, but when I press him to name his favorite episodes, he accurately recounts two of them.

"It's all nonsense, of course, but that's what fairy tales are all about," he says. I can't bring myself to ask where and when he'd actually seen these episodes. I haven't seen the show on television for years, so he must have caught it in the late seventies. At least I know that he had a television at some point.

I am curious about his political leanings, hoping that might reveal something about his past. He claims not to follow politics, as Democrats and Republicans "seem the same."

Towards the end of the meal, I ask why he is so hard on his students and, more particularly, why he shouts at them. He looks at me with the utmost seriousness and proclaims, "Mister Meyers, do you think Bruce Wayne could have built the Batcave by failing mathematics?"

I nod approvingly, but don't ask where he thinks the Joker went wrong, especially in regards to his stupidity when he explains his plans to Batman before leaving him to whatever trap he's designed that week.

I make certain to have my credit card charged prior to the meal to force him to accept this meal as my thanks. The next morning, outside the door of my parents' home, I find a case of the very same wine I selected. Although there is no note attached, I know it is from him. I am blown away by the generosity of the gift, but also mystified by it. The wine is unnecessary, and a case of it even more so. Is he sending me a message? Is it because he does not want to feel indebted to me for the dinner? Did I say something so profound that he felt the need to reward me? Is it because I demonstrated how adult I was to choose a good wine? I have no answer, but am left to contemplate the gift along with two other impressions from our meal.

The first impression is that his very specific questions generated a great deal of thought after-the-fact. He seemed to suggest that the sciences might not be the right occupational choice. I know I want to make movies and tell stories, and everyone in my dorm poked fun at the "engineer-filmmaker." And yet, I do find math and physics and chemistry interesting in a grander, more philosophical sense. I think the message is that he wants me to consider my future very carefully, so as not to err.

His eyes also strike me. This is our first social encounter, and I see a different side of him. His eyes hold tremendous power, second only to his voice. They aren't merely expressive, but prohibit anyone else's gaze from penetrating his own irises. They are always focused and stern, never straying from their subject. However, when I saw Mister Barlow tromping through Greeley, his eyes did not appear to be viewing this world. They were unquestionably focused on his inner world, the dark interior caves wherein lurked any number of mysteries personal and mathematical.

Yet, I see and feel something behind his impenetrable gaze, and it isn't just wheels turning. It has the same delicate texture of my autumnal melancholy, it is spiced and bitter, but does not reek of anger or resentment.

It is pain, I think. Maybe even anguish. I can't be sure because I only sense it subliminally. I know one thing now about Mister Barlow. The waters run deep within him, and they are anything but still. He might laugh and dismiss such a subjective, speculative assertion. But is my perception any different than his implication about my chosen career path?

*   *   *

The rest of the summer passes far too quickly, as summers often do, and I return to Cornell. Calculus becomes increasingly complex, though somewhat more interesting as we focus more on theory. Organic chemistry proves to be as tricky as its reputation predicts. I have trouble conceptualizing electricity and magnetism in my physics class. B-minuses and C-pluses do not a chemistry career make. The damnable hotel students pour salt in my wounds each night, when I return to my dorm and their "food chemistry" delights.

The message is clear and I need to act. At semester's end, about to leave for Christmas break, I decide to leave the Engineering school for the College of Arts and Sciences. I have completed sixty percent of the Chemistry major requirements, so it seems silly to back out of it this late in the game. At least as an "Artsie" I can take more electives, and thus more interesting classes.

Cornell makes this as difficult a transition as possible. Rather than just switching colleges within Cornell, a student must slog through a kind of purgatory, known as the "Division of Unclassified Students," or "D.U.S.," where they are presumably washed of the sin of changing majors. D.U.S. members are further given a de-facto ultimatum: You may stay in DUS for two semesters, maximum. If you achieve a "B" in his first semester, your transfer will be permitted. If not, you get one more chance. If you don't maintain a "B" in your second DUS term, you are summarily kicked out of the university altogether!

Considering my GPA so far had been a 2.67, just shy of a "B-," this absurd grade requirement will prove to be a challenge. So I supplement my chemistry and calculus classes with two easier electives.

I also learn that D.U.S. carries a stigma. When I meet someone at Cornell, one of the first questions asked is which college I belong to. When I reply "D.U.S.," I receive one of two reactions. Most ask what the hell it is, assuming it is a special program for the mentally handicapped. It takes a lengthy explanation to bring them up to speed. Others crinkle up their nose as if I am some kind of foul-odored hunchback, and then vanish into a crowd. These are usually sorority girls.

I feel like I am the sole non-believer, the heretic, the castaway. I am neither form nor substance. I am betwixt and between, a spirit in the material world, the empty space between atoms. I am neither here nor there. I am <u>unclassified</u>.

Upon hearing this during a visit over Christmas break, Mister Barlow quotes Gertrude Stein in reference to my unclassified classification. "'There is no there, there.' And yet, Mister Meyers, the paradox is apparent. You are there even though they say you are not. And you paying tuition for the privilege, I might add." He criticizes the university, proclaiming that it is shirking its moral responsibilities by distracting a student's intellectual development with petty matters.

"Emotion is logic's greatest enemy. Mathematics and the sciences are no place for them, Mister Meyers. You have enough pressure, and these blockheads are creating obstacles which pollute your thinking." He offers to write a letter excoriating this absurd penance, but I decline. I appreciate his offer, but it isn't his fight, and he won't win anyway.

I take Mister Barlow's advice and purge my emotions for that semester. I devote myself to my studies like a monk to God. I go for extra help to the T.A.'s. I succeed almost immediately. After the term concludes, I score the necessary "B" average. Relief washes over me. The rest of college will be a much more pleasant experience.

But my experience in D.U.S. has also stirred other feelings. All my energies had been put into my studies that term and I am no happier at the end. After fighting to get into Arts and Sciences, is it really worth pursuing a Chemistry career? I have been told that the best jobs don't go to students with average grades. I don't even know what the best jobs are, and I'm not sure I care. These thoughts are on my mind as I sit down for dinner this summer with Mister Barlow.

"Are you familiar with Kant's categorical imperative?" Mister Barlow quizzes me as he fixes me with a gaze suggesting that this is a topic of utmost importance. I confess to ignorance to Mister Kant and his imperative.

"Kant's Metaphysics of Ethics, to paraphrase, holds that all actions must come from a sense of duty. The categorical imperative itself dictates a course of action that must be followed because it is both right and necessary."

"Can you give me an example, Mister Barlow?"

"As I told the Greeley Tribune a few years back, I believe that everyone is born with a vocation that suits them best. Some people need to discover what that is, and the way to find it is to reason out what sense of duty you have."

"To whom?"

"To society. To you," he grumbles impatiently.

"But those aren't always mutually inclusive," I press.

"Perhaps not. But it is an ideal to strive for. For myself, I have to teach. It is right, it is necessary and it is my duty to myself and to the students of the Chappaqua school district. To that end, I am content within my chosen vocation. What I hear you saying, Mister Meyers, is that you are not happy with the path you are following. So you must ask yourself: what is your categorical imperative?"

"I'm starting to think it isn't chemistry."

"Now that you've left the single digit exam scores of the engineering school behind, you should have plenty of opportunity to discover what that is."

I tell him I am torn between the sciences and storytelling. Yet filmmaking not only seems to make little use of my scientifically inclined mind, but also appears to be a dead end in terms of achievement, prosperity, and practicality. I sense a struggle between two different sides of my personality, each battling for dominance. Reason and thinking are going hand-to-hand with sense and emotion.

"Fortunately, you have two more years at Cornell to figure it out, Mister Meyers," he says. I sense a whiff of displeasure in him. I know that Mister Barlow champions the mind, thought, and reason.

Still, he parts with these words: "Don't forget your Aristotle, Mister Meyers. 'If happiness is activity in accordance with excellence, it is reasonable that it should be in accordance with the highest excellence'."

*　*　*

Having entered the Promised Land of the School of Arts and Sciences, my disposition brightens. Two significant moments occur during the semester that help shape the rest of my life.

Teacher of the Year

During one of my twice-weekly laboratory sessions, I conduct an experiment involving the notorious Grignard Reaction. It is one of the more vexing reactions in chemistry because it is difficult to get the chemicals to react properly. All the other students get their reactions chugging along quickly, while I am consistently frustrated. After ninety minutes of this torture, I walk out and enroll in the Introductory Film-making class for the spring semester. Finally, I do something for myself. It is not logical. It is purely emotional, and it feels great.

A few days into winter vacation, having again managed B-minuses in the chem classes, a car plows into me while I cross a street in Mount Kisco. For the next two months, I sit in bed, waiting for my fractured pelvis to heal, for my concussion to do whatever it is concussions do, and for my knee to just stop hurting. My parents worry endlessly. The nurses rub my bottom with baby powder. I watch enough of The Price is Right to peg the cost of a Dodge Sunbird to the dollar, and a can of Chef-Boy-Ardee Ravioli to the penny.

Although Mister Barlow politely declines to visit because he "doesn't like hospitals," I have time to consider my categorical imperative. I want to write, to make movies, or at least tell stories in a visual medium. The only thing chemistry does is kill me, literally and figuratively. Every autumn all I want to do is write down my feelings, to find a way of translating what stirs inside me into something expressive. It is right. It is necessary. It is my duty to do what makes me happy. Perhaps, if I am good enough at it, society could even benefit...though that seems like youthful naïveté at the time.

But how will I accomplish it? I am a chemistry major. I am too far along to quit. I peruse Cornell's offerings, and discover that I can fill out the rest of my matriculation with film production and criticism classes. Following graduation I will apply for a graduate position at a film school. I realize this career change will worry my parents, but that they'll accept my choice.

And yet, it isn't my parents who concern me. What will Mister Barlow think? He suggested in no uncertain terms to find what vocation suited me, but is this what he expected?

CHAPTER SIX

A Final Decision, A Final Goodbye

"I've decided to finish my chemistry major at Cornell, but then apply to film school graduate programs. This is what I've wanted to do all my life and it seems foolish to keep wasting time on something I'm not good at."

Mister Barlow takes another sip of ginger ale at our customary restaurant. "Well, perhaps that is the vocation you were born for." He smiles broadly and lets out a chuckle, "But I'll tell you one thing, you won't change the world by making movies, Mister Meyers."

Even in my wildest imagination I don't think that I can change the world doing much of anything. I explain that my interest in storytelling is the only way I can express myself, and to find some kind of truth about the human condition. He smiles at my grandiose aspirations and counters, "if it's truth your after, there are a number of first-class philosophers that have spent much of their lives on that topic, without the help of a movie camera".

"Yes, but I bet they didn't have as much fun as I will".

He chuckles knowingly, but his attitude frustrates me. He tells me to find my categorical imperative, and when I announce I have, he dismisses it. I ask if, because of his vocation, he doesn't take artists seriously. His eyes transform into those familiar billiard balls.

"Make no mistake, Mister Meyers! I take everyone seriously. It is their thoughts that I may take less seriously than others. The thoughts of an artist or a politician or a car mechanic will not have as much meaning for me as those of a mathematician or philosopher."

A Final Decision. A Final Goodbye.

"Isn't there something to learn from the artist, though?" I press him on this matter because I can't believe he is this closed off to any educational source.

"From their thoughts, it is unlikely. But an artist is not concerned with his thoughts. He is concerned with the senses, and transforming that sensory information into a form interpreted through his own filter. I can admire a piece of art, but I cannot learn from it."

Reaching the end of my philosophical rope, I tell him that for some inexplicable reason, artistic expression holds just as much importance in understanding life's grander questions. I can't say exactly why, though, and this frustrates me. Mister Barlow asserts that thinkers, not artists, have always preceded all great human progress. Art is, to him, an interesting diversion but holds no real value. Still, he reminds me that we are all born to a vocation and that if one pursues it, then one will not be unhappy. What other things we derive from that vocation depend on each individual's dedication.

* * *

Senior year finally fulfills the promise of college life that my Cornell classmates have already been experiencing for three years. The fall semester is filled with courses I enjoy and that do not make unwelcome demands on my time. From film criticism to production classes, I revel in my newfound freedom.

The film production professor allows us great latitude in our assignments, permitting us to stumble and learn how to express ourselves in this medium. She is the very antithesis of Mister Barlow, and her approach to our artistic endeavors encourages all of us to soar. The projects are clumsy, but they are our projects and everyone feels a sense of accomplishment. I score straight A's that term, and make Dean's List to boot. The autumn colors seem brighter. I have time to linger in awe at the hundred-foot-long icicles in Cascadilla Gorge. The sheath of white that covers the Arts Quad in early December is more beautiful than I've ever remembered.

The spring term of senior year is divided between the enjoyable advanced classes in filmmaking and criticism, and the more onerous requirements of Physical Chemistry II and Experimental Chemistry III. The professor in Physical Chemistry distinguishes himself in a dubious manner after his first lecture. Because I missed the previous spring semester due to the car accident, the sequential Physical Chemistry courses are being taught by a different professor, who covered more in Physical Chem I than my professor had. The result is that my new professor begins three chapters ahead of where I had left off.

I politely ask him for suggestions on how best to deal with this matter. He barely looks at me and says, "Oh, you're too far behind. You'll never catch up."

The other students within earshot stand with their mouths agape. This professor, a Fulbright Scholar no less, pulls a George Patton—slapping a soldier in full view of his troops. The only difference is that he isn't required to apologize. So much for dedication to one's profession!

I still manage a "B" in the course, my highest chemistry grade during my Cornell years, and to this day I utilize the Evil Chemistry Professor as the villain's name in whatever piece I'm writing. It will take me years to realize it, but despite my travails at Cornell, I leave with a hell of a work ethic.

A Final Decision. A Final Goodbye.

I tell Mister Barlow this during our final dinner together that summer. The conversation at this meal is different than the others. His health is definitely bad. Although he is as sharp as ever, he seems very tired. We banter further about art versus science, and the values of each. I don't score any major victories, except to steadfastly lay out my plans for the coming year.

I will apply to film schools after taking the required Graduate Record Examination, with intent to matriculate the following fall. This will allow me a semester at Cornell as an extramural student, where I can make another film to beef up my application and experience. There will be no pressure for grades, just a chance to have fun in my field of choice. In the spring, while awaiting acceptances, I plan to travel the U.S. and Europe. A storyteller, after all, needs to have some stories to tell, and Chappaqua is just another provincial suburb.

I'm not certain, but I think I detect a momentary wistfulness in Mister Barlow's eyes as I tell him of my grand plan.

"Then we will no doubt meet again after you've made a few movies of your travels. But if you want to make your mark, Mister Meyers, you'd better be sure to cause a ruckus here and there."

I smile at the irony. He expects me, the student who couldn't handle the burden of not going to the library that day in study hall, to raise a ruckus. I tell him I will do my best. He insists that when I apply to film schools that they are "first-class" and I assure him that will be the case.

At the end of the evening, we part as we always do with a firm handshake. His stubby and calloused hand shakes mine a bit more firmly this time and he wishes me the best of luck. I feel how coarse his skin is, and how tiny his hand seems in mind, almost like a dwarf's, as if his hand and the rest of his body are so much smaller than the intellect that resides within.

I realize in this moment that Mister Barlow has spent hour upon hour with me eating dinner or tutoring me or hearing my complaints, and he never once turned me away. At first I believe it is because he is so isolated, he is glad to hear of any predicament involving the real world. Perhaps each interaction we have serves that purpose for him. And yet, I think it goes deeper still.

Mister Barlow does not simply listen to what I say. He _hears_ what I say. He also offers something beyond simple replies. He _serves_ his responses to me, as if each sentence is presented upon a platter, honoring each and every word as being divine, reminding me of the sacred art of true conversation. I am reminded of a saying in Judaism that one should always greet another human being as if a retinue of angels precedes him. This is how Mister Barlow handles our every encounter. I believe each time he meets with someone in need, he responds in whatever manner will help that individual. If that is not divine, what is?

He turns to the right and I to the left, and we part ways. As I walk towards my car, I can't shake an odd feeling about our meal. It felt almost as if Mister Barlow was a priest bidding farewell to one of his flock. Perhaps he is disappointed in me, or that he feels that he has somehow failed because a promising young Thinker has chosen a path different from his own.

I don't know why I turn around at that moment. I rarely act impulsively, but nonetheless stroll back around the corner and search the parking lot for Mister Barlow. I catch a glimpse of him settling into his car, which is parked down the street. I guess I just want to make certain he makes it off safely. But his car does not move for quite a while. I lean against the building, trying to stay hidden lest he think I am spying on him.

76

A Final Decision. A Final Goodbye.

Something compels me to stick around. Some twenty minutes go by and I become worried. I walk towards his car, and when I finally arrived by the driver's side window, I peek in.

He is fast asleep.

Against all decorum, I stand by his window for two or three minutes, just watching him. If he awakens, it doubtless will cause both of us embarrassment. But I can't take my eyes off of him. In this moment he seems, for the first time, human. Vulnerable. An old man snoozing.

I don't know how long I watch him, probably only for a minute or two before I return to my car. I glance at the moon, which passes behind a cloud. A light breeze kicks up, offering a moment's respite from the humidity. The only sound is of the occasional passing car and my shoes scraping against the asphalt.

It is the last time I ever see Mister Barlow. A few months later, after I travel the country and move to Los Angeles to begin graduate studies at the University of Southern California, he dies.

I want to return for his funeral, but I have a final exam the same day. I know Mister Barlow would never have wanted me to miss a moment of my work for his service. Instead, I take time to reflect on my association with him.

It is the most unusual relationship I've ever had. I don't call him a friend, because we barely spent any time together and he never shared any of his intimate thoughts. I can't think of anyone else in my life that I was initially petrified of, only to later turn to him for advice and hold him in such high regard. He wasn't a parent or relative, yet took the kind of interest in my development that a parent might. A "mentor" is as near a description as I have for him, and yet I don't think he'd have called himself that. "Hero" is another word that frequently comes to mind, and yet I couldn't specify what made him heroic. A lot of other students wouldn't describe him that way, to be sure.

What he did, through subtle means, was to help me find my path in life. At first, in the classroom, his methods helped build my confidence. He recognized the manner in which I excelled and left me to it. He also set a standard for respect in the classroom. It wasn't just the teacher I should respect, but my own mind. I admired his devotion to assisting me without any request for compensation. He also seemed to have a specific viewpoint about life. The idea that someone has a personal philosophy from which they do not waver is respectable. I don't feel that he was capable of hypocrisy. He also showed humility when he confessed his ignorance about compact discs.

I think, though, the biggest impression I was left with is how he seemed so totally dedicated to his profession. That is what I most desired to emulate.

When I return to Chappaqua the following winter, I review my notes from his class. It hasn't been very long since I last studied mathematics. Some of the material is already fading from memory. I wander through the empty Greeley campus and peek inside L-111. Empty chairs, dutifully lined up in rows, await the return of their students. The blackboard has been washed clean. The desk and chair I had grown so accustomed to seeing in the back corner is gone, as it has been for years since Mister Barlow had relocated.

Every corner, every courtyard, every hallway of Greeley lies silent. There is no learning here today, no mischief to make, no Crush for which to long. I pass from building to building, like some disoriented wraith, searching without reason for an era long gone.

The distant horn of a Metro-North train blares.

And it begins to snow again.

Part II

The Mister Barlow You Knew

Introduction

"Dry the tears from your eyes

And try to realize

That the best things in life

Maybe ain't free!!!"

- Class Motto, as dictated

to Mister Barlow's algebra

students, Fall 1957.

I interviewed hundreds of Greeley graduates and faculty. Most students offered the same rumors I had heard countless times. But every so often, an insightful anecdote would surface concerning a classroom antic that carried with it a profound lesson, an encounter between student and teacher outside of class, or something that shed light on his attitudes or life outside the classroom. In a few rare instances, people came forward that had something approaching a friendship with Mister Barlow. I collected what little documentation existed about Mister Barlow from his sole surviving brother, Albert (more on him later).

Viewed individually, none of this information offered much insight into this elusive character, just as one would be unable to divine the image of a completed jigsaw puzzle from one piece. However, after organizing the testimonials, a portrait of Mister Barlow, in the gestalt, appeared. It was impossible to completely reconstruct Mister Barlow's life, but what did emerge was a puzzle with many missing pieces—one that had enough of it filled in to get a sense of the whole.

Part 2 Introduction

Just as some integrals cannot be solved without approximation tables, I could only fill in these gaps with educated guesses. In order to do this, however, I had to enter Mister Barlow's mind. I had to become an FBI profiler, and use my own knowledge of him and the human psyche to specify his motives, behavior, and emotional landscape. Once I placed myself in his shoes, I gained a clearer understanding of who he was.

Thus, the narrative approach in Part II is intentionally reminiscent of Citizen Kane. The only way to truly fathom Mister Barlow's depths was to see him from many different angles. Some of these angles are culled directly from specific testimony. If a name is mentioned in an anecdote, then it is a direct written account from that person, which has been edited for length, drama, and voice. Actual quotes are properly attributed. Letters and other correspondence are unaltered. Most names have not been changed, although a few have, if the person is portrayed negatively.

The narrative style will change. Some of the story will be from Mister Barlow's point-of-view, some from those of others who knew them, some of it from my own perspective.

We can never know exactly what Mister Barlow did or thought or felt in any particular moment. But using this storytelling approach, we can imagine much of what his life was like.

CHAPTER SEVEN

Welcome to Horace Greeley High

September 1954. Mister Barlow did not pause for even a moment as he approached the stone building where he would begin teaching. The time for reflection had passed. Today, work was to begin. Although the building was called Horace Greeley High School for the moment, the entire school population would soon be relocated out of downtown to a patch of clear-cut land where a proper campus was being erected.

A bit of a shame, Mister Barlow thought. He liked the enormous building. It had three floors and a multitude of classrooms. There was a large gymnasium for the athletes, and a common room with a stage. The whole package reminded him of a cathedral, with its high ceilings and lengthy hallways. There was even a church next door, constructed from the same type of stone. Its bells resonated in his heart. They always did. They were a draught of elixir every morning, a call to action, a call to discipline. His students would learn that soon enough, as well. That was his first and primary goal: establish expectations—his of them and vice-versa.

A few steps out the school's front door put him on the main street of the tiny hamlet of Chappaqua. The little village had been founded back in 1720's by the Quakers and, even today, consisted of only one main street with its assorted delicatessens and family businesses, a train station that took commuters to and from New York City, and a healthy number of affluent homes. Although provincial in geographic terms, its plethora of wealthy citizens and its heritage more than made up for its size. The idea that he was settling into a community founded by Quakers comforted him. Its serene setting amongst the trees and creeks of Upper Westchester seemed commensurate with the Quaker way of life. After all the bad business of the 40's, after all he'd been through himself, a Quaker-associated community (even if only in history) would be a welcome respite. Perhaps even the Demon would be calmed by the sleepiness of the town.

* * *

Principal Don Miles vigorously shook Mister Barlow's stubby hand. It was a pleasure to be finally working for Don, for whom Mister Barlow had tremendous respect. Don was a fellow intellectual who brooked no nonsense. He only cared about education. He never hired a teacher without performing meticulous research. He traveled great distances to observe candidates in a classroom. He gathered recommendations. He did what any motivated Principal would do.

He first heard of Mister Barlow when the applicant had been nominated for a teaching position at Greeley by Dana Cotton, the Director of Placement at Harvard. She noted in her letter that Mister Barlow, who graduated with an A.M. in Teaching in 1952, "is one of these people who tends to his knitting, is very conscientious, very hard working and very much interested in working for the best interests of students in the school and not watching the clock and having the feeling that he is being abused. There is something about these boys that either lived or worked in Maine or New Hampshire that contributes to a rather wholesome attitude when it comes to rolling up your sleeves and spitting on your hands and working."

Don didn't stop there. He probed Mister Barlow's employers at Hinsdale High School in Vermont. Chester Lees, the Superintendent of Schools there, wrote a glowing recommendation: "Mr. Barlow is a superior teacher. He is without question one of the best teachers of Mathematics and

Physical Science that I have observed. His class standards of achievement are high. Such high standards maintained by some teachers would be a deterrent for pupils to select their courses of study. With Mr. Barlow, however, such is not the case. His pupils have the utmost respect for him and his methods. He is a keen student with a profound grasp of his subject matter. He is a throwback to the taskmaster type of teacher who at the same time is perfectly at home in a modern school setting. His personal scholarship is on the highest plane."

When Don came to observe one of Mister Barlow's classes, he also questioned Hinsdale Principal Robert Girardin, who wrote another hymn of praise: "Mr. Edwin Barlow is an exceptional teacher. His command of that area is which he is employed is one of decided breadth and depth. He is held in very great respect by our pupils and respected most highly by his fellow teachers. His adherence to ethics of his profession is most commendable. Mr. Barlow has established himself as a student in his willingness to pursue further study at every opportunity. I would deem it a privilege to have my daughter study under his guidance and supervision. Mr. Barlow is, in every respect, a gentleman. I would dislike losing him but will offer every encouragement for his advancement in his profession."

Don wanted a superior teacher, and he had found one. Mister Barlow, like the rest of the faculty, was different from the "professional teacher" which Don loathed. There were no Teacher's College graduates on the faculty and that was by design. If someone was hired to teach a subject, then in Don Miles' eyes he had better be an expert on that topic. Don refused to have a homogenized faculty, where individual personalities and teaching styles were to be subservient to some arbitrary set of rules. To that end, many of the Greeley faculty regarded him as a visionary educator. The teachers were given enormous power, including the right to choose their own textbooks. They were cut loose to instruct as they pleased until there were complaints—and there were very few complaints. It took extraordinary damage to a child or the school to secure a reprimand from Principal Miles.

*   *   *

Mister Barlow walked up the stairs to the third floor, stopping to admire the sunlight streaming into the courtyard in the school's center. It was in marked contrast to the utilitarian architecture of the school's interior, all done up in industrial browns and linoleum, and smelling perpetually of dust. Surrounding that heavenly square on each side were tiny chapels of knowledge, buzzing incessantly around the structure's eternally serene core. The Holy of Holies, he thought to himself, a private joke few would understand.

He let out a disapproving grunt when he found his classroom. He'd explicitly told Don that his desk be located at the back of the classroom. He'd discovered this strategic positioning two years ago when he began teaching at Hinsdale High. Mister Barlow had recalled his boyhood church and how, when he closed his eyes, he could feel the Lord's words echoing through the church and through his very soul. Those were the moments where he lost himself. The kids needed to lose themselves, too. Not to daydreams, of course, but to the work.

Mister Barlow would never be so prideful as to think himself a God, but the classroom was akin a church and he, its priest. The students needed a strong voice, an authoritarian voice, a directed voice, and the less they could see of its owner, the more powerful the message. He also figured that his presence at the front of the room was a distraction to the lessons on the blackboard. Additionally, the students would feel more vulnerable being exposed in front of their peers. Therefore they'd be more susceptible to verbal reprimand and focus more on the day's lesson, to avoid such a lambasting.

There was also an unadmitted by-product of this approach, and to staying hidden in the back of the room. It allowed Mister Barlow to disappear into the back of the room, where he could avoid the stares, and the thoughts behind the stares. It allowed him to maintain his persona of the all-powerful teacher, and not reveal the doubts within.

At any rate, he'd have to move the desk, and best that the students not see their instructor grappling with unwieldy furniture. There'd be no reclaiming respect after that, and he'd worked too hard to achieve this level of royalty. He scanned the hallway. It was empty, as he'd arrived two hours before the students would. He spread his arms wide and barreled his bulky frame against the desk, shoving it along the side of the room. The legs moaned as they scraped across the floor. He winced at the noise, but better for it to moan now, than outright snap in front of the class.

He positioned the desk so he could see the door, the blackboard, and every single seat. He paid no mind to his black tie, which had rumpled as a result of the unexpected athletics. He set his books on the desk and considered the lighting. Incandescent bulbs hung from a high ceiling.

Didn't the architects confer with physicists before building this place? Nobody in their right mind would pair 60-watt bulbs with high ceilings in a classroom. A light's brightness fell off at twice the rate of the distance it traveled. By the time it hit a student's desk, a 60-watt bulb may as well be a candle in the darkness. He'd have to turn to the windows for salvation.

These confounded panes of glass were always double-edged swords. On the downside, they provided ample means of distracting his charges. Then again, the kids needed both sunlight and fresh air to stay focused. Dark, stuffy rooms could cause some to drift off beneath heavy eyelids. The ventilation was sufficient in the room, but it was still September and that meant the occasional hot day. A hot classroom was the worst. He'd hold their attention as he always did, but on those blistering days it was solely out of fear rather than interest in mathematics. He elected to open the windows and let in the breeze.

I'll see how this bunch does, he thought.

*   *   *

Freshman Tom Holmes dragged his feet into school that morning, nervously anticipating high school. His white shirt constricted his neck. He wanted to open the top button, but then he'd stand out from the crowd and be a prime target for the upperclassmen. He stuck two fingers between the collar and the neck and vainly tried to stretch out the starched fabric.

He congregated with his peers in the auditorium for the opening assembly. Everyone related tales of summer vacation, desperately trying to dissipate the anxiety of freshman year amidst casual conversation. Everyone squinted and tilted their head for a look at their new teachers.

The most interesting character had a determined jaw and an outfit consisting of black tie, black jacket, jet-black hair and white shirt. He was impossible not to notice. Following the introductions and words of greeting from Principal Miles, Tom noted with astonishment that this oddly dressed man was his math teacher. He gathered his books and joined his compatriots in Mister Barlow's classroom, for their first class of high school.

Everyone spoke in quiet voices, warily eyeing their instructor, who sat motionless in the back of the room, reading <u>Alice in Wonderland</u> at his desk.

A few boys whispered nicknames they thought suited Mister Barlow best. "Blackie" proved to be the most popular, and the name stuck for decades thereafter.

Tom watched with astonishment as, "the classroom clock's minute hand struck the exact moment the class was to begin, and Mister Barlow slammed and locked the classroom door—preventing six or seven students from attending this first class. He glowered at us and announced, 'This class begins at nine A.M., not 9:05 or 9:03 or 9:01—it starts, with you or without you, at nine A.M.' He waved away those staring incredulously and slack-jawed in the window of the locked door, as they realized they were to be hopelessly abandoned in the hall.

Then, he said seriously, 'Some of you may inadvertently survive this year-long test of your puny intellectual capacities, a test for which you are poorly equipped and unlikely to wish becomes repeated'. We were mesmerized. We were in absolute awe. We were scared shitless and listened to his every word from that moment forward."

Mister Barlow had everyone open their notebooks, and on the front cover asked them to transcribe this dictation: "The Boy Scouts have their motto, 'be prepared.' We will use the same motto. This always means that our notebooks will always have sufficient vacant paper for our uses in class, before we start class. We always, further, have our pencils sharpened, our pens full of ink, before the class starts. The reason this teacher objects to our preparing ourselves in any way for work after class starts, is that the number of individuals who have the habit of so preparing themselves is always less than the number who are prepared, and therefore it is impolite for us to demand that a whole group wait for us."

The math class departed in haste at period's end. By the time Mister Barlow's first physics class began—at exactly the appointed hour—word had already spread not to be late to Blackie's class. Everyone was entrenched in his seat as freshman Terry Raymond took his.

"He had this manic stare; tree-full-of-owls look; strange cadence, enunciation and timbre in the voice; frequent hiss at the end of words and sentences and lips tight against his teeth. He was like a salivating pit bull. I think most of us were mesmerized, terrified and fascinated. At one point, one of us used 'speed' instead of 'velocity' after Mr. B had emphasized the difference. We were told to write out 25 times: 'Velocity is a vector quantity. It has both magnitude and direction. Speed is not a vector quantity. It has magnitude only'. The next day we turned in our writing. Jay Overocker had written his out on toilet paper. Mr. B accepted the writing, noting that he had not ruled out that possibility."

* * *

Once classes finished that first day, Mister Barlow felt confident that he'd made the desired impression on his youthful congregants and firmly established expectations. His third class had also arrived early, and everyone already knew to keep their hands (but not elbows) on their desks, to speak only when spoken to, and maintain eye contact with the board or one's notebook at all times.

Yes, his methods shocked them. Some parents might even have a few words to say about them. But his approach worked, and it was based on the time-tested theories of the <u>Summa Theologica</u> itself. He removed his copy of it from his briefcase, as well as Walter Farrell's <u>Companion to the Summa</u>. He flipped to the page he had bookmarked regarding fortitude and read it to himself. He read it to himself before and after each year's first class day as a reminder of his mission.

"A man must make the conquest of fear before he can begin to live. He must sustain that conquest of fear as long as he hopes to continue to live humanly. For he is surrounded, indeed, penetrated with dangers; if he shrinks from those dangers, he is forever paralyzed. The dangers will not be dissolved by his cowardly attempts to escape them."

He closed the book and nodded to himself. The kids might be frightened, but it was for the best. They might not appreciate it now, but they would someday.

Mister Barlow dreaded the after-school faculty meeting. He disliked meetings, and today each teacher was to be assigned an extra-curricular activity to supervise. He'd known about this requirement before accepting the job and even admired Don Miles for the concept. Despite his own reluctance, he considered it unfair and lower-class to deprive the kids of supervision in activities in which he had experience. Ma and Father Don would have agreed, so he acquiesced to this bothersome requirement. He just hoped he'd be assigned something in which he was reasonably competant.

He let out an audible chuckle, stifled it, and replaced it with a sly smile. If his terrified students had only known the past of their imperious instructor! On his Harvard Placement Office transcript, following his graduation from the teaching program in 1952, he listed numerous activities in which he participated, none of which any student would associate with their own Mister Barlow. These activities included school publicity and civic organizations.

But his students would likely find it all the more bewildering to learn the activities he was proficient in directing. These included "camping," "playground," and "gymnasium activities." Oh, what laughter it would provoke for them to imagine their teacher pitching a tent in the wilderness, roasting marshmallows over a fire, and bounding through the scrub with backpack attached. But he'd done that, and more—far, far more and under circumstances he wished never would repeat. He never agreed to do a task that he could not devote himself to entirely. Anything less than complete devotion just wasn't right, especially if it involved kids.

He'd been told that even Don had raised an eyebrow at his extracurricular experience. Had Mister Barlow not been such a forthright and ethical gentleman, Don never would have believed him. Don knew Mister Barlow well enough after the interview to know he was a man of his word. So he believed him, when he stated in his application that, "I have had three summer's experience in camping, which I feel qualifies me to assert as I do concerning the activities of camping, playground, and gymnasium activities. The nature of my collegiate training I feel qualifies me to assert as I do concerning the other activities I have checked. It would certainly be quite unreasonable of me to desire to be a teacher and be uninterested in the kinds of activities I have checked."

Unreasonable, indeed. It was exactly this firm sense of ethics, coupled with Mister Barlow's teaching acumen, which made him such an attractive candidate. Mister Barlow knew that. He was not a man of pride—pride had caused quite a stir up in Heaven that one time—but even he popped a button off his vest when he read an evaluation of his work by the Executive Director of Boys' and Girls' Camps, Inc., two years earlier. "I have observed his work as a camp counselor with children in our camp and have found his work to be far above average. He has a very wholesome influence upon youngsters and is respected by them. I judge Mr. Barlow to be a high type of person, of excellent character, and appreciative of humor."

Mister Barlow wasn't terribly pleased with his assignment of Junior Varsity Basketball coach, but at least it involved athletics as opposed to home economics. He had some appreciation for athletes, though not nearly as much as for a good scholar, and had always been impressed by what a person could achieve physically if properly motivated.

Supervision of the Debate Team would have been ideal—he thrived on intellectual debate—but those more interesting endeavors were given to faculty with seniority. He understood and was not bitter. Despite having very little knowledge of the intricacies of basketball, he would read up on the sport and do his best.

When he finally began as coach a few weeks later, he realized he was in over his head. He had little interest in the sport itself, even less understanding of it, and did not feel his contribution would be of much value. But like dear old Holden Caulfield, he despised phonies. So rather than fake his way through coaching, he relied on his method of classroom teaching: Let the kids be self-directed and learn self-reliance. He entered the gym on the first day of practice, his briefcase overflowing with books and papers to be corrected. He sat in the bleachers, read from a book about basketball and let the three star players lead their own practice. When the actual game came around, he let the same experts conduct the strategy. During time-outs or at the half, he huddled with the team and asked them what they thought they should do and let them roll with it. They didn't win many games, but won enough to earn a trophy, which a beaming Mister Barlow accepted at a school assembly. He even accepted the trophy by telling the students, "Good morning, ladies and gentlemen. This is your good friend 'Blackie' Barlow speaking." He immediately won over many students, showing his sense of humor and dumbfounding them by showing knowledge of his nickname.

* * *

After receiving the JV coaching assignment, he strode out to his green Chevy in the parking lot and headed over to Mount Kisco. Don had told him to investigate the culinary delights at the White Horse Restaurant, a whitewashed building located near the railroad tracks in the center of town. He sat down at the bar. The hamburger was, as promised, oversized and delicious. He paid no attention to the juices that dripped onto his white shirt and black tie, or the splash of beer on his jacket. A fine meal. He would make a point of returning here often.

As darkness crept over town, he started up his car and drove out of town along Route 117. There were papers to correct and, with luck, still some time left in the evening to read. He drove home, his headlights winding along the road, the forests pressing up against the asphalt. Nobody knew where he lived and nobody ever would.

That was just how he liked it.

CHAPTER EIGHT

Mister Barlow Slept Here

It was time to move again. Word had gotten out that he had a room at the Kittle House. He never would've chosen to live so close to Greeley, just a mile away, but had to because of the broken leg he'd suffered in the car accident. He'd been healed for some time, but liked the restored Colonial hotel because it reeked of class. He didn't want to leave.

But that's how it always worked out. He left when they got too close. When he was last without a vehicle, following the first car accident, some teachers would offer him a ride to and from school. He would usually accept the offer, but never got picked up at his actual home. He would walk anywhere from several yards to a full mile to a prearranged spot. He recalled one teacher, Charlie Pollock, who lived near the duck pond in Chappaqua, and picked him up on the corner of South Greeley Avenue and King Street every morning. This went on for a week or two, it was wintry and cold, and he waited for Pollack to ask the inevitable question. He finally did, saying, "You don't have to stand here on the street corner waiting for me every morning, I'll pick you up at home."

Mister Barlow didn't say anything. Not a word. He could feel Pollack's awkwardness at the lack of a response. The drive to school was quick, and thus the tension short-lived. The next morning, Mister Barlow did not appear on the corner. He moved two days later. Nobody could know where he lived. It wasn't right. It was an invasion. It was impolite to enquire after this information. It was nobody's business.

He'd gone to great lengths to protect his abodes. Mail was always delivered to his official address: Horace Greeley High School, 70 Roaring

Brook Road, Chappaqua, New York, 10514. Rent bills came there. Tax returns, too. Utility bills were sent to this address, as was his paycheck.

Another check came here as well. It came every month, was never late, and always came from the same official government address. Nobody ever asked about it. Nobody ever asked how he'd earned it. But he had earned it, a long time ago, and he was rather proud of it. And nobody, but nobody, ever dared to steam open his mail. The repercussions would be far too disastrous.

At any rate, he'd found an apartment out of town. It meant a much longer drive to school, but the new place was rent-controlled and it would keep the prying eyes away. He began packing his belongings. This never took very long because he had so few. It wasn't only because it allowed him to up and leave at a moment's notice. It was because he didn't really need very much. He had almost no clothes. The "Blackie" of old had given way to "Friendly Ed," so the multiple sets of black suits had all but vanished. Irene Berns always sewed up the torn and ragged outfits that he still had. He hadn't purchased a new wardrobe since the incident with the sports jacket, and that was almost ten years ago.

He had books, but most were borrowed, save a few of his favorites. He had his liquor, but that was easily replaceable. He had one suitcase, a beat-up brown Samsonite whose straps were falling off. But that was all he ever needed. These things were of the material world, and the material world had little to offer him.

Even money made no sense to him. He had little need for it, and only recently kept closer track of it because someone had broken into his car and stolen all the change he'd left on the console. Of course, they missed the two thousand dollars he had in the ashtray, but it was a wake-up call he thought prudent to heed.

He paused and examined the few pieces of paper he ever bothered to keep. The letters from Don served as the best reminder of why he'd come to Greeley and why he had long since decided that the school was to be his permanent home. Every expectation he'd had for the place had been fulfilled, due in no small part to the implementation of Don's progressive vision. Don remained resolute in his approach to education, and both appreciated and protected Mister Barlow's perceived eccentricities. He enthusiastically granted him tenure after only three years. Mister Barlow held a letter Don wrote to him on April 19, 1956, in which he stated that he was impressed by "the tenacity with which you follow through on your responsibilities to every individual."

Don did have some criticism, as well, which Mister Barlow would normally not have tolerated. Don, however, was his intellectual equal and deserved the respect Mister Barlow had afforded him. Specifically, Don noted that, "There is a need for developing in our students a self-reliance and independence of thought which, when coupled with adequate studying technique and proper motivation, will prepare them for college. The very effectiveness of your teaching might pose a problem, perhaps best defined by the following questions: Does the thoroughness of your teaching leave insufficient room for the development of student initiative, originality, and ingenuity? Do your students have ample opportunity for assuming responsibility for what they learn and how they learn it? I look forward to some lively discussions along these lines in a supervisory conference to come."

Don was half right in the end, Mister Barlow thought. On the one hand, high school mathematics had no room for ingenuity or originality. There were very specific parameters and approaches for solving problems. However, the more advanced disciplines of mathematics were where such talent was required. Still, he was eager to please Don, and so he loosened his style a bit and it seemed to work better for the kids. Don also made a reasoned point regarding the assumption of educational responsibility. He altered his approach just slightly to accommodate this idea, but in such a manner as to let those students who were capable of such advanced thought discover it for themselves. Naturally, they did.

Mister Barlow set the note down, and picked up another from Don. "Some students indicated that they had come into the course with no particular love of mathematics but now they considered it their most exciting and rewarding subject. They were unanimous in saying that one of the biggest differences between this course and regular courses was that they were being self-directed rather than teacher-directed, as a result of which they felt that they were learning more, understanding it better, and making more rapid progress."

He poured himself the last ounces from the Chivas Regal bottle and sat in his chair. It had worked out perfectly. Don understood him. The kids did, too. Horace Greeley turned out to be a fine place to teach, a fine place indeed. He took a sip and reflected on his younger days, about how close he came to resigning after the close call with the Russians.

*　*　*

By 1956, the school had been moved a few miles away, onto a sprawling campus by high school standards. A number of brick buildings had been constructed on clear-cut property adjacent to the Saw Mill River Parkway and across the street from the famed castle of the Reader's Digest headquarters. It was possible to traverse the entire campus without being pelted by rain or snow, thanks to covered walkways that filled the voids between buildings. The athletes had a massive gymnasium, tennis courts, a track-and-field course and two enormous fields to practice their budding talents. Best of all, in L-building, every teacher had their own classroom with lower ceilings, more incandescent bulbs, and an adjacent room for private discussions.

Mister Barlow had settled comfortably into a routine, which was a good thing because he was not fond of either chaos or spontaneity. Rigidity and structure were his hallmarks. They meant an uncomplicated life, and the ability to focus on matters of the mind.

Then came January 1957. The argument was fierce and had passion on both sides. The reformers wanted to toss out the science and math curriculum entirely, even though they couched their plan in the word "revise." One teacher wanted to get rid of textbooks and use other instructional materials like films and activities. Another teacher emphasized modes of scientific inquiry. Problem solving in mathematics was more important than theory.

The other side wanted the status quo. The hysteria surrounding Sputnik was overblown, they thought. America was strong. America was progressive. They should not toss out a program that had worked for years simply because of a little ball in space. It would be even worse if the government got involved. They'd throw all kinds of requirements at us. Besides, while everyone here knew their subjects well, future generations of teachers would be difficult to hire if they followed traditional paths of knowledge and we veered in a direction where that no longer applies.

Mister Barlow didn't particularly care which way they decided to go. He taught his way. Don would permit him to do so, or thought he would, until Don spoke up.

"The world is changing and we must change with it," he said. He received resistance from the chorus of groans by those supporting the status-quo. A dagger went through Mister Barlow's heart. He did not sign up for change. He had signed up to do as he pleased. He never spoke a word in faculty meetings, but now he was forced to, feeling that Don had suddenly betrayed him.

"Principal Miles," Mister Barlow said, always using Don's proper title in contrast to everyone else's use of his first name. "My concern is for the students. Some will simply not be up to the task."

Several of the reformers chimed in. One teacher named Klein disagreed. "Not true at all," he said. "We're not suggesting they learn Russian. We just want to shift the focus of their studies."

"One cannot be all things to all people," Mister Barlow replied. "Some students who are not inclined towards the sciences or mathematics will not be served by this program. There are some weaker students for whom this will be inappropriate."

Another teacher nodded. "Ed is on to something there. And I have to say that education is about the development of these kids, not about competition with the Reds."

That earned nods from almost everyone. Mister Barlow felt relieved. At last someone was making sense. He watched Don closely. These next few moments might decide his future at Greeley. Finally, Don broke his silence.

"Well, if it ain't broke, don't fix it. But that doesn't mean we can't also build something new. What if we offered accelerated studies to those who wanted to teach those classes, and for those who wanted to take them?"

That seemed a good compromise, Mister Barlow said. Teach four years of math in two years. There would be takers. Some of his brighter students would enjoy the challenge. Other expressed support for the idea, and offered to teach accelerated classes as well. Mister Barlow turned to Mr. Klein and added, "And to cover all bases, I shall be delighted to teach Russian after school."

*   *   *

Mister Barlow took another sip from his glass. Those were good times, challenging times. He got a lot from his students. He still did, of course, but was so proud at how many of them had stepped up and tackled the challenge of accelerated math. He liked the students for the effort they showed. They liked him, as well.

He recalled how his reputation amongst both faculty and students had grown to mythic proportions. He realized that much of it was done without real effort. Much of the carnival mask had been fashioned from an honest desire to keep people out of his personal affairs. The students seemed fond of this myth, not only for its entertainment value, but because he subtly encouraged prankish anti-administration activities. He never consciously pandered to the kids, which was unbecoming, but shared their disdain for authority. Don always ran interference so he never got in trouble.

He perpetuated the mystery as to his lodgings, taking all necessary steps to insure his privacy against amateur detectives and nosy faculty. Except for the occasional deliberately misleading reference to weekend trips to Boston to see "my 88-year-old grandmother" and "truck driver brother," almost nothing was revealed of a personal nature. Of course, he had neither such relative in Boston. His grandparents were long gone and his brothers were a distant memory, if that.

His weekend trips to Boston had been the subject of much speculation over the years. Some said he taught poor kids at an inner city school. Some said he had a house up there. A few believed that he tutored Harvard students for extra pay. Nobody bothered to guess anything as simple as a visit to his mother's grave. He'd stay overnight at some flophouse, visit with the Imp in one of his preferred pubs, and be back at Greeley by Sunday morning.

He thought about the image he perpetuated in the late seventies. As a prank, a student had given him tickets to see The Who at the Fillmore East. He'd enjoyed the performance. He also was convinced he'd gotten high because of the secondhand marijuana smoke, and had been startled by the woman who stripped naked and bounded over him to dance in the aisle. Afterwards, he wore love beads at school, while sporting a Tommy T-shirt and playing music from the band on his LP phonograph before classes began.

The myths had recently gotten outlandish. He had never been keen on providing the yearbook with photographs, and had let it be known that pictures of him were off-limits. Everyone said it was because he'd lost his wife and kids in a terrible auto accident, that he felt he'd died along with them, and thus could never stand to have his picture taken. He'd let them believe that, along with all the other rumors they'd concocted. They'd gotten him all mixed up with the unfortunate Sam Rutigliano. Poor fellow had actually suffered that tragedy, but somehow the loss had been projected onto Mister Barlow instead.

The other issue he had with photos was that problem in '72. The rain had subsided that day, and he had been scurrying to get to his class, manila folder in one arm, teeth gritted. He remembered this image because it showed up in the school paper. That blockheaded pseudo-paparazzo had the nerve to snap a candid picture of him hurdling one the many puddles in his

103

way that morning. There he was, on display for all to see, with that awful expression on his face, dancing in mid-air, hair in the wind.

He let everyone know about his displeasure. He was especially hard on his students those days, ranting and raving over the insulting and degrading photograph. It wasn't just that he had to make his point to them, but it truly was a personal affront. It was an invasion of privacy, presented as a joke. When he discovered it was one of his own students, it was the final bitter pill. He boiled over in front of Principal Hart, demanded a personal apology from the student, as well as a printed apology in the paper. Everyone obliged. They had no choice, because he'd made sure they would have no choice. He let out an annoyed sigh at the memory. The nerve of that student. His parents must have been cretins.

That did it. He could feel the anger rising. He was definitely going to move. Nobody had the right. Where he lived and what he did was his business. The rudeness, the arrogance—familiarity breeds contempt.

He caught sight of a classroom evaluation Principal Hart had delivered to him recently. "The teacher I saw simply communicates to the students that the business of learning is the single most important thing while they are in that classroom and he establishes a firm expectation for them to behave accordingly. The students sense that some of the things that are done and said are simply for effect and are intended to keep them alert. You soften the experience a bit by engaging in moments of mischief and by asking them questions about interests they have outside the classroom."

The anger subsided. Emotions mean nothing. It's about the kids. That's it. Besides, they liked his sense of humor. The whole mystery about his abode had been the source of endless amounts of fun.

He always watched his rear view mirror when he departed Greeley and on a few occasions, he'd notice a car following him. With a knowing smirk, he'd lead his intrepid pursuers on wild goose chases all over Westchester County. Most got bored and gave up, he evaded several others with carefully negotiated maneuvers through confusing neighborhoods, and one pair even ran out of gas while tailing him. On that occasion, he'd driven onto the highway headed for Boston. When the kids ran out of gas halfway through Connecticut, he pulled over, ambled over to their vehicle (enjoying their terrified expressions), and handed them gas money to get back home.

He liked to keep the students off-balance, never really knowing what to expect from him. So despite his reluctance in revealing his own domicile, he would occasionally assist students in returning to their own. Many needed the transportation after receiving tutoring for an upcoming Regents exam. For some, of course, it allowed him to accomplish two tasks at once: helping out a kid who needed a ride, and providing himself an opportunity to play a little joke.

He recalled a trio of his students—Stuart Jorge, Jeff Boemerman and Tom Holmes—who were in White Plains one afternoon preparing to take the train back to Chappaqua. He spotted them, and offered a personal ride to each of their homes. They gladly accepted, partly because they were scared to death to refuse, and partly because they thought that accepting his charity was a sign that he might favor them in his classroom treatment.

He patiently and carefully drove each of them up their respective driveways, dropping them off as near to their front doors as possible. The whole time he acted like a chauffeur under their direction and made the most formal, respectful, and obsequious discourse. He had no doubt that the kids would immediately phone each other, rubbing their hands together, gleeful at

105

their apparent good luck at having somehow miraculously become favorites of the vaunted (and previously intimidating) Blackie Barlow.

The next day in class, their unrealistic hopes were brutally dashed as he exposed each and every one of their singular failures in their homework, the very work for which they were certain he would go easy on them. That was a good prank, and he enjoyed letting those students know that life would give them no such free ride, either.

He finished the last drops from the glass, and equivocated about moving. Being here did provide a few moments of amusement, even if a few kids had discovered his abode. There was Jim Benkhe, who would show up with his homework from time to time. He would try to discourage this practice by making Jim wait at his door for 20 minutes. There was a knock every five minutes, he'd answer, "Just a minute, please," and continue reading. Eventually he'd open the door, take the homework, and duck back inside. He knew Jim wouldn't blab his location to other students or risk losing this exclusive delivery option. Jim wasn't cut out for math, and they both knew it. Still, he permitted this intrusion because Jim applied himself and tried to succeed where they both knew he would fail. Jim also saw through his so-called eccentricities, and that meant he was a cut above most of the other blockheads.

There was also Barbara Telesco. She had not been particularly good at math, but had responded well to his teachings in Geometry. She'd also been warned by her older sibling about what to expect from his class, and she never flinched at his remarks to her or other students. Additionally, she saw the brilliance of <u>Alice in Wonderland</u>, and that put her miles ahead in his book.

He knew she worked as a chambermaid at the Kittle House after school. She probably thought he had no idea that she attended to his room, but he knew everything about his students. She also showed great attentiveness to his room, and that was something he appreciated, even if it didn't ultimately matter how clean his room was on any particular day. She would make the bed and turn down the sheets, wash the bathroom, leave a clean glass, and dust around the box of very expensive brandy and advanced calculus books. She probably figured out it was her own instructor who inhabited the room when she saw the gigantic copy of <u>The Annotated Alice</u> on his night table. That was the day she also began polishing the mirror, and hanging up his ties on a daily basis. They were very kind gestures. Barbara was also an upstanding young woman and would never spill the beans about her guest.

He chuckled to himself as he remembered the one other Peeping Tom who appeared at the Kittle House. This intrepid student has actually raised a ladder outside his window. The kid nearly fell two stories when he reached the window, completely unaware that his prey was lying in wait. Mister Barlow shouted, "Boo!" just as the student reached the ladder's apex, and so frightened the poor nut that he quickly retreated with his ladder.

His eye caught a glimpse of that same window. He walked over to it. Outside, Christmas lights twinkled from nearby homes. When the holidays rolled around, he always felt a twinge of regret about his chosen isolation. He never really minded being alone. What hurt were those few times that he *felt* alone, and Thanksgiving and Christmas had exactly that effect on him. These days always meant that families would come together. Kids would return from college. Relatives from different cities would congregate. Brothers and sisters would make pilgrimages to their parents. Houses would become homes, fires would burn in hearths, colorful lights would shine both outside and in, and stockings would be hung on chimneys with care.

He would drive past these homes after Mass on Christmas Eve, and feel the warmth that emanated from their windows. He would see families sitting at long tables enjoying their meal. He would watch as parents put their little ones to bed, snuggling them tight against the winter's frost, listening to their excitement at Santa's imminent arrival.

These were the hardest times. He always thought of his brothers this time of year. He always thought of the tiny Christmas tree in their Springfield house, with the few makeshift toys Ma could afford to put under it. He always mourned the loss of those precious instants in time, and thought about how just a few seconds of childhood could so overcome him, and make him curse the choices he had made and could not rescind.

He would go home and drink, as he always did on Christmas, and try to forget.

He looked back to the well-appointed room. It felt cozy. It felt almost like a home. Would it really be so bad to stay just a bit longer?

His eye drifted to the empty Chivas bottle.

The Imp materialized next to it.

Yes, he decided, it would be bad. It was time to move on.

CHAPTER NINE

What They Thought

Al and Claire Damon sat on the couch, setting their china cups down onto the coasters. They were careful not to let the coffee slosh over the sides. One was always refined when visiting Irene Berns. That's the kind of person she'd always been. She was the one who opened up her home on Greeley's Community Night—which everyone hated—and threw the dinner parties in the 60's and 70's. They were always lavish affairs. It reflected her own sense of sophistication, an aura of class, about which she had endlessly tutored her Russian language students. If you wanted to exhibit class, you took Russian. If you wanted to be a slob, you took Spanish. That was Irene. She took the Russian students to Russia every spring, and filled them with the kind of cultural enhancements that only a devoted teacher could.

"Have some cake." She offered a tiered tray of sweets to her guests. They all knew it would be impolite to refuse, and she'd harangue them the rest of the night if they didn't indulge, anyway.

Steve Frauenthal and Rosslyn Zook joined them in the living room. They'd all enjoyed each other's company for years and, now retired, didn't find a reason why that should change. They all shared the same teaching values, had universally strong reputations with their former students, devoted themselves to the school and the kids, and would never miss one of Irene's parties, if at all possible.

And, of course, they all knew Ed.

"Why did he stop coming to the parties after all those years?" Rosslyn wondered aloud. Ed had always shown nothing but deference to

Rosslyn. She enjoyed how he lengthened out the double-O in her name. Each morning as she walked towards her chemistry classroom, they'd pass each other and he'd say, "Good morning, Mrs. Zooooooook".

"Why this? Why that? With Ed, there was never a why." Irene shrugged.

"There has to be a reason." Rosslyn replied.

"We'd have to trace his social history, and the answer lies there, I think." Steve was a mathematics teacher. He knew there was an answer for everything, one just had to find the way to solve the problem. Steve continued with his thought.

"I first saw him outside Greeley when some of us would congregate on Friday afternoons at Pines Bridge Lodge. Do you recall? It was this turn-of-the-century frame house that got converted into a bar and restaurant."

"It was no White Horse," Al said.

"Be that as it may, I saw him there in the late 50's. Some days Ed didn't want to talk to anyone and sat at the bar nursing his martini, reading. But there were days when he was considerably more talkative. So, for a period of several years we would meet him, and he became a regular. There were other interesting regulars, including a gentleman who worked at IBM, who had a major involvement in the space program. And this fellow seemed like a drunk, but he had a command of his discipline. Ed was always amused to see the man make phone calls from the bar at Pines Bridge Lodge, and give advice to people at NASA while flights were going on. It was people like that who attracted him. These were people whose intellect was interesting enough for him to be around."

Claire took a sip of her coffee, and reached for the sugar.

"I recall a few students saying he'd appear briefly at their wedding and then duck out. Beyond that, I only ever saw him here for the Community Night parties."

This annual event, in which parents were invited to attend miniature versions of their children's classes, was generally regarded a waste of time. Only Irene's pre-parties made them bearable because the food was good and the liquor flowed.

"I hated those evenings," Al and Claire said simultaneously, and then laughed. Al shook his head.

"Ed told me his life was not about putting on dog and pony shows for parents. It was about educating their children. Rambling on to parents about some mathematical concept they would neither remember nor have utility for was a poor use of his talents and his time, he always said."

"Irene, what was that dish he always loved that you made him?" Steve asked.

"Tomato Provençal. Breadcrumbs and parsley, butter, olive oil and heavy garlic. He couldn't get enough of those, and he'd say, 'Good, we'll go and I'll breathe garlic at those parents.'"

Steve laughed out loud, and put his hand to his balding head.

"Were you there the night told his classes that he would refuse to show up unless each parent brought him a martini? He got fifteen of them. Or the year he didn't show up at all, and parents came in and found a table with a bottle of gin, a martini glass, and a note, 'I'm home having a martini. Why don't you do the same?'"

Al jumped in, "Or when he went on and on presenting some complicated mathematics theory to the parents, and they just sat there clueless?"

Rosslyn's attention had wandered to the window. A light snow had begun to fall. For reasons she could never explain, snow made her nostalgic. "But how does that answer the question? Why stop being social?"

"I don't think he was ever social, not the way we think of it." Irene replied. She rose and refilled Steve's coffee.

"He was at your other dinner parties," Rosslyn said, turning her attention back to the group.

"It wasn't about being social. Steve has it right. It was about what we had to offer him. You know he dabbled in Russian and Chinese, and so he found me to be a source of knowledge. My parties were always split between the entertainers and the entertained. Ed was one of the latter. Again, it was what he got from us, not what he gave socially."

Al recalled, "He loved listening to Hal Rennhack."

"Who wouldn't? He was a dandy! He had the stories. He'd seen it all, knew it all, done it all. The man knew seven languages, for Heaven's sake! And Hal helped Ed, who was a meat and potatoes eater, develop a taste for the finer things."

They all thought about Irene's words. A moment passed in silence. Irene whipped out a crumb scraper—seemingly from nowhere—and scraped the tiny bits of cookie that had the courage to fall onto her tablecloth.

"Ed wanted to have what Hal had, knew he couldn't, and that there was no way he ever could. No matter how much he observed Hal, he could never be like him. No matter where Ed went to eat, he would never understand the difference between eating and dining. . .and Hal always would."

She dropped the crumbs into the trash and wiped her hands on a towel.

"You want to know why he suddenly stopped coming?" she pronounced. "The parties lost their utility. He'd heard all the stories after awhile, discussed the same topics, and got bored. Everyone was pleasant enough company, but company was not what he sought. And he would never say that to a host, certainly not to me, so it was always better to accept an invitation and not show up. He knew the invitations would stop coming and everyone would be spared embarrassment."

Claire sighed. "It makes me feel a little used."

Al shook his head and put a hand on her arm, saying, "Don't be. That was Ed. It was never anything personal. Well, except for Patrick. That was personal."

The doorbell rang.

* * *

My plane had just landed and I drove over to Somers to speak with Mrs. Berns and her friends. Of the group, I'd been a student of Mrs. Zook, Mrs. Damon, and Mr. Frauenthal, thinking them all worthy of their great reputations with the kids. I only knew Mrs. Berns as being the head of the language department and only after graduating Greeley did I regret missing Mr. Damon's American History classes. As we became acquainted, I admired his intellect and forthrightness.

I asked about their impressions of Mister Barlow as a teacher. There was general agreement that they appreciated the progress he made with certain students, but disapproved of his tactics. They all felt a kid should never be humiliated, especially in public, unless they'd done something humiliating to someone else. Only Mr. Frauenthal could speak to whether he was successful as a math teacher, and he felt he was. When I asked if he thought Mister Barlow had a net positive or net negative effect on the students, he replied, "Oh, without a doubt it was positive. I say that with conviction because of what one of the principals that I worked for said to me. He said the worst thing that can befall you as a teacher is to not be noticed and forgotten. It's much better to be intensely disliked, than it is to be so bland and so indifferent, that you don't have any affect on your students.

"And I'll tell you something else. Larry Breen told me that Ed never missed a single day of school, not a single one. He would never chisel on the kids. He also insisted that if he was to teach the highest-level course in a subject that he teach the lowest-level course as well. He didn't want the weaker students to think they were weak and, therefore, only be entitled to the worst teacher. It was far better for their confidence to demonstrate that they were important enough to have the advanced teacher."

I told them that Larry Breen, the Vice-Principal, seemed to hold Mister Barlow in high regard as well. Larry had told me of his first visit to Greeley, where he observed Mister Barlow's class.

"I had never seen anything like him in my life. So much electricity in the room, and everybody sitting with feet on the floor and hands folded. I remember coming out of that AP class and saying, 'Why doesn't this guy teach at Harvard? Why doesn't he teach at MIT? What is he doing here?' And that was the first time I'd ever seen that whole business, no textbook, kids writing everything on the blackboard, him sitting in the back dictating. And the references to literature and to comic strips, it wasn't all this highfalutin' stuff. It was really unbelievable. I went home and I was so shook, I said to my wife at the time that I could never teach there."

Steve chimed in, "Well, that just shows the disparity of views. John Lee had the opposite experience. He had visited Frank Bauer's class at first, and could not believe what a boring class it was, and how there could not have been a worse teacher. Then he went into Ed's class and, as he put it, realized there *was* a worse teacher. John felt that Ed was the cruelest, most pointless teacher he'd ever run across. In later years, he told me that he'd inherited a few kids that had been with Ed the previous year. They had gotten B's and A's from him yet hadn't a clue as to what even the beginning of the previous course was about. So they'd come to John thinking they had learned the previous course when they hadn't even started it, and it distressed him. On the other hand, the kids did have a willingness to confront John on certain issues that certainly gave them an internal strength a lot of kids didn't have."

This made perfect sense to me. I had been a student of John's, and his approach was commensurate with the societal attitudes of 1969, when he began teaching at Greeley. He was laid back, soft-spoken, very patient with the kids, and had a jovial giggle identifiable from considerable distances. I got a lot out of his class, and I'm sure his approach was more appealing to some than Mister Barlow's.

I decided to play Devil's Advocate, challenging their assertions about whether or not yelling at the students had any value. I told them what Preston Trusler ('75) had written me.

"Public humiliation at the hands of his verbal ridicule was one of the most powerful motivators to force our brains to understand the impossible— mathematics of a higher level than The New Math and long division. I differentiate 'ridicule' from 'abuse' because abuse makes people <u>cry</u>. He never made anyone cry in the years I had him. At worst, all one could do was sit there, stare straight ahead and take it like Lyndon Johnson at a press conference. Most times, it was difficult not to laugh when I was the victim. For sure, we would all laugh for days about one of his verbal disembowelments from class."

They unanimously responded that if even one kid was harmed by his outbursts, then that was one kid too many. I realized that trying to assign a definitive value to Mister Barlow's tactics—that the odds were in his favor in motivating the majority of kids—wouldn't hold water for them.

I moved on to Mister Barlow's behavior outside of class. The consensus was that all of Mister Barlow's behavior—his entire mythos— aligned some faculty against him. There was no shortage of people in that camp, and some outright refused to have anything to do with him. One way or another he had offended some of them, either by his teaching tactics, because of perceived favoritism shown to him by the administration, because of how he treated female students, or because of perceived arrogance on his part. Or maybe they just didn't like all the attention he seemed to garner.

Because of his attitude at faculty meetings, he did not win many friends. He often sat silent, believing meetings to be a waste of time, ignoring the proceedings until a particularly asinine issue was raised. In these instances, his subsequent outbursts were electric, powerful, and full of vitriol. He never considered that he came off to some as a two-year-old raging against the world. None of this mattered to him, of course. He wasn't there to please his colleagues or to make friends with them. He was there to teach and believed any teacher worth their salt would pour every ounce of strength into the same endeavor. Administrative matters were a drain on everyone's intellect, and any idiot who actually enjoyed those parts of the job "should have gone to work for the government".

He made this point abundantly clear early on, when Don Miles asked each teacher to present a report on a conference they had each attended. Mister Barlow began at the moment he woke up that morning, carried everyone through his morning routine, every bite of cereal he took, and every subsequent minute detail. He had not even described his arrival in the conference parking lot before Don cut him off and thanked him for the report. Nobody was asked to deliver any more reports of any kind after that.

Of course, being an anarchist, anytime he could needle the administration, he did. He quietly approved of an occasional prank or two, especially from his agent provocateur, Don Daggett. He never told Don what to do, as the boy had far more imagination than he on how to drive the Powers That Be nuts. Instead, he would pull the kid aside after some a notable bit of mischief. The day Daggett was caught urinating in the soap dispensers, Mister Barlow told him, "Mr. Daggett, what you have done today makes this place more interesting. You have become the talk of the teacher's room. Wonderful, just wonderful."

I asked about an enmity between him and an English teacher I briefly had named Patrick Halstrom. Claire was in the same department as Patrick, and the story was that the men had gotten into an argument over a point of grammar, that Mister Barlow had been dismissive of Patrick's argument, and this so enraged Patrick that he pointed his finger right at Mister Barlow's nose and said, "If you ever speak another word to me again, I will punch you in the face as hard as I can."

And they never spoke another word to each other over the next thirty years.

I nodded. "Yes, Patrick told me that story himself. I wanted to corroborate it. He also said that he felt Mister Barlow's methods were 'sick', and that he chalked his popularity up to those students who required a disapproving father figure to succeed, even if that figure was the same as "that guy at Jonestown."

"I think that may be somewhat hyperbolic", Al cautioned, "I don't think it gives our very bright student body enough credit to recognize when a teacher is harming them and when he's helping them."

That brought me to ask about how parents viewed Mister Barlow. Surely the kids came home telling stories about him, especially if they felt put upon. The group offered up a couple of revelatory interactions.

During the summer of 1974, student Adam Steier had had enough of being berated in front of the class, and told his father of his experiences. His father went to class the next day and met Mister Barlow outside of the class, as the eyes of every student were glued to the board. A quick glance to the hall revealed that Adam's father and Mr. Barlow were actually getting along! They shook hands, followed by Adam's father departing. Thereafter, Mister Barlow went a little easier on Adam, although he announced to the entire class that he only did so because Adam was "so sensitive."

Another parent found Mister Barlow standing on their doorstep one evening, having walked the three miles from Greeley to their house, to discuss why their child was unhappy in his class.

In a classic moment from 1957, Mister Barlow remembered how a parent came in ninety minutes after dismissal looking for her child. This parent said to Don, "I want my kid out of there." Don replied, "No, I don't think you do." The parent opened the door to the classroom where Mister Barlow was shouting at the kids. The parent told his kid to leave, and this kid didn't move. The kid wouldn't even look at her. He was looking straight ahead at the board, just as he'd been taught.

Al mentioned that, if any family epitomized how revered Ed could be, it was the Brooks family. Mister Barlow taught four of their children. He enjoyed tremendous respect and admiration from the entire clan, so much so that during the early 60's, he was a frequent guest at their home. So austere was Mister Barlow's presence that Lynda Brooks, even at age ten, struggled to make a good impression on her brother's legendary instructor during one dinner visit. Mister Barlow watched with awe, and then concern, as the young girl cleared all six fancy Limoges plates following the meal, and tripped on the rug. She fell flat on her face and broke the china. He knew the dishes had been used in his honor, and so he tried to make the youngster feel better about the accident, which both she and her parents appreciated.

Indeed, Mister Barlow had been extremely successful with the Brooks kids. Don had shown Mister Barlow a letter from the family in June of 1960:

> Dear Don:
>
> I want to again express the appreciation and gratitude of the Brooks family for the work of Mr. Barlow. Last year he prepared Danny for Princeton in a fashion that has permitted Danny to enjoy among the highest marks in his class in physics and mathematics in the engineering school. This year he was willing to exert himself in a manner far above the call of obligation and duty to pull Byron out of a hole mathematically, and in the process he has taught Byron, as he taught Danny, how to study and how to enjoy the mental disciplines that are an integral part of a sound education. May I congratulate you for exposing our children to a man of Mr. Barlow's unusually strong character and his magnificent professional talents.

The hour was getting late and the snowfall had picked up. We all hated to drive in the storm at night, so the meeting was adjourned. Hats and coats were assembled, and the entourage made its way out the door. As I put on my coat, Mrs. Berns eyed me askance.

119

"Did I have you as a student?"

 "No. I took Spanish."

She crinkled her nose and made a face.

"*Spanish?* Why would you do that?"

"I guess I was too stupid to take Russian."

"Ed Barlow would never let you off with that excuse."

"No, he wouldn't. Thankfully, Mrs. Berns, you're no Ed Barlow."

"Who was?"

And she ushered me out into the cold night.

CHAPTER TEN

Mister Barlow's Best F(r)iend

The Imp took on the form it usually did. Mister Barlow knew it did that simply to vex him, but since that was the *modus operandi* of demons, he expected nothing less. He could see it out of the corner of his eye, sitting in the passenger seat, as he wound his way towards Mount Kisco along Route 117. As usual, it sat quietly, egging Mister Barlow to start the conversation. Finally, the Imp got impatient, so it started to sing *Deutschland uber alles*, in a soprano that sounded impossibly young and innocent.

"Will you please shut up," Mister Barlow intoned. The Imp—Demon, Speakeasy—whatever name he called it by didn't matter, the damn thing was the only entity unmoved by Mister Barlow's powerful voice.

Surprisingly, the creature quieted. They sat in stony silence a moment longer before it piped up again.

"Edvin, I thought ve were friends"

"Allies. That's different from friends."

"Don't hurt my feelings, Edvin".

Mister Barlow shot a look to the boy. That's all he was. Maybe 21, short blond hair and blue eyes, dressed in his spotless *feldbluse,* his helmet glossy and bright, even at night.

"That's Mister Barlow to you".

The Imp pulled out a hankie and polished the Iron Cross on his chest, *"All these years, I think we know each other well enough—"*

"Absolutely not. Familiarity—"

"Yes, yes. But I'm not afraid of you, so what's the harm?"

Mister Barlow remained silent as he drove into the parking lot at the Mount Kisco train station. The White Horse was just down the street.

"I was thinking. Vhat do you say ve make an exception? Just this once. You don't need to be at school tomorrow."

Mister Barlow shot him a withering glance. "We have an arrangement."

"Temperance never got anybody anywhere."

Mister Barlow leaned in threateningly. "We have an arrangement." He opened the car door.

"Tomorrow is just one day. Big deal."

Mister Barlow slammed the door shut, and recited <u>Ephesians</u>, "Do not get drunk on wine, which leads to debauchery. Instead, be filled with the Spirit—"

"Tomorrow. Just one day. They won't miss you."

Mister Barlow bolted across the parking lot, stalking towards the White Horse, defiantly reciting, "Let us behave decently, as in the daytime, not in orgies and drunkenness, not in sexual immorality and debauchery—"

The Imp materialized behind him, leaning against the car, arms folded, singing again, that chilling song from that movie: *"Now Fatherland, Fatherland, show us the sign—"*

Mister Barlow pressed on, "He must abstain from wine and other fermented drink—"

"Your children have waited to see—"

"—And must not drink vinegar made from wine or from other fermented drink—"

Two other Imps appeared beside the first, both wearing the uniform, both with guts hanging from their exploded abdomens, forming a chorus, *"The morning will come when the world is mine—"*

"He must not drink the fruit of the vine, nor consume it!"

Then five more Imps, blood and guts and brains from smashed heads, standing tall and proud, altos and tenors, *"Tomorrow belongs to me! Tomorrow belongs to me!"*

He pressed his hands to his ears, shouting Aquinas, *"omne agens agit sibi simile!"*

The chorus was thirty strong now, their voices rising in volume, bass and mezzo-soprano filling out their shrill and triumphant mockery, *"Tomorrow belongs! Tomorrow belongs! TOMORROW BELONGS!—"*

He flung open the door to the White Horse, a single hissing and slippery whisper replacing the vibrant chants...

"To meeeeee"

Inside, the Bartender looked up and offered a smile.

CHAPTER ELEVEN

Chivalry and...Sexism?

Ever since the 70's, Mister Barlow had heard whispers about him being a sexist. "Sexist." Such an odd word. All his life he defied categorization, except as the quality of teacher that he was. Now this. Preposterous, of course. Nothing could be further from the truth.

Even back in the 50's and 60's, he'd shown deference to women at every turn. He thought about Helen Thompson, back in 1958, and how she had asked him to be the Faculty escort to a Drama Club outing on Broadway. That evening, he'd presented her with a dozen yellow roses and from then on, she referred to him as her "medieval knight." It was the same year he actually allowed his picture to appear in the yearbook, and he signed his picture for Helen, "What remains to be said after I remark that it would be impossible to find a more excellent student? Helen, you would be a compliment to any class. Do a good job. Look forward to seeing you on Broadway. Mr. Barlow."

He even showed up at Maureen Brown's wedding reception in '69 with a gift of napkin rings. Women held a special place in his heart and his spirit.

He suspected that those who thought him sexist were the same lot who couldn't handle his class. There was no shame in that, of course. Instilling students with fortitude meant putting the kids through the wringer. After all, a lot of boys couldn't handle his class, either. The verbal ridicule was dealt out equally, as far as he was concerned. He had specific attacks prepared for both boys and girls. For every, "Mr. Jones, stop scratching your chest, you're not a gorilla," there was a, "Ms. Jones, only prostitutes wear purple, get out of my class!"

The women, in particular, had to understand that the classroom was his classroom. He set the standards. He decided what was and was not a distraction. Skirt-wearing girls who crossed their legs were disrespectful to him and distracting to the boys. That drove him nuts. He'd holler, "Ms. Jones, kindly uncross your legs, this is not a 5th Avenue beauty parlor!" or the more gentle, "Only girls that sit on pianos cross their legs!" How could someone take offense to that?

When Miss Ashton crossed her legs, he blurted out, "Miss Ashton, you have the manners of a cockroach," which was soon followed by, "Mr. Jackson, you have the manners of a cockroach, and not even a high-class cockroach like Miss Ashton." If the girls didn't understand that their behavior was offensive and distracting, and if they couldn't understand his jabs at humor, then it was their problem. They would face a lot worse in the real world.

True, he called on the boys more than the girls, but that was strictly a function of intellectual capability. He never discriminated against a brilliant student. My God, there was Stephanie Strickland, valedictorian of the class of '59. Brilliant, just brilliant. First student to turn in the 128 integrals. Only girl member of the informal club of "Blackie's Boys," a group of intellectually minded kids who hung around with him after school. He never once discriminated against her.

He also had had enough experience to know that many girls preferred to excel quietly. He called on those girls who showed a willingness to speak in front of the class. He made certain to call on them to help the slower boys, for Heaven's sake!

In his current class there was even a redhead, Jane Quinn, whom he frequently sent to another person's desk to help them out. Some of the girls were athletes, and his respect for them immediately doubled. Girls were rarely handed his occasional punishment assignments, either. The idea of a young lady writing something two thousand times just wasn't proper. He reserved it only for truly unforgivable transgressions.

Every student in his classes had the same need for education. It made no sense to discriminate.

Sexist? Ridiculous. Hasn't anybody in this school read the <u>Summa Theologica</u>?

*　*　*

Mister Barlow had a far greater impact on Elissa Grossman's life than he should have. She had always, without apology, described him as the only person whom she had ever completely hated. She did so with a purity of sentiment that lasted for fifteen years. She also hated the irony that he was instrumental in both her choice of career, and how to pursue it.

She took Advanced Placement Calculus with him as a high school junior, during the 1984-85 academic year. Her initial reaction was that he resembled the bastard child of Ludwig van Beethoven and Benjamin Franklin. She was awed by his reputation and couldn't believe a teacher got away with calling students "vegetables" and "clods." She also initially reacted with false bravado, deciding that if he ever lit into her, she would muster her dignity, gather her books, and exit the room, never to return.

Despite that, she was frequently stricken with a palpable fear before each class, to the extent that she'd vomit in the bathroom every morning before class.

As it turned out, she was one of the students upon whom Mister Barlow regularly called. He asked her at least one question a day, often ones that others had already gotten wrong. If she provided the right answer (and she was geeky enough that she often did), he'd send her over to the incorrect person's table, saying, "Ms. Grossman, please walk to Clod Boy's desk and show him how to calculate the integral."

Despite this attention, Elissa felt victimized. She couldn't handle the pressure of making a mistake. For her, he was the worst possible instructor. She hated him so much that she unwittingly torpedoed his entire educational strategy of motivation through fear by doing the minimum necessary to pass the class. While math had always been her strength, she stopped paying attention and refused to study for the AP exam, ending up with one of her lowest exam scores ever.

Philosophically, she disagreed with his teaching methods. She felt that no one should be motivated through fear. While most teenagers share streaks of defiance and self-righteousness, Elissa belonged to an elite few from Greeley who stood by their principles, regardless of the ultimate outcome.

She felt conflicted about her instructor. She should have dropped the class, given that she'd not earn college credit by sabotaging herself on the AP exam. She saw that coming early on, but stayed the course. A part of her wanted to undermine Mister Barlow, and beat him at his own game. She didn't enjoy being picked on in every class, but another secret part of her loved the compliment. She'd formed a strange dependence on him, a corollary to the Stockholm Syndrome. So she felt betrayed when Mister Barlow ambushed her on a day in late May.

She'd been one of the early deliverers of the yearlong assignment to solve 128 integrals. At the start of class one day, Mr. Barlow wrote one of the integrals on the board. He turned to Elissa, saying, "Ms. Grossman, you didn't show any work when you solved this integral. So I expect you to answer it without doing work now." After a few seconds of silence, he launched into a rage-tinted speech that it wasn't humanly possible for anyone to solve this integral without doing paperwork, and that she'd committed a heinous crime by failing to do so. Colleges would always require work to be shown, and a student could be slapped with an accusation of cheating if it wasn't. He went on and on about her transgression and he finally simmered down.

Until Elissa promptly gave him the correct answer.

The room went silent. Time hic-cupped. Elissa heard the blood course through her body, pounding in her ears. And then it all rushed to her face when Mister Barlow opened his mouth. As he spoke, her desk itself vibrated from the harmonic resonance in his enraged voice. As red as her face was turning, it was no match for the deep purple of Mister Barlow's. He was so infuriated that she'd actually solved the integral and thereby undermined his point, that he lost all control. It was never a good idea to challenge Mister Barlow in class. She knew that now, and she was going to pay.

He turned to the board and put up a new integral, one that she had no hope of solving in her head. He just stood there fuming, waiting for her to give him an answer. Even though she rationally knew that none of this would ever matter in the long run, it felt to her like the Earth was about to fly apart.

He would periodically interrupt the silence with his cutting voice, each word a knife slash across her body. "Well, clod girl? Can you do this one?" "Come on, vegetable girl. Solve it!" thrown in with a gratuitous "You cloddess." She got progressively more upset and said she couldn't solve it.

But Mister Barlow wouldn't let up. Nobody could usurp his power in the class. Nobody. He ratcheted up his abuse. She stopped hearing the

128

words. She felt small. She felt alone. The classroom felt cold. Slowly, quietly, she began to cry.

This just provoked him even more. He spent the entire period hurling abuse her way, at one point reading aloud the volumes of criticism he'd written in bright red ink on the initial integral in question, even though the criticism had been proven unjustified. She never gathered herself or her dignity and walked out of the room. She just cried. All he did was bellow, "Ms. Grossman. Stop leaving salt stains on my carpet!"

She was a mess the rest of the day, and angry with herself for melting down. She thought she wouldn't be able to ever return to class. But she had to. For herself. And she'd walk out if he uttered a single word to her. He spent the first 20 minutes of the class doing some more yelling. And she spent the first 20 minutes of the class doing some more crying. So much for fifteen-year-old moral outrage.

When class was over, she left herself. Pushed by something inside her, moving without thinking beforehand, she summoned up the courage to approach him. She glided across the classroom, ready to be firm and confident, expressing her opinion and trying to shame him.

She cried through all that, as well. She managed to sputter out that he'd been rude and unfair and couldn't understand why anyone would treat another person in that manner. His response was delivered in a calm and reassuring voice.

"Ms. Grossman. You told me once that you want to go to Harvard. If you want to go to Harvard, you'll need to be tough."

Mister Barlow never called on her again. Despite sandbagging the AP exam, to which a student's grade was rumored to be pegged, he gave her a top grade. This mystified her. The only reason she could think of was that in her moment of crisis, her courage to confront him earned his respect.

She saved that one contentious integral. The page it was on was filled with his excoriating red ink. So integral number fifty-seven sat in a bureau drawer, carefully folded in half, as a reminder of the sort of person she never wanted to be.

Many years later, long after Mister Barlow had died and integral fifty-seven had been discarded, Elissa went to Harvard to pursue a Ph.D. and to become a teacher. She ran headlong into a young female professor who seemed like a reincarnated Mister Barlow, one with a different personality, but who held fast to her belief in building "toughness" by making life intentionally more difficult.

At one point, Elissa got feedback on an assignment that she thought was unnecessarily nasty. So she went to the Professor's office to discuss it. As much as she wanted to treat the situation with dignity, quietly gather her things, and walk out of the room, she failed.

But she did not cry.

Instead, she went on the offensive, comparing the Professor to the nefarious Mister Barlow and his negative, emotional impact. This time, though, it was Elissa who was cruel. She was angry. She was unfair. But she had to tell this Professor what impact she was having on a student. She could not stand silent as she did those many years ago.

For just a moment, out of the corner of her eye, Elissa was convinced she saw Mister Barlow standing beside the Professor, watching her tirade. The look on his face was the same one he'd worn during her confrontation: that of watching someone making a discovery about themselves, the intent stare of man listening very carefully to her every word, and proud of her every word.

The conversation took a turn. Elissa and her professor had a long talk about what sort of teacher they each wanted to be, whether teaching was about making people learn the course content, about making people feel inspired and self-confident, or about allowing people to realize their potential. Up until that point, Elissa never thought about how deeply her experience with Mister Barlow had shaped her commitment to teaching, or to prioritize the type of relationship she would form with students.

Ultimately, she decided to leave Harvard's Ph.D. program in favor of UCLA's. After having several opportunities to teach, she became much more confident in her abilities because of the thought that Mister Barlow fostered. The greatest irony of all was that her teaching style was interactive. In fact, her style is all Mister Barlow, without the abuse. She is deeply committed to a philosophy that's supportive of students, and that people should only learn to be tough when it's necessary. Education, in her opinion, was about caring and encouragement and motivating through enthusiasm.

One day after class, she stirred her coffee outside a Starbucks in Westwood, a stone's throw from UCLA's campus. Students filed by. She scanned their faces. Just like every campus, some of the kids were happy, some morose, some lugged tons of textbooks across the street. One of her students spied her, smiled, and waved. She waved back.

She wondered, if she saw Mister Barlow today walking down the street, would she smile and wave? She wasn't sure. But what she did know was that he would have proud of her, of how she stood up for herself, and how she found her own path and philosophy of education.

CHAPTER TWELVE

Student Becomes Friend

Every year in homeroom, Mister Barlow singled out one person who became his pet. In 1962, it was a lackadaisical fellow named Bill, who was charged with reading the morning announcements. Mister Barlow would let Bill get away with just about anything. This was, of course, all a clever ploy to lead poor Bill into overstepping his boundary. Ten days in, Bill did just that by mimicking a silly Southern accent as he was reading the announcements. Mister Barlow interrupted in a put-upon rage, lighting into Bill.

Then he lit into the class, "I can't believe you people! Of all the classes I've had, you people have kept me waiting for ten whole days!"

John Willard was the only student who laughed at this prank. Nobody in the freshman homerooms ever understood the joke, which meant they would never understand Mister Barlow. The fact that John saw through it, and cast a smile at Mister Barlow, demonstrated John's intelligence. In that moment, Mister Barlow decided he liked John Willard.

John further proved himself by being the most capable student in his freshman algebra class—forever diligent, attentive, and articulate. Some mornings, before homeroom, Mister Barlow would listen to a cheap LP record player with his latest musical find, perhaps the old English folk songs as sung by countertenor Alfred Deller or the lightly salacious German lyrics of Marlene Dietrich. He would occasionally drop the needle on the latest top-40 teenage fare, which he dutifully kept abreast of via car radio, and appropriate titles like "Big Girls Don't Cry" ("and by extension, big boys don't either!") to reinforce classroom lessons.

132

He not only appreciated the music, he also carefully orchestrated their playing to further baffle students and faculty. Some mornings he would catch a glimpse of John outside his classroom. John would smile wryly, acknowledging that he was in on the joke, that he understood exactly what Mister Barlow was doing and approved of it. Mister Barlow enjoyed having inside jokes like this with the few truly intelligent students.

John saw eye to eye with his instructor, so much so that they shared classes together for three of John's four high school years, along with a voluntary summer school calculus class in 1964. Mister Barlow couldn't name many students who would subject themselves to mathematics for grins, during the summer no less, and that sent John's stock through the roof.

Anonymous morning greetings gave way to more casual conversation. They chuckled over Mister Barlow's frequent use of a rubber-stamp collection, pounding the black-lettered words "YOU BLOCKHEAD" or "YOU VEGETABLE" across a student's quiz paper.

They also found common ground on the subject of Egyptology. In 1964, Mister Barlow had given John an 'A' for the course for knowing the difference between Tut-Ankh-Amun and Tut-Ankh-Aton, while a classmate was punished after mentioning "King Tut" ("How dare you call my favorite pharaoh by a nickname!"). By 1964, John had also known Mister Barlow well enough to present him with a birthday bottle of green Chartreuse and glasses, much to the teacher's surprised joy. John knew his preferences ran to Pall Mall cigarettes and Tanqueray gin, but decided to go with the Chartreuse to add a little color to Mister Barlow's life. He wanted to see Mister Barlow quit smoking, so he deferred from offering up any cigarettes.

Mister Barlow had become fond of John and was disappointed to see him go on an exchange program to Germany his senior year. He had become friends with this reckless pupil and missed his wry, anti-authoritarian commentary regarding the administration. Much to his own surprise, Mister Barlow took up a weekly correspondence with his wayward charge. To himself, he professed to do so merely because he thought John would feel mentally isolated without a correspondent. There was no telling what the level of intellectual accomplishment his German counterparts had achieved, and wanted to be certain John's mind did not soften during his time abroad. Simultaneously, he did feel a stirring in his soul when he read John's letters, a twinge of the road not taken. Mister Barlow was not one for regrets. He quite enjoyed his life. But he was human and occasionally wondered where alternate paths might have taken him.

As the correspondence continued, Mister Barlow came to regard John as a surrogate experiencer of life, not unlike the relationship between the title characters in Herman Hesse's Narcissus and Goldmund. He found great resonance in the contradiction between the two characters, and found many similarities between himself and Narcissus. That character was a 13th-century monk, devoted to the cloistered life, religious pursuits and tenets of Aristotle.

John was reflected in the young boy Goldmund, brought to a cloister by his father, who believed that his son must repent for the acts of a mother who overindulged in sins of the flesh.

Early in the story, Narcissus noticed that Goldmund was not one for the cloistered life and encouraged the boy to seek out his heart in the world. In fact, Mister Barlow had done the same with some of his students. In John's case, he dismissed convention and authority, and was a restless soul.

Mister Barlow dog-eared several pages in the book, to remind himself that not every student was cut out for the life of the mind. In one such passage, Narcissus told Goldmund:

The soul-oriented, the dreamer, poets, lovers are almost always superior to us creatures of the mind. You take your being from your mothers. You live fully; you were endowed with the strength of love, the ability to feel. Whereas we creatures of reason, we don't live fully; we live in an arid land, even though we often seem to guide and rule you. Yours is the plentitude of life, the sap of the fruit, the garden of passion, the beautiful landscape of art. Your home is the earth, ours is the world of ideas. You are in danger of drowning in the world of the senses, ours is the danger of suffocating in an airless void. You are an artist; I am a thinker. You sleep at the mother's breast, I wake in the desert. For me the sun shines, for you the moon and the stars.

Mister Barlow was always disappointed when his students did not fit the mold of a classical intellectual. The world always needed Aristotles, and always found a place for an Aquinas. Yet he knew perfectly well that God did not grant those gifts to very many students. To that end, he always looked again to Narcissus. Every person, every student had value and a place in life where they would find both happiness and a way to serve. He always read this passage near the end of each school year, when students came to him, asking what career they should seek:

Perhaps I did ruin a future monk in you, but in exchange I cleared a path inside you for a destiny that will not be ordinary. . .Never do I wish to find myself in the position of meeting a strong, valuable human being and not know what he is about, not further him. And let me say this to you: whatever becomes of either of us, you'll never find me heedless at any moment that you call on me seriously and think that you have need of me. Never.

He even inscribed that passage in a note to John. He wanted to remind the boy that he was always there for whatever assistance he might need. He didn't like to advertise that fact. Students should be self-motivated. But John was special. He didn't want John to become too lost in the world.

His concerns about John were always unfounded. This was best illustrated on one particularly ugly morning, the kind of cold and rainy day that put a lot of Greeley folk in sour moods. Mister Barlow received some correspondence from John that kept him bright and relatively cheerful the entire week.

John was enrolled in a math class in Germany, and his instructor had foolishly told the students that it was impossible to determine the formula for the area and the width of an ellipse using a definite integral, that it could only be done with integral approximation tables. John disagreed and did a proof using trigonometric substitution. He came out with the formula of an ellipse in about seven or eight steps, which the instructor himself had difficulty following.

Mister Barlow proudly held John's letter in his hand that morning, Marlene Dietrich crackling beside him on the phonograph. John was one of his best, and Mister Barlow's teaching was effective to the point of humbling a European scholar.

Each week produced new letters between the men. John expounded of his wanderings in Germany, the cultural differences between their countries, and the teaching methods of his German counterparts. None of them compared to Mister Barlow, nor did any of them have the same success with students. In return, the reserved Mister Barlow limited his handwritten insights to discussions of students in his own classes, or in response to John's experiences.

* * *

John was a thoughtful person, and knew that Mister Barlow would particularly appreciate unusual gifts. Sending the usual trinket from a foreign country would not only be an insult, but of little interest to Mister Barlow. So, John found a jeweler in Berlin, and took with him a cartouche of Tutankhamen. He had the jeweler fashion a set of custom silver cufflinks, which he sent to Mister Barlow for Christmas. On that Yuletide, Mister Barlow's heart was moved more than the Grinch's and Scrooge's combined. He occasionally received gifts from former students and appreciative parents, but not once in twelve years at Greeley had anyone presented him with such a carefully crafted, and specific, present.

Quid Pro Quo. Mister Barlow felt these were words to live by and most certainly, in this case, an absolute necessity. What would John appreciate in return? Perhaps a variation on a theme. One night, while sipping brandy in his reading chair at his usual undisclosed abode, he was struck with an inspiration. Cufflinks would be the choice, but fashioned from gold. They would contain cartouche, but one nobody could replicate. He arose early the next morning, and shuffled into Greeley. He rummaged through a stack of math papers from the previous term. He thought the students had collected them all, but a Janitor had lovingly placed the forgotten ones in a classroom cabinet, knowing Mister Barlow would not have wanted them discarded.

He discovered one of John's math papers and smiled. He tore off the top of the page, placed it in his pocket, and at day's end hurriedly left campus for Mount Kisco. He'd seen a jewelry store by the White Horse many times, but never had use for it.

Three weeks later, John received a set of gold cufflinks, with his initials engraved on them just as he always had written them on his math papers.

John's year abroad came to an end and he reunited with his mentor that summer. John would soon graduate, but would still be accessible, because he'd taken a job as a custodian at Greeley. He wasn't too pleased about the line of work, but he needed the money. He thought Mister Barlow would be disappointed, but the teacher was pleased that he'd have the opportunity to see his student. The thought of a friend being a custodian brought up an ugly memory from his childhood, but perhaps John would redefine that memory now.

"Besides," Mister Barlow told John, "one can never judge a custodian. Who knows what progeny might spring forth? Remember, some have entertained angels and never known it."

* * *

In August of 1966, Mister Barlow finished his customary round of beers at the White Horse and, as he usually did, made the poor choice of driving immediately afterwards. Every time he sat in a car he knew he might pose a menace to others because he simply couldn't keep his mind on the road.

Traversing the same rural roads every day allowed him to develop a near-perfect sense memory. Driving became an automated chore, allowing his mind to engage in more fruitful conceptualizations. He'd already had two accidents by then, and this humid summer night added a third notch to his car's fender. As usual, nobody was hurt because it was far too late for normal folk to be cruising the suburban town. A broken leg and multiple contusions landed him in Northern Westchester Hospital, where he remained, until school started in September.

As Fate had it, John Willard found himself in the same facility, due to an unusual brain blockage in one of his arteries. When he learned of Mister Barlow's sojourn in the same hospital, he arranged to have them share a room. Those five days went quickly for both. Mister Barlow was glad to have the company, as was John. They had several enjoyable days, as John would choose some poems and have Mister Barlow read them aloud, engendering long discussions about the interpretation of some of the more obscure choices.

John took the opportunity to introduce him to the Symbolists, a group of nineteenth century French and German poets who reacted against both realism and naturalism in favor of impression, suggestion, and imagination-as-reality, often with heavy doses of decadence and morbidity. He knew these passages would appeal to Mister Barlow, and was rewarded when Mister Barlow entered this inscription in John's yearbook (in French).

The Owls
by Charles Baudelaire

In the black yews where they arbitrate
The owls perch in a range,

Seated like deities strange,
Darting their red eye. They meditate.

Motionless they sit and wait
Until the melancholy hour
When, at sunset taking power,
The shadows dominate.

Their attitude instructs the seer
That in this world it's wise to fear
Tumult and movement;

One drunk with a passing shadow's race,
Suffers lifelong punishment
For venturing a change of place.

John didn't need to ruminate much on the poem's meaning to Mister Barlow. He'd always thought of Mister Barlow as a wise owl, always motionless, always deep in thoughtful meditation or complex calculation, that would never forgive others for letting their minds stray to decadent thoughts.

In 1971, John and his family relocated to Long Island. The friendship endured, but contact was far less frequent. During their final meal together before John moved, he asked Mister Barlow about the future. Could he remain a teacher forever? Would he always be Narcissus to John's Goldmund? Mister Barlow leaned forward and in his usual deep staccato voice, quoted Hesse:

My goal is this: always to put myself in the place in which I am best able to serve, wherever my gifts and qualities find the best soil, the widest field of action. I want to serve the mind within the framework of my possibilities, the way I understand the mind.

"And that," Mister Barlow said, "is that."

CHAPTER THIRTEEN

Sunday Chats with Bob Gluck

Robert struggled with his career dilemma for several weeks following the lunch. Part of him had a decided interest in the law. Yet, he'd already been a musician for several years, and could feel the tug of passion roping him in that direction. He did not want to disappoint Mister Barlow. Yet it wasn't Mister Barlow's approval that he sought, so much as the man's willingness to allow him into his life. Robert had never encountered someone so brilliant and austere, and it was a privilege to be afforded the enormous respect Mister Barlow gave him. Mister Barlow made him feel wise beyond his years. It made him feel worthy. It made him feel cared for in a unique, parental way that no parent could ever truly show, for they were always too invested in their children.

What would Mister Barlow say when he announced his decision? Would the Sunday meetings that Robert so enjoyed come to an end? He feared so. Mister Barlow could be unforgiving. It would be a real blow to lose Mister Barlow from his life.

*　*　*

It was another Sunday morning in 1974 and Mister Barlow sat in his classroom, New York Times crossword puzzle in hand, ready to make mincemeat out of the paper's wordmeisters. He was endlessly fascinated by language. Many people didn't see the similarities to mathematics, but they were there, primarily in the sets of rules that accompanied each tongue. Verb conjugation, particularly in the Latin-based languages, followed very logical

142

patterns. It didn't matter if one had an ear for the spoken word or not. If one had a mathematical mind, it was easy to learn a different language.

As for the crossword, the words didn't always leap immediately to mind, but after some thought, some process of elimination, and a healthy knowledge of both Latin and English syntax, even the more obscure words were filled in. It was a rare occurrence to be defeated by the literary checkerboard. Once in a while he might need to consult a dictionary. He disliked this maneuver's dishonesty, but since it was only a game and it enhanced his knowledge, he permitted it.

Sundays were the best time to be at Greeley. He'd arrive at six in the morning, and correct papers or prepare lessons in addition to the crossword. Nobody would bother him here this early, and it was better than staying at home. The other enjoyable thing about Sunday was Robert Gluck. He would show up soon, and he always had something interesting to say. He'd had Robert for senior year calculus and was one of his better students. What really caught Mister Barlow's attention, however, was that Bob had gifted him a rather interesting early edition of <u>Alice in Wonderland</u>. Mister Barlow eternally appreciated customized gifts, regardless of who sent them, and the thoughtfulness of a student who knew his fondness for Lewis Carroll had to be rewarded. He made no attempt to hide his pleasure at the gift, and the ensuing conversation demonstrated their mutual interest in supernatural horror fiction. Mister Barlow had been a fan of H.P. Lovecraft in his youth, and appreciated Robert's newfound interest in the same.

He mentioned to Robert that he was at Greeley on early Sunday mornings and it was always a good time to chat. Robert took him up on it for next several months, through the summer, until he went off to college. He'd arrive at around seven in the morning, glance at some of the challenges from the day's crossword, and then move on to whatever topic seemed to be of interest.

Mister Barlow was always polite, careful to first ask after Robert and his studies, and then permit the boy to direct the discussion. Literature was the primary topic at first, ranging from the classics to the beloved horror fiction. World events would come up in conversation from time to time, but never in much detail. Mister Barlow didn't have much interest in politics, as all politicians seemed the same to him.

There were several discussions about the challenges of teaching all the dunderheads that inhabited his classrooms. Mister Barlow admitted a certain degree of frustration, for most of his students came from privileged backgrounds and had access to endless resources. Yet so many of them acted like idiots. The situation often confounded him, and that explained some of his explosiveness. He just didn't think these kids should need extra motivation given their circumstances, and took their parents to task for raising such lazy kids.

Despite his frustration, however, he always remained resolutely focused on his task. The bright but lazy kids deserved the verbal lashings they received. But even they sometimes had trouble understanding the material, and he always gave them the help they needed. There were other kids, of course, who still had the privileges but just weren't the best students. Robert sensed that Mister Barlow had assigned himself a mission to serve these particular kids to the best of his abilities.

Later in the morning, the school would begin to populate with athletes practicing for whatever competition loomed that week. Mister Barlow felt like he was in a fishbowl in those moments, so he would clear out.

After several Sundays, Robert invited Mister Barlow to his home. It was a purely altruistic gesture on Robert's part, a feeling that he'd like to open his home up to his mentor, a show of respect and gratitude. Although he expected to be gently turned down, Mister Barlow surprised him by agreeing. He said he would enjoy a lunch with Robert and his parents, who were obviously high-class people given the polite gentility of their son. He asked that a particular menu be prepared, one consisting of finger sandwiches with tea. Mister Barlow's specificity mystified Robert, but he was happy to accommodate his austere guest.

The only reason for such a menu, Robert considered, was that it was a classic and sophisticated manner in which to receive a guest. This made him think that Mister Barlow came from a well-to-do family, one whose matriarch frequently hosted near-royalty, Victorian gentlemen, or literary giants for a weekly salon. Even if this was not the case, it meant that either Mister Barlow saw himself as a guest worthy of this presentation, or that he thought highly enough of Robert that his family would be able to handle such a regal arrangement.

Mister Barlow arrived the next Saturday and met Robert's parents. They greeted him heartily, having heard much about him, and invited him in. They enjoyed polite discussion as Mister Barlow sipped his tea and took genteel bites of his finger sandwiches, neither a mouthful nor a nibble.

On previous occasions, Robert had thought to venture queries about Mister Barlow's home life, and on this occasion, given his presence in the Gluck home, the topic itself could naturally arise. But just as he did each previous time, Robert demurred. If Mister Barlow wanted to broach the topic, he would have done so. Otherwise, prying would be impolite. While it might satisfy some of Robert's enduring curiosity, it would likely mean nothing to Mister Barlow.

Instead, the focus of the discussion turned to college.

Mister Barlow had already shown concern about Robert's leaning towards a music program. Music, in and of itself, was a perfectly pleasant diversion as far as Mister Barlow was concerned. However, the idea of anyone becoming a musician, particularly someone as bright as Robert, was anathema to him. Yes, music had elements of mathematics in it. Yes, it required great dedication. And yes, listening to a fine piece of music was a lovely way to spend some time. But a student with such motivation, and a willingness to devote the time and energy necessary to become a first-class musician, would be better served to apply himself with the same gusto towards a more intellectually superior profession. Music rested with the Goldmunds of the world, and Robert was far from a Goldmund. If anything, Mister Barlow saw a budding Narcissus in the young man and fervently hoped he would at least steer himself towards the pre-law program that he was also considering.

He dared not speak his true mind regarding possible occupations for Robert while in the presence of his parents. This was not, after all, an ambush. Nor did he denigrate Robert's interest in music during the luncheon. Rather, he subtly inferred that Robert's intellectual talents were as close to the pinnacle as he'd seen from twenty years of Greeley pupils. Wouldn't using them to become a lawyer be a fine use of such talents?

Robert groaned internally at the statement. It would make the announcement even harder now. Still, Robert knew that Mister Barlow would not show displeasure in the presence of his parents. He felt it disingenuous to make the announcement then and there. At that moment, though, he'd decided that if Mister Barlow couldn't accept the choice, then he wasn't much of a friend.

When Robert finally got up the courage to tell him that he'd chosen to follow the musical path, Mister Barlow nobly congratulated him on the choice, knowing that to do otherwise might harm the boy's confidence. A youth should not have to look for approval from a teacher for his choices, but since many did, he accepted the responsibilities that came with it. He would write Robert a stellar recommendation, and make certain he entered the school of his choice. The fact that Mister Barlow went easy on Robert elevated the teacher in his mind. He cared about Robert, period.

Robert went to college and studied music. He would always visit Mister Barlow, always on Sunday morning, and Mister Barlow would always ask after his studies. Still, with every visit, Robert knew Mister Barlow did not approve of his choice. This always sat poorly with Robert, as if there was always an undigested walnut sitting in his stomach. However, following his college graduation, things changed. He was a musician and always would be. But he'd heard another calling in the meantime, one he'd never mentioned to Mister Barlow, but one he felt sure would garner a more enthusiastic endorsement from him.

The gastrointestinal walnut dissolved instantly when he announced to Mister Barlow that he would be going to rabbinical school. This thrilled Mister Barlow to no end. A broad smile crossed his face. His eyes expanded into billiard balls.

"This is a noble endeavor," he told Robert.

Their Sunday convocations now were focused on theology and comparisons between their respective faiths.

As Robert was about to be ordained, Mister Barlow could not contain his glee. He offered Robert two presents. The first gift was a very generous check. The attached card nearly moved Robert to tears.

"The only thing more important than teaching is becoming a member of the clergy. And of course, rabbi means 'teacher'."

147

Robert knew that Mister Barlow cared about him, but this note inferred so much more. Despite the obvious paradox of his surface behavior, that of the slave-driving and demeaning classroom maniac, Mister Barlow's caring for his students (and for Robert in particular) was endless. And it was unconditional. He tried to think why he, of all people, was so deserving of such attention from Mister Barlow. Countless students flowed in and out of his classrooms. Why Robert?

His answer came further down in the card. This portion of the card was more akin to a thank-you note. There he said that Robert had brought back to him the things he'd loved most from his childhood. The Lovecraft stories were but one example. It was Robert's demeanor that also reminded him of the days long since past—so full of curiosity and of fascination. Mister Barlow revealed that he was once an altar boy with dreams of the clergy. That, more than anything, is how he saw himself in Robert.

The second gift was a copy of one of Mister Barlow's favorite books, The Catcher in the Rye. Robert really appreciated this gift, almost more than the other, because he saw this as an attempt by Mister Barlow to reveal more of himself through indirection. Like Holden Caulfield, here was a man who put up huge walls around himself and wanted people to stay away. And yet, part of him really didn't want that to be the case. The fact that Robert decided to act as if those walls weren't there made a huge difference to Mister Barlow. He decided that, for whatever reason, Mister Barlow would never have leapt that wall on his own. The fact that Robert met him on his own turf may very well have been one of the greatest gifts he'd ever received.

Robert didn't have the heart to tell Mister Barlow, many years later, that he'd left the clergy to follow music full-time. His relationship with Mister Barlow was, hands down, one of the most special things of those years of his life. Why ruin it for him?

CHAPTER FOURTEEN

The Drunken Memories of Eddie Dearborn

January 4, 2001. Eddie Dearborn received no callers save his whores. There were few whores in Mount Kisco, but they all found their way to Eddie Dearborn. They weren't the streetwalking type, since the town could fit on the head of a pin, and they would stand out. No, the whores came from the more respectable escort services, and Eddie had made a few friends, given his occasional use of their wares. The way he figured it, he had two-and-a-half years until retirement and if he lived, he lived. If not, tough shit for him. He had to have sex, and he had neither girlfriend nor wife. Blackie Barlow wouldn't have approved, but then, Blackie Barlow was dead and probably hadn't had sex a single time in his life.

Eddie had his reasons for staying drunk the past sixteen years, but they were his reasons and never felt obligated to share them with anyone. The liquor kept him company, and it was good company, aside from the whores. It could always be relied on, never let him down, and was there for him when he needed it. It was all the things a best friend should be and more. Not that he gave short shrift to his other chums—the two or three packs of smokes each day and a hefty daily dose of red meat—but if had to rank them, alcohol came a decided first.

Of course, he could not leave out the LP's, stacked from floor to ceiling on every wall in his one-bedroom apartment. They'd been with him a long time also, and several made frequent appearances when he and his best friend sat down for extended parties. They were mostly jazz and blues, as befit both his taste and image, but with a healthy portion of classic rock. No self-hating, self-destructive individual was worth his salt if there wasn't some classic rock in his repertoire.

Eddie was morose this wintry evening because he really wanted a burger at the White Horse along with a scotch and soda. Alas, another mediocre restaurant had replaced the venerable eatery years ago. He thought about how annoyed Blackie would have been at that. He cracked open a bottle of Jim Beam, threw Albert Collins onto his beat-up Harmon Kardon spinner, and thought some more about Blackie. Yeah, he missed Blackie. They were strictly Elmer Fudd and Bugs Bunny through the years.

* * *

September 21, 1956. 8:45 AM. Freshman Eddie Dearborn was talking during a fire drill. The reason Eddie Dearborn was talking during a fire drill was because he didn't give a shit about rules, especially ones like, "do not talk during a fire drill." It's also the reason why Blackie Barlow scared the shit out of Eddie Dearborn. Blackie took down Eddie's name and promptly chewed him out with such ferocity that his tirade would have made Cotton Mather look like Donny Osmond. Someone had finally put the restless Eddie Dearborn in his place, and Eddie Dearborn immediately wanted to get to know his new tormentor better.

Another encounter proved elusive until the new Greeley opened in 1957. There was a bum door between C and D buildings on that September morn. Eddie charged through it, the door burst open due to its malfunctioning mechanical restraint, and he nearly bowled Blackie over. The two men stared at each other. Eddie froze. Blackie straightened, then stiffened. There was a momentary silence, and Eddie could actually see Blackie suck up every atom of energy in the vicinity to fuel the upcoming blast. The two of them stood there, in a vacuum of time and energy, before Blackie's brow furrowed and he demanded to know Eddie's name.

Except Blackie damn well knew Eddie's name from the fire drill incident. Still, he demanded it from the boy. Eddie, who frequently had little to lose in any situation, proudly announced that he was "Lowell Zack," who was in truth some kid from his 1953 Catholic School class. Blackie stared Eddie down, another millisecond of silence passed.

Then Blackie giggled and trotted off down the hall. Blackie knew Eddie was shitting him, and he loved it.

* * *

As the liquor found its well-worn dimple in Eddie's brain, his memory of the next couple of years vanished into a customary fog. There was a flash of a twice-failed typing class, probably the only Greeley grad with that dubious achievement, though nobody knew what Attention Deficit Disorder was back then. Somewhere in there, he'd failed algebra three times. There was also summer school in 1959, which he got kicked out of, but could not recall why.

It was fine that he couldn't remember. That way he wouldn't be able to dwell on the damage done when home life unraveled in '57. Or was it '58? Either way it sucked, it fucked him up for life, and there was no changing a single godforsaken thing about it.

* * *

Geometry. That's when he ended up with Blackie. Yeah. 1960. By then he was a bona fide wiseass party guy on the five-year plan at Greeley, and destined to clinch the bottom rank of his class. Not that he minded school so much. He was just fucking up to spite his parents. They deserved it for what they did. Hell, he couldn't wait to go to school, for <u>funzies</u>. If anything, Blackie's class would be the most fun he'd have.

Eddie made no secret that he was a brilliant student, deliberately sandbagging his own fortunes. Blackie knew it, and never once challenged him on it, because Blackie sensed he would never respond to authority. So, as Blackie browbeat, cajoled, manipulated, and verbally abused the other students, he always addressed Eddie with total politeness, and otherwise completely ignored him. On those occasions when Eddie was asked to perform and did so incorrectly, Blackie displayed patience, kindness and understanding.

It took Eddie a few weeks to figure out Blackie's plan. Why did he receive this kind treatment while everyone else was wrung through the mill? Then he caught on. Blackie must have known his shtick wouldn't fly with Eddie, so he took the opposite approach. This was Blackie's way of being a testicle demolition artist—a ball buster!

Eddie engaged in his own mind games. He sat straight up, folded his hands at his desk, and performed the best Eddie Haskell routine he could. Blackie barely suppressed a smile when he did this. The game was on. How would Blackie respond?

A few days later, one February afternoon, Blackie asked the class if anyone knew where the Dodececonese Islands were. No one raised his hand. As the islands' name sounded Greek to Eddie, he raised his hand, and said matter-of-factly, "Yes sir, Mister Barlow. They're off the coast of Greece."

Blackie responded, "Ah, excellent, Mr. Dearborn"! Blackie had the class face him, bow, and deliver a standing ovation. Then it was back to the silent treatment.

In that instant, Eddie knew Blackie was beat. He was using a reverse-double-whammy, and Blackie couldn't behave any differently lest it destroy the "nice guy" ruse he was using on Eddie. He knew and Eddie knew, that Eddie has bested him. The bow and ovation from the students were merely a proxy for Blackie that day, as if to say, "I tip my hat to a fellow prankster. You have bested me, sir!" Blackie subsequently passed Eddie with a 65, so he could graduate.

* * *

The alcohol had filled the dimple and slopped over onto the rest of his brain cells now. This was always a good transition moment, a fine time to add a little nicotine to the mix, so he wouldn't fall asleep. He pulled the cigarette from its crinkled pack and chucked the waste into the basket, five feet away.

As he lit up, a Metro-North commuter train pulled into the Kisco station, spitting out the good people of the world with their wool coats, briefcases, and wedding rings. He took a nice long drag, filling his lungs with that blessed crap, and looked out his window at them. They scurried to their cars, anxious to escape the chill, and drove from the lot, past the new restaurant. Yeah. The restaurant. The White Horse. He thought it was '64 when he ran into Blackie there the first time.

* * *

1964. They never used each other's first names, per Blackie's custom. When Eddie saw him in the bar that evening, chowing down on a burger, juices dripping onto his coat, Eddie bounded up with glee, shouting, "Hi Blackie!" Without missing a beat, Blackie growled, "Mr. Dearborn, don't come near me

153

when I'm eating, it's bad for the digestive system." So Eddie obliged, and whenever he spotted his rival at the restaurant, he dutifully ignored him, leaving him to his continuous rounds of Miller Beer. Blackie got a kick out of this response, but never said a word.

The good-natured rivalry escalated a few months later, as Eddie couldn't let too much time go by without upping the stakes. Blackie would have been disappointed otherwise. It was a warm spring morning and Eddie was strolling down South Moger Avenue, not far from the train station. He always walked because he never owned a car, which he knew delighted Blackie to no end. Just as that exact thought crossed his mind, he caught sight of his prey leaving the Mount Kisco Diner, trundle down the steps into the parking lot and enter his car. Knowing Blackie to be a man of discipline, he figured this was a daily event.

So the next morning, Eddie hid behind a parked car, waiting for Blackie's exit. When it happened, Eddie screamed at the top of his lungs, "Blackie!" It scared the crap out of him, and he growled, "<u>Dearborn</u>," feigning anger, shaking his head. Yeah, Bugs Bunny and Elmer Fudd. Tit for tat. Rabbit season. Duck season. Rabbit season. Duck season.

Random encounters. That was life with Blackie. They'd bump into each other at other local saloons. Despite Blackie's veneer at the White Horse, they always engaged in conversation elsewhere. Eddie would amble into the saloon *du jour*, find Blackie downing a Miller at the bar, and would be greeted with, "Ah, Mr. Dearborn. Please sit down, and to what do I owe this pleasure, etc. etc." These were mutually beneficial encounters, for they enjoyed each other's company.

The topics weren't terribly grand, as Blackie usually grilled Eddie for his take on former students. Eddie wasn't sure why he got the third degree on those people, but the line of interrogation suggested a need for reassurance that he'd analyzed his students correctly, so that none of them had received sub-par attention from him.

But of even greater concern during bar chatter were the wasted talents of former students. This, more than anything, was disappointing and upsetting to Blackie. He'd shake his head, lean forward with that intense gaze and ask Eddie a question he never had an answer for himself. "How could they turn out like that? Didn't s/he realize what they had?"

Eddie didn't understand why Blackie harped on the topic so often. Spilt milk, as far as he was concerned. Besides, he always thought that one hundred percent excellence was never good enough for Blackie. Why care about those who fell by the wayside? From time to time, he even thought Blackie was addressing him directly. He never pried into Eddie's life, but could see the waste he'd become. Eddie never took the bait, though. They were drinking buddies. Best to leave it at that.

Then there was that one student—what was his name—the one Blackie went on and on about? It was too long ago, and his head too numbed to remember. But that student went to Tufts—no, that wasn't right—he went to an Ivy League school. Yeah. And that student was thrown out for running a prostitution ring. Of all things to be tossed out of school for! Still, Eddie was surprised by Blackie's disappointment in the kid. Blackie was a renegade himself. Was it the prostitution angle that upset him? Maybe. Was it the waste of the intellectual talent? That seemed more likely. It took a few more mentions of this fallen angel before Eddie realized the boy had been a protégé of Blackie's. Then it made a lot more sense.

* * *

It started to snow. Eddie liked the snow. He liked how even the ugliest object could be transformed. Even a mangy drunk, fermenting in his run-down apartment, might look halfway decent if viewed from afar, through a blizzard.

He let out a laugh. He remembered it was snowing when he gave Blackie the scare of a lifetime. It was, shit, when was it? Had to have been towards the end. Not <u>the</u> end, but towards it.

* * *

Late 80's. Blackie was in Northern Westchester Hospital again. Eddie worked there as an orderly, always knew when his chum was there, and always dropped in on him. This time it wasn't a broken leg from a car accident, like it usually was, but for something internal. Eddie didn't care. It gave him the perfect excuse.

He purloined some surgeon's gear, a cap, gown, and gloves. He took off his glasses and marched into Blackie's room, "sterilized" hands in the air. There was Blackie, looking out the window, sitting in a chair with his glasses on the table. Eddie let loose with a deep, bellowing voice with a heavy German accent, "ED-VIN, it's time!"

Oh, man. Blackie just shit! He fumbled for his glasses, put them on and screamed, "DEARBORN!" Eddie burst into laughter. Blackie shook his head and couldn't control his own laughter. Blackie got a kick out of that, oh yes. But Eddie knew, and Blackie knew he knew, that Blackie thought he was going to the O.R.!

* * *

Eddie laughed as the snow fell. There were tears in there also, the kind where he was never sure if they came from laughing or crying. Blackie did that to him, always did that to him whenever he got drunk enough to remember. Goddamn. What was Blackie's deal, anyway? He'd analyzed him from every angle to figure what made him tick. It was still a crapshoot as to whether or not Blackie's shtick was real, or some grand version of living theatre. He revealed nothing but still left a lot of openings in ways. He could have been a master spy. He could read motives immediately. He created and promoted a false image of himself. Eddie knew it was false, anyway. A lot of people weren't sure. He knew why Blackie did it because he pretty much did the same thing. What easier way to retreat from a world that had fucked him up years earlier?

Oh, man. That was too deep a thought for a drunken man. The Albert Collins record came to an end. He rose as quickly as he was able, preventing the needle from tearing into the center label.

He flipped on the TV. There was that flick he liked. <u>Men of the Fighting Lady</u>. He dropped back into his chair. He was getting woozy now. His half-closed eyes caught sight of the wind-driven snow, and it was picking up in intensity.

Walter Pidgeon's voice emanated from the TV, "Where do we get such men?" Yeah. Where indeed?

Eddie's eyelids lost the battle with gravity. As the snow merged into the darkness behind his eyes, just as he fell asleep, he thought, "My only regret is that Blackie never called me a blockhead."

CHAPTER FIFTEEN

An Interview with The Greeley Tribune

February 17, 1984, conducted by Greg Feldberg and Corey Robin.

Q: Mr. Barlow, tell us about your educational background and how it influenced you as a teacher and as a person.

A: I received my Bachelor's Degree in physics at Holy Cross, and my Master's Degree in education at Harvard. Neither experience did anything for me as a person. I was the same person when I went into college as when I came out. As far as teaching, I knew I was going to be a teacher. The question was whom I could emulate when I became a teacher.

Ralph Beatley, a mathematics professor at Harvard, was worth emulating. This guy knew his stuff cold. One particular instance in his class demonstrates exactly what I mean by education. There was a student who asked me what Ralph Beatley had just said, because he had not heard. I told him, and then Ralph Beatley demanded, "Is there a problem?" Ralph Beatley ran the class. If there was a fire, and the student next to me was burning, I wouldn't say a word.

In my household, no one dared say anything during supper. We had to read books, or newspapers. It was all academics in my household. My mother was a teacher. My parents were interested only in academic excellence.

Q: What made you decide to become a teacher?

A: Well, I believe that teachers are born, not made. To put it in a philosophical context, I subscribe to the theory that everyone who shows up in this world has a vocation. If you fight that feeling, you'll be unhappy. If you don't, you won't be unhappy. It's like the categorical imperative of Kant (the German philosopher of the 19th century): I have to teach.

Q: What do you like most about teaching?

A: That it exists. Miss Gertrude Stein, when asked about her childhood in California, replied, "There is no there there." I think that's a very provocative statement that applies to why I teach. For me, teaching was there.

Q: Why were you chosen Teacher of the Year two years in a row?

A: Well, there are a lot of ancillary reasons that add to the totality. But the main reason is the freshmen, who must be buying what I'm selling. I have four freshman classes and one upper level class. The freshmen must have supported me, and the upperclassmen must recall their earlier experiences.

Q: Do you consider yourself a good teacher?

A: Oh, and how! I consider myself an excellent teacher. It would be obscene to offer something less than first class. You may know what you know, but I know mathematics. Whatever the categorical imperative is for me, has to be done first class.

Q: You seem to intimidate students, Mr. Barlow. If you do it purposely, why? If you don't, why are they intimidated?

A: Well, as far as high school, it's done deliberately. I am entitled to respect. When I was at Harvard, I had to take a biology course in a lecture hall where there were 350 students. When that professor walked into the hall, there was absolute silence. They didn't have to be silent; he would have never known who was talking. They just gave him that kind of respect. Well, if Greeley is supposed to be a preparation for Harvard, Princeton, etc., then I should be accorded that same respect. In my class, I won't even debate the issue. I expect it from the beginning.

Q: What do you think of your students intellectually and as people?

A: Oh, they're first class. As people, well, they're thoroughly delightful. For instance, a few years ago, I was driving through Hawthorne, and I ran out of gas. One of my students was behind me, and stopped and insisted on getting me gas and filling up my car at no cost. The next day in class I was as nasty as I could be. Emotion means nothing to me. All that matters in intellect. Sometimes I get annoyed but not in the everyday sense. I get angered by students who are not responding as intellectually as I expect them to. I demand one hundred percent achievement.

Q: How would you like to be remembered by your students?

A: I would like them to be aware that I provided them with what they needed, whether or not they wanted it. If they want to continue in mathematics, they have the preparation for it. It is better to have it and not need it than to need it and not have it.

Q: Are you deliberately more open and friendly with students who are not in your class?

A: Oh, yes! I accept the New England definition of association between student and teacher: "familiarity breeds contempt." In class, that's my way; outside, I go much further. You can't let students forget their place, and the teacher can't forget his place. I guess you can't teach an old dog new tricks.

Q: Could you tell us a little about what you did before you came to Greeley?

A: I taught in New Hampshire for two years before I came here. I had wanted to teach at the Boston Latin School, but I needed two years of experience before I could apply. I had to take an examination as part of my application and I had the highest score. At the same time, I had been offered a position at Greeley. I spoke to my advisor at Harvard, and he told me that Chappaqua was a small school system. Boston Latin was a big school, very impersonal. Oddly enough, I chose Greeley because it offered personal associations on my terms. For instance, at Boston Latin, if I had a student, I would never see him again after class. At Greeley, I can see students outside of the classroom. That is sort of an oddity because while I try to avoid close associations with students, I chose a school where they could happen.

Q: Why did you choose teaching at a high school over college?

A: I chose high school over college because in the lower grades, a teacher only deals with the personal aspects of education. In college, the emphasis is purely intellectual. At high school, there is the perfect balance between the two.

161

Q: How have you seen Greeley change through the years? Specially, what was your response to the student activism of the sixties?

A: Oh, Greeley hasn't changed. The students are still bright and motivated. I didn't even notice all that fuss about protests. I wasn't affected by all those riots, demonstrations, and flag burnings.

Q: Mr. Barlow, you said last year in the <u>Tribune</u> that your philosophy of education can be found in <u>Alice in Wonderland</u>. Could you please elaborate?

A: Everything that I read in the story is mathematical. Carroll never lets a word or idea go by. There is complete precision and control in the book. Carroll was in fact a mathematician. There's logic in the book, which applies to mathematics. Mathematics is a completely totalitarian subject. There's no democracy in mathematics. That's one thing I like about his country—I can have totalitarianism in my classroom, but outside the classroom, there is democracy.

Q: You are considered to be a very enigmatic person. Could you tell us a little about your interests to shed light on yourself as a person?

A: The one thing that I find most intriguing is that television program <u>Lost in Space</u>. It is thoroughly delightful. I also like <u>Sesame Street</u>. I like to imagine the way kids are reacting to that show and if they're getting what they're supposed to get. Everything I do relates back to education. I also like reading for pleasure. I enjoy good spy novels, and I think I've read every single book written on U.F.O.'s. They're adult fairy tales and, of course, they're all nonsense.

Q: Who is your favorite character in literature?

A: I like Moby Dick, and I don't mean Ahab the captain. That whale personifies so much. Who finally won in the novel? The whale did. I am with the winner. You remember what that coach of the Green Bay Packers said? "Winning isn't everything. It's the only thing."

Q: What character in fiction and in history would you compare yourself to?

A: If I could be anybody, it would be Charles Lutwidge Dodgson, that is, Lewis Carroll. In fiction, I would compare myself to Goethe's Faust. He's concerned with what it's all about.

Q: How have you changed as a teacher since you came here to Greeley?

A: I have become extremely liberal in my extra-curricular associations. I would never have allowed this interview in my first ten years. I was convinced that I was right—I would have had nothing to do with students outside of the classroom.

Q: Do you have any interest in current events?

A: No. If I were to have an interest in current events, it would have to be a first class interest. I don't have time for that. When I retire, I might be able to form an interest in it, but not now.

Q: Do you vote?

A: I used to automatically vote Democrat. However, when Reagan's new tax plan was ratified by both parties, there was no longer any difference between them in my eyes. Democrats become Republicans when they're elected to Congress.

Q: What plans do you have for the immediate future?

A: Very shortly, I'm coming to that time when I have to retire. When I find that my health makes it impossible for me to meet my responsibilities, I will retire. After I retire, I want to go somewhere where there's no snow. Florida, California, or maybe Europe. Then I'll get a job teaching at college, maybe one or two classes a day. I have no outside interests. I plan to stay in education for the rest of my life.

Q: Do you read any newspapers or magazines?

A: The only newspaper I read is the <u>Greeley Tribune</u>.

Q: What do you think of the state of education today?

A: In this community, it's in good hands. So much as been constructed here; it's more than money alone can build.

CHAPTER SIXTEEN

The Glory of Arlington National Cemetery

Mister Barlow had the <u>Tribune</u> photographer meet him in the faculty office of J Building after school. He decided that since this was to be an exercise in vanity and for posterity, he might as well try to look presentable. He went to the extra effort to have his hair cut at the barbershop in Mt. Kisco. He even washed his hair that morning. He wore his customary (for that winter) green striped sweater with his customary (for that and the three previous winters) blue down jacket.

He considered mercilessly berating the photographer as he went about his business as a joke, much as he did a few decades earlier to a yearbook photographer. But doing so would only sabotage his fifteen minutes of fame, so he decided against it.

He had settled on three different poses. He knew the first one was a mistake as soon as the photo was shot. Two fingers on his right cheek, two curled fingers on his mouth, head resting on the chin. But the eyes were wrong. They were open and wide, as if hiding a smile.

The second one was more of a classic pose modeled after Rodin's "Thinker." Thumb on the corner of the mouth, the rest of his hand curled up like a fist, his chin resting on it. The stare was just right, something that said, "I'm always watching you and I'm thinking seriously at the same time."

The final one, which he ended up selecting for the paper, had him resting his head in his hands, elbows on the table, with a look of frustrated and exasperated annoyance on his face.

Mister Barlow was uncomfortable with his enjoyment of the award. Still, it had a hold on him, probably because it was his students that had bestowed the honor. He knew he was a great teacher, but to hear it from his students in such an overt way. . .well, it moved him.

The faculty, of course, did not pay the matter any heed whatsoever. Not a single colleague congratulated him. He didn't really care, but noticed it nonetheless.

So now there was the honor and the photograph in the newspaper. They gave him a strange kind of comfort. There was really only one other thing he truly desired, an honor higher than this one, but it was taking forever to receive. In fact, he wasn't sure if he'd receive it at all. It wasn't given out to just anybody. He went through a lot of red tape to apply for it. He always struggled with the whole idea of it, especially considering the sacrifice he'd made. But he finally came to the conclusion that it was the path that God had chosen for him, and that as God's gift, he should embrace it despite all the suffering he endured as a result.

He received the letter a few weeks later, in the school mailbox where he received all his mail. He tore it open right there in the front office, read it, and then stuffed the letter back in the envelope. He hurried from the room. He had to tell somebody. Who could he share the news with? None of the faculty would appreciate it. None of the students would ever understand, and if he shared it with them, it would shatter another myth.

He went straight to C Building, into Likeu Lee's office. She had taken the job of teaching computers that nobody else had wanted. Mister Barlow always respected her for that. More to the point, she was a kindred spirit. He never could figure out why, but she just felt like someone he could occasionally talk to. And he did. Although every time he did, he would vanish for weeks before appearing in her classroom again.

"Mrs. Lee, I am to be buried at Arlington National Cemetery," he announced.

He felt giddy, as if he were thirteen again, with all the energy and pride of winning a math medal. Mrs. Lee had not even known Mister Barlow to be a veteran, but was even more surprised that he'd chosen her to which he revealed this news.

"How wonderful, Ed. What an honor."

He rambled on in his familiar staccato about how he wasn't sure if it really was ever going to happen. He'd served his country in the war, been wounded in the process, and received a few medals. That alone should have been enough to qualify. But there was always government bureaucracy to deal with. But no matter. He had been granted his wish, one of the few wishes he'd ever really had.

"Well, have a nice day," he blurted out, and left.

Mrs. Lee was very happy for him. She also had no idea exactly which war he had served in to earn him this honor. She had to wait several weeks before he turned up again in her classroom to learn it was World War II.

Part III

THE MISTER BARLOW NOBODY KNEW

INTRODUCTION

"Show me the child at seven and I will show you the man"

- A Jesuit Proverb

Receiving confirmation that Mister Barlow had been a wounded veteran of World War II shattered the persona he'd created. There were obviously many details to seek out about his service, but the idea that he had a rifle in his hand and shot at Nazis some forty years before I'd met him cast him in a new light. This was a man who had seen hardship and death, had probably been close to it himself on more than one occasion.

His classroom demeanor made sense now. He was an educational drill instructor, the steel sergeant assigned to whip us kids into shape for war, to face the mortars and grenades of the most unforgiving battlefield— the real world. One just didn't waltz into Harvard, after all. One had to be trained, armed, and briefed on the enemy. We would be alumni of Barlow's Special Forces Corps, the toughened intellectual elite with a work ethic that would shame our competition. That was how he saw his task. It also made sense that, without a family, the only tangible thing he could leave behind was a gravestone in Arlington emblazoned with his name.

* * *

The story of Mister Barlow's earliest days were provided to me by his sole surviving brother, Albert. Greeley Vice-Principal Larry Breen had done some detective work to find Al following Mister Barlow's death. As executor of the

170

will, he required himself to scour the country for surviving relatives and found Al living with his wife in North Carolina.

Larry put me in contact with Al, who I discovered to be a soft-spoken and gregarious man with an impish laugh and an attention to detail. When I told him I wanted to research his brother's life, he could not have been happier or more grateful. Apparently, Mister Barlow had severed all ties with his three brothers in 1950, shortly after their mother had died. Edwin Barlow had ceased to exist, and never replied to any attempt by the brothers to contact him. Thus, Al was eager to learn all he could about his long-lost kin, beyond the stories and legends that Larry Breen had provided to him.

Al was my window into Mister Barlow's life from birth through age 28. He was the last eyewitness left on earth who could share what Mister Barlow's childhood was like. Here, of course, lay many answers to who Mister Barlow was, and how he developed into the man we all (sort of) knew. Al and I had many lengthy chats on the phone. I gave him lists of questions and asked him to record his answers into a tape recorder. Each memory sparked others, and after many months, a complete picture of life in Depression-era Massachusetts came into focus.

Even more significant, however, was that Al was able to use Mister Barlow's social security number to retrieve his World War II records. This was the code to learning everything about his military service. Certain pieces of information came easily with this magic number. With it, I was able to call the Veterans Administration and learn that he received a 40% disability payment every month, which ran contrary to the myth that he received 100% pay.

For the most part, however, obtaining important details about his service involved a very time consuming reconstruction of history—not just Mister Barlow's, but of his entire unit's.

To begin with, it was only by a stroke of luck that I learned any specifics of Mister Barlow's service. It seemed oddly appropriate that his war records were housed at the Army Personnel Records Center in St. Louis, which suffered a terrible fire in 1970. Thousands of files had been destroyed. I feel almost certain that Mister Barlow willed that fire to happen to frustrate future biographers.

Remarkably, the Army sent along what they did have, which were six pages of documents all of whose edges had been singed or burned away. By some miracle, the most important information remained intact: his troop identification, where and when he'd been wounded, his induction and discharge dates, his rank and serial number, his medals, and where he'd seen action. With the help of the late Colonel Robert Dwan (Ret.), I was able to decipher the Army codes and all of this information. The troop identification turned out to be vital. Using it, I was able to track exactly where Mister Barlow had been in World War II.

Once again, through some mysterious twist of fate, his troop participated in a part of the European Campaign that has been largely ignored by history: the Brittany Campaign. Only one book existed about this part of the war, and even it had few details. History books focused on the fighting immediately following the invasion and the push towards Germany. Securing northwestern France had little interest to historians, despite the fact that General Patton was involved with some of this campaign.

The Brittany Campaign today remains a controversial aspect to the Allied assault on Europe, due to the commitment of valuable troops and supplies following the Normandy invasion. Patton wanted to push into Germany immediately upon his arrival and was prevented from doing so. Nonetheless, some historians postulate that had the Germans been confronted with only minor forces in Brittany, they could have caused tremendous havoc against the Allies in this region and prolonged the war. A few accounts had been written which summarized the campaign in very broad strokes, but offered no details. Extensive internet searches turned up almost nothing. The children of a few veterans had tidbits to offer, but again, there was little in the way of specifics. One soldier in a sister troop managed to collect many photographs of his unit's operations, as well as a few accounts of what the men endured. I used this as a basis for understanding what Mister Barlow had been through.

Even despite the Army's propensity for requiring enormous amounts of paperwork from its units, I still had to turn over every rock to even find the notes known as "After Action Reports" to determine exactly what Mister Barlow's troop did. When I did find them, most of these reports had been photocopied so many times that the type had nearly faded from existence. I spent hours with a magnifying glass reading these reports, and had to call upon all my talents with syntax to fill in sentences that had been truncated by the poor copying.

Finally, I was able to obtain rosters. Some of these had not been updated in ten years and many veterans had since died. Other rosters were just plain incorrect. But I finally found a few men who were in Mister Barlow's troop, and enough were still alive to attend a reunion every few years. Almost nobody recalled Mister Barlow, but a few did, and I either got eyewitness accounts of Mister Barlow's actions, or first-hand accounts of their own. Together, it was enough to extrapolate what life in Mister Barlow's troop was like. Time was not always friendly to me, though. On several occasions, some of these heroic soldiers died before I was able to place follow-up questions to them.

The final, most important answers about Mister Barlow's life were finally available to me.

CHAPTER SEVENTEEN

Young Edwin Barlow

Once again, Edwin's father did not come home from work. The family had long grown accustomed to this, and when they sat down to dinner, his absence was always the elephant in the room. Nobody spoke about it, yet everybody knew what it meant, and they all tried to blot out what the rest of the night would bring as a result.

Edwin took his customary dinner table seat by the window. His Ma, Agnes, had managed to get a day-old chicken from the butcher and roasted it in the oven. Although Danny was two years older than Edwin, he wasn't enthusiastic about saying grace, so Edwin always got the duty. It was fine by him. He enjoyed it. The family dove into the meal, supplemented with potatoes from the market and wild blueberries.

This was the season for blueberries. The four boys often ran to the end of their street, a dead end where a they negotiated a steep embankment before reaching the bounty. They rumbled back down the hill, hands and tongues stained blue, and dashed back to 40 Everett Street with a wooden bucket full of fruit.

Albert, the third son and three years behind Edwin, slurped every ounce of meat off his chicken leg. The legs were his favorite. The dark meat had more flavor. After he'd cleaned off the bone, he tossed it on the floor to the bulldog.

The poor animal had sat patiently in the corner, desperately eyeing both the roast chicken, as well as the nearby cat, hoping for a bite of either. He'd never have a chance with the cat, though, and he knew it. All he'd ever done was kill cats. There wasn't a cat to be found in the neighborhood.

Then, Ma bought that orange and white cat home to handle the mouse problem. Nobody knew what gymnastics she had performed, but she made that bulldog accept the cat as part of the family. That was Agnes. She ran the household and made sure everybody knew the rules.

The dog clomped his teeth around the chicken bone, and trotted out the front door to sulk.

Edwin raced through the meal. He was hungry—they were all hungry because it was the Depression—but he was more interested in the apple pie cooling on the windowsill. Once a week, fifty-two weeks a year, Ma baked that pie. She collected the apples all week, one by one, picking up the bruised ones that had fallen off the grocer's cart and paying the discounted price. Sugar was easy to come by, and very cheap, and the pie crust was her mother's recipe.

Agnes knew the pie was Edwin's favorite. When Edwin came home from school, there was no better greeting than the aroma of fresh baked apple pie. Very few things ever tempted him, but on many occasions he thought about taking that pie and eating it himself in some alley. He'd tell Ma that someone must have stolen it from the windowsill. He not only knew better, but knew it would put him in heaps of trouble with both her and Pa.

The pie and blueberries sweetened an otherwise lousy evening. The boys roughhoused before bed. Ma read stories to Al and Dave. Edwin had outgrown that ritual, but still longed for his mother's lap. He peeked into his parents' bedroom, where Ma sat with Dave, reading nursery rhymes. Dave lay his head against her bosom as she read him the nonsensical ditties. His eyelids drooped. He'd be asleep soon.

Edwin watched his mother. If God sent the Four Horsemen upon his family, he knew exactly where to go, where no demon could ever touch him, where neither famine nor disease could afflict him.

175

Edwin went to bed in the same room as Billy. In the next room, Ma lay the sleeping Dave in his bed, pulled the covers up to his chin, and kissed Al goodnight. The house was quiet. Billy went right to sleep. Edwin lay awake, though, waiting for his father to come home. He would be awoken by the shouts anyway, so it never made sense to try and sleep. Sometimes, though, the day's excesses defeated him and he drifted into a light doze and dreamed. The dream, unfortunately, was always the same and it always upset him.

A man with thinning gray hair, wearing a tattered green jumpsuit, shoveled coal into a furnace. The room was small with steep pipes running overhead. The furnace roared, its fire gobbled up the oxygen. There was a single light bulb overhead, swinging from a single electrical wire, buffeted by the hot air blowing from the furnace. The man's face was beaded with sweat and black with soot. He could have been a coal miner. He shut the furnace door and set the shovel against the wall. He reached up and steadied the swaying light, then moved to check the temperature gauge on the boiler. The needle was well into the red, and before the man could take another breath, the boiler exploded. The man's body was blown to smithereens, as if a grenade had been thrust into his gut. His body erupted into ten different directions, arms and legs separating from the torso, head popping high.

Edwin woke up, and wanted to tell himself that it was only a dream, but it was all too real. The man was Edwin's grandfather, his Pa's father. He had been a janitor of a large apartment building not too far away and that was exactly how he'd died. Pa took over his post, and the boys often helped him take out the garbage or tend the furnace. The roaring fires terrified Edwin. He never went in the boiler room alone, usually dragging an unwilling Al to help. He could never get the image of his grandfather being utterly destroyed out of his mind. He didn't like to look at the fire in the furnace, either. It made him think it was a doorway to Hell.

The shouting began in the other room. Billy woke up and then heard Al and Dave stir next door. Edwin sighed. His Pa, William, never failed to come home in a bad mood, and was almost always drunk. Prohibition hadn't stopped him, either. He just went to his favorite speakeasy to drink and gamble away his wages. Rumor had it that William played poker there and, being an easy target, the owners and patrons made sure he never won. That meant coming home late with empty pockets, but filled with both drink and anger.

And boy oh boy, did Pa have a temper. The screaming between him and Ma scared the boys to death. Pa had never hit Ma nor any of the boys, but everyone felt that it could happen. They'd made a pact to protect Ma at all costs, and that if Pa ever laid a hand on her while they were home, they'd come running and fight their father for all they were worth. They knew they could do it because he'd be drunk and couldn't handle all of them at once. They all prayed this would never happen and, so far, God listened.

So the boys listened to the arguments. When Pa shouted, Edwin could almost feel Satan in their home. Pa's voice had an unnatural quality. He could raise it far above that of his Ma, and his deep and resonant tones could vibrate furniture. Sometimes he would hiss, and Edwin imagined the Devil's forked tongue licking out from Pa's lips. They all knew the voice because they'd all been on the end of many verbal reprimands. The whole neighborhood knew when William Barlow was upset with his boys.

The argument ended the way they usually did. The screaming reached a crescendo and then both parents went silent. Then they heard Ma's firm, strong voice. She shamed Pa, and because he was so tired, he brushed past her and collapsed onto the bed. Within minutes he was asleep.

The boys, thankful they did not have to intervene, went back to bed. Edwin, as always, kneeled by his bedside and prayed. When he did, he sometimes felt himself levitating. He always kept his eyes closed, but knew for certain that his knees were no longer on the floor, that God was lifting him a little bit so Edwin could be just a little bit closer to Him. He always felt better after he prayed.

Then, and only then, could he sleep.

CHAPTER EIGHTEEN

Edwin and the Church

Ma and the boys went to Sacred Heart Church every Sunday. Pa never bothered. He'd never been a religious man and there was always work to do at the apartment building.

Edwin could not think of a better place than church, save his mother's lap. He was an altar boy, and knew it made his mother proud. He liked the smell of incense, and it made him feel pleasantly woozy. The sweet aroma filled his lungs, chasing away the dusty, sleepy feeling of the church. The priest's voice would echo in his head. Edwin would look up at the crucifix and it would seem so monumental, as if it were reaching up to Heaven itself. It never felt imposing, though. It felt more like God was so big, he filled the church and Edwin stood by his knee. Edwin would catch his mother's eye from time to time and she would smile at him. Her beaming face made his heart soar.

After the service, Edwin opened the collection envelopes in the rectory, diligently counted every penny and made an accurate report to Father Don. Al had once asked if he'd ever been tempted to take just a little for himself, and Edwin shot him a look that cowed his brother for a week. He would never do such a thing. He could only imagine what Ma would think of him.

Then there were the priests. He needed them. To violate that trust would put him right back out in the cold. He'd become a real fixture at the church, spent some of his free time there, and talked a lot to each priest. Recently, he'd even asked about becoming part of the clergy.

179

*　*　*

Father Don took particular interest in Edwin. They had long talks about God, what it meant to be a priest, and the devotion it took. Father Don never pushed him, but spoke freely of the benefits of being a clergyman.

Of particular interest to Father Don was Edwin's honesty and earnestness. He'd heard many children talk about becoming a priest with the innocence all children have. But Edwin was different. Father Don had seen the pattern before, and had fit it himself: Difficult home, poverty, a strong mother to guide and protect, and an intangible but genuine interest in helping others. Edwin inherited that from Agnes. She was known across several neighborhoods for mending and sewing garments and refusing to accept payment. Despite the Depression, despite the desperate need for any mother to collect money, she stood fast by her Christian beliefs.

Edwin admired this so much that he took it to the next level. The boy showed more interest in helping people than playing in the street. He tended very much to his knitting, was a superior student, and never complained. He had a giving heart. He showed far more interest in the church than the regular pasttimes of boys. He liked baseball, but not enough to go to a game. He liked popular music, but not enough to make it a hobby. He played checkers and yo-yo's and street games, but none seemed to ignite any passion in him.

In addition, the boy was brilliant. Absolutely brilliant. He learned the entire catechism, in Latin, at age eight. He was also mindful of sin. Edwin had shared an account of his visit to a magic show, and how he'd covered Al's eyes when a scantily clad women came onto the stage to be sawed in half.

Edwin and the Church

Father Don saw himself in Edwin, and spent extra time with the boy, hearing him out, listening closely for the telltale signs of a young man who's heard the Call. There were signs of a potentially celibate lifestyle in Edwin.

He recalled that Al had told Father Don about this one teenage girl. "She was the oldest of this one family, and she was a real beauty. I just thought she was something else. So one day she came to me and said something cryptic like, 'Your brother Edwin is really smart, isn't he?' And I got the feeling that this girl really had the hots for Edwin, and that she was looking for me to tell him, 'Hey, Bernice needs help with her algebra.' But Edwin took this literally! He goes to her and says, 'I understand you need help with your lessons,' and never returned her flirting."

After a few years, Father Don was convinced Edwin had indeed heard the Call. He met with the priests and talked seriously about helping Edwin along this path. God would gladly welcome this young man to become his servant here on Earth.

CHAPTER NINETEEN

Pa is Dead

Ma did not know what to make of the letter that arrived from Detroit. At first, she knew it couldn't be true. It just wasn't possible. She inspected the envelope for signs of a hoax. The letterhead seemed genuine, but people had ways of faking that kind of thing.

The letter was also much too long. The police never wrote such long letters. She went across the street to church and asked to see Father Don. She was gone about an hour, and then came back home to the boys, who had sat quietly in the tiny living room waiting for her. They were worried. As soon as she returned, she secreted herself in the bedroom for two long hours.

Then, she sat them all down at the kitchen table.

Edwin knew something was very wrong because his mother never looked pale. She always had color in her face, even after arguments with Pa. Now, there would be no more arguments.

Pa was dead.

The letter from the Detroit police said they had found him in a gutter and rushed him to a hospital, where he died shortly thereafter of a cerebral hemorrhage.

Ma really didn't believe the letter, even though Father Don said it was genuine. The letter said Pa's body would be shipped home, but Ma didn't believe he was dead or that any body would be shipped home. Then they'd all see that this had just been a mistake. She told them to get washed up for dinner, and prepared the meal. The boys looked at each other. They did as they were told and washed up for dinner, which was eaten in utter silence.

Afterwards, Dave and Billy went out to play. Al sat down with Edwin, who'd retired to his bedroom to read.

Pa had gone to Detroit to live with his sister, and to look for work at one of the auto plants. He'd been fired from his job as building janitor, and then again from Smith & Wesson, all due to his drinking. The boys were, at first, ecstatic about his departure. There was no more fighting or shouting, no more being dressed down, and no more worrying about Ma. But when the letter came, Edwin knew that Al felt guilty. He knew how Al felt—that Pa wasn't all that bad, that he did some good things, and that Ma did love him, after all. He knew that Al was angry because his three brothers just didn't seem to care about Pa dying. Edwin said that since Ma wasn't upset, why should they be?

Al thought about it, thought about why nobody seemed to care. He realized that they had not come home and found Pa laid out in the middle of the room. He had died in a whole other city, days before they ever found out. He thought everyone would've felt differently if he had died right in front of them.

Plus, the way they had been told just didn't seem right. He bet that nobody in the family really believed Pa was dead because people just don't have those hemorrhage things out of the blue. Al just didn't believe what the police had said. He knew his Pa had probably gone drinking and gambling, flashed some money, got followed out and was mugged and got his head smashed in. He brought it on himself, there was no doubting that.

Heck, even when Ma went to the morgue to identify the body, she still refused to believe it. She went on about Pa having a mole on his arm that the dead man didn't have. It was a useless argument because, of course, it was Pa.

Gradually, Al knew that everyone had accepted Pa's death. Nobody ever spoke about Pa, about him being away or when he was coming back. He just knew that everyone understood and decided there was nothing to talk about. He could hear Ma sobbing at night sometimes, so that's how he figured out that she knew the truth.

The pressing concern was that, even though Pa was never mentioned, they all knew there would be no money coming from him anymore. Ma had always insisted that "welfare" was a dirty word and she would never allow her family to live that way. Something had to be done.

At this point, Billy was twenty, and old enough to join Roosevelt's Civilian Conservation Corps. The program was becoming weak after a full decade of tremendous success. Still, it paid thirty dollars a week, which Billy sent back home to Ma. He was assigned to a camp that built fire roads and planted trees in Massachusetts. Al and Dave took what work they could find in between their schooling.

Once Edwin graduated from high school, he got work at Smith & Wesson to help out Ma. Al knew Edwin didn't want to work. He wanted to enter the seminary, but there just wasn't any money for it. He still attended church regularly, and even went to Mass every single morning.

Father Don had told Edwin that God's plan was not always clear, and that right now He needed Edwin to help his mother. Al felt bad for his older brother. Sure, they were all having tough times, but he knew Edwin was cut out for better things and he had evidence to prove it. He had found a student-created summary of school events of the 1939-40 school year. It lay on Edwin's bed the day he graduated. In it, Edwin was listed as having made the honor roll and was named as one of four "Best Boy students," one of four "Most Dependable Boys," and as "Most Generous Boy." He was also mentioned as being the boy with "The Most Missionary Spirit," one of the five

"Most Thoughtful Boys," and one of the three boys who had "Done the Most for the Class." Also in this summary, class member Robert Fay wrote a short essay entitled "Class Prophecy," in which he imagined what students would be doing in 1950. He described an operating room in an American hospital where stood, among other alumni, "Dr. Edwin Barlow, busy preparing a hypo for the patient." In the class' "last will and testament," it was announced what each student would leave to the community. "Edwin Barlow leaves his missionary spirit to anyone who has hopes of invading the Chinese and Japanese war front on an errand of good deeds."

Al was flabbergasted at the praise heaped on his brother. All those accomplishments, and Edwin was working in a gun factory. It just wasn't right. Yet Edwin never complained. He never said a single word about him being unhappy, and that was because he liked helping Ma. But that was Edwin. Nothing could drag him away from Ma. Even if did become a priest, he knew he'd have his congregation right across the street if he could.

CHAPTER TWENTY

Drafted

The draft letter was not unexpected. Billy had already been swept into the service, and Al had joined the Navy because he'd heard it was the safest branch. The worst part about being drafted was that Edwin wouldn't be able to help out Ma. He'd be able to send home his pay, but he'd be so far away from her. There was an out, though he wasn't sure he should attempt it. Still, he felt in his heart that he might qualify, so he went to see Father Don.

The tenth commandment had multiple interpretations. Some believed it meant that one should never kill another man, regardless of circumstance. Some believed it was acceptable to God if killing happened during a just war, such as the war on Hitler. Edwin asked Father Don what he thought about it, and Father Don put the question back to him, "What does God tell you?"

Edwin knew killing was wrong, period. God had commanded it, and making excuses for wars was not something God would do. Father Don said he would write the draft board and vouch for Edwin as a Conscientious Objector, if that was what Edwin wanted.

He told Father Don, "God wants me to become a priest. I know that. I could never be a priest if I was willing to kill another man, no matter what the reason."

Father Don nodded in agreement, but Edwin had already heard about life as a Conscientious Objector. For starters, CO's did not just walk off into normal civilian life. They had to perform services for local communities. For these services, CO's did not receive any pay whatsoever.

186

This would make things all the tougher on Ma. At least in the army, he could send his pay home.

As a CO, he would have no choice about where he was sent. He might end up a medic on the front lines, and not have a gun, even to defend himself. He knew nothing about medicine, though the prospect of helping wounded men did stir something in him. Still, that would send him overseas, again without pay.

Worst of all, though, were the stories he'd heard about CO's. He had been called "yellow" many times for not having volunteered. He'd heard that an entire town in New Hampshire burned down because nobody was willing to call for help from the nearby CO camp. They'd been trained as firefighters, but the citizens preferred to let their town burn down rather than use the CO's. Edwin was afraid of being branded the rest of his life.

Father Don reminded him that Jesus experienced the same persecution, and He would look well upon any man who took the path of pacifism.

The words floated in and out of Edwin's ears. He'd already made his decision. As awful as killing was, the Conscientious Objector path would make life much harder on Ma. As a soldier, there was no guarantee he would see combat, either. Maybe he'd be stationed Stateside. He might even be able to see Ma on weekends.

The more he thought about it, the less frightening it became. Father Don understood. He pulled his chair closer to Edwin's and looked him hard in the eyes. "If this is to be your choice, then you must commit completely to it, as you did with us here. There will come a time when many young men will depend upon you to do your duty, when their lives and yours will be at stake. At that moment, you must do what you will be trained to do."

Edwin realized that he could not join the Army, and perform at less than one-hundred percent, anyway. A Barlow never did anything halfway.

CHAPTER TWENTY-ONE

Boot Camp & The *Queen Mary*

Edwin had thought that nobody could hold a candle to his Pa when it came to dressing someone down. That changed when Sgt. Cerrone began training his unit. Pa never got in your face the way Sarge did. Edwin watched a lot of his comrades tremble, stutter, or outright wet themselves when Sarge read them the riot act. Edwin was used to this kind of treatment, so when Sarge lit into him at point blank range for dropping his rifle during march, Edwin just stood quietly. When Sarge was done, Edwin shouted back, "Sir, yes, sir!" and that was that. Sarge seemed both pleased and shocked at how unflappable Edwin had been.

It was a strange life at Fort Devens boot camp. Everything Edwin had been accustomed to had been stripped away from him, even his hair. There was no Ma to run home to each night. He missed her terribly, even though she was only fifty miles away. The eats were at least more plentiful here, if not tastier. There was no library to whittle away the hours at, nor time to read books anyway.

The physical demands were tough. All that running for mile after mile, wriggling under barbed wire, leaping through obstacle courses while Sarge screamed like a maniac. There was, however, something attractive about the push for perfection. The way Sarge inspected their uniforms and bunks, the way he insisted a rifle be held, the way to speak and respond— Edwin admired the discipline and precision.

Every day was the same. He liked the structure. It reminded him of all the rituals he'd learned in church. He even got to like Sarge a little bit, liked the firmness with which he controlled his troops. Edwin understood that all this training was arranged so they wouldn't get killed, and he appreciated Sarge's devotion to that task.

His troop was filled with a lot of boisterous Boston boys. Although most were two or three years younger, even Edwin's contemporaries lacked maturity. They all swore too much, talked about things his family never discussed in public, and spoke disrespectfully of ladies and girlfriends.

Edwin was the quietest of the bunch, and he thought that only five or six others were church-going folk like himself. Nobody paid him any mind until he began to excel on the firing range. "Outstanding, Barlow!," were the words most often heard from Sarge during target practice. Edwin had surprised himself at his skill with a gun. He had a steady hand and perfect eyesight. He also felt an inner calm when he had the rifle in his hand. It made him uncomfortable to hold the thing at first, but Father Don's words echoed in his head. "You must commit completely."

Sarge molded plenty of these reckless youths into fine soldiers. Some even had a natural affinity for it. They just liked performing when told. Others were very competitive and wanted to be the best. Sarge could tell who they were and egged them on. Edwin just liked boot camp because he knew what was expected of him, just like back home, and he was eager to please. So he did.

In fact, by the end of boot camp, Sarge called him one of the best soldiers in the unit and awarded him the top level of three rifle badges, "Expert." He wasn't ever really scared during the whole thing, except towards the end. Sarge had some of the NCO's throw dynamite gourds near them while they were crawling under barbed wire in full pack. Live ammunition was used. The sound of every gunshot made his heart leap. He knew that here in camp nobody would get shot or blown up, and that this was just preparing them for the worst, but when something exploded close by, it was hard not to be scared.

After running the drill several times, Edwin got used to the sounds, stayed focused, and kept his eye on the finish line. That must be the trick, he thought. Just put all of it out of your mind. He thought he could do that if and when the time came for real.

He finished boot camp just in time for Thanksgiving, and the boys all got three-day passes. Edwin appeared proudly before Ma in his uniform, and she doted on him that whole weekend. They hadn't gotten their orders yet, he told her, but Sarge expected they would soon. He kissed her on the cheek at the end of the weekend, and was already missing both Ma and his own warm bed as he hitched his way back to camp.

Edwin's unit caught a string of good luck. They stayed at Fort Devens for three more months, kicking around, waiting for orders. They didn't have to do much. Sarge had moved on to train new recruits, so another staff sergeant took over and ran them through marching and rifle drills to keep them sharp. Edwin thought he might be able to make it through his entire two-year tour without ever seeing combat. Even if he did, he felt pretty ready for it. Sarge had taught them well. None of the other boys seemed worried, but rather, full of bluster. How bad could it be, anyway?

The word came down in mid-February, and soon thereafter they were all sent via train to Camp Shanks, about 30 miles north of New York City. Before leaving, Sarge addressed them one final time.

He said some of them might not be coming back, that there will be many times they'll be in the thick of it, with a hell of a lot of action going on around them. In that moment, not even God, their mothers, or their fear will get them out alive. The only thing that would save their ass was their training, so they damn well better remember it or he'd see them in the Great Hereafter and let them have it.

On February 29, Edwin boarded the Queen Mary in New York City, along with thirteen thousand other soldiers and crew. He marched through the cramped passageways and stowed his duffel bag with thousands of others, then made his way to a massive room where the bunks were housed. Edwin couldn't believe his eyes—row after row of bunks, as far as he could see. It took him almost a half hour just to jostle and squeeze his way to his bunk. He passed the time during logjams by glancing over the ship's Standing Orders, which explained emergency procedures should the ship be attacked.

He finally located his bunk, and was about to drop onto the lower one, but stopped. He thought about the size of the boat, the rough sea, and that very few of these boys (himself included) had probably ever gotten their sea legs. The likelihood that vomit from any of the surrounding bunks would fly onto him seemed high, not to mention that there was only eighteen inches He clambered, with difficulty, onto the top bunk and tried to relax. They would not ship out until tomorrow, given the sheer enormity of the troop movement.

He knew these next six days would be a bore, and he was not disappointed. Even though the ship flew across the ocean at twenty-six knots, easily able to outrun any German naval vessel, time seemed to drag on forever. There were few diversions. Meals were seved twice a day, but Edwin avoided them after the second day. The ballrooms had been converted into mess halls, and they served kidney stew for breakfast. Edwin didn't mind the meal so much, until they hit rough seas and everyone got seasick. After that, Edwin followed the example of one comrade and stuck to candy bars.

The Daily Orders announced all activities. A band might be playing topside, or a film would be showing somewhere in his section. He took part in these festivities, along with attending Mass, whenever possible. He even participated in impromptu calesthenics exercises up top. He did this primarily to escape the unbiquitous odor of smoke, vomit, and thousands of unbathed men. He'd obviously foreseen the seasickness problem, and there was no room for either showers or water for them. Space was at such a premium that even the bar in the tourist-class ballroom had become a pharmacy, stocked with pharmaceuticals.

He hoped for warm weather, but knew that early March in the North Atlantic would not yield such a bonanza . During such weather, the men got to sleep on deck two nights of the six. It would've been nice. He could imagine going to sleep while hearing the ocean slosh peacefully against the boat, and he could stare up at the stars.

Instead, he had to endure the bunks. Besides the awful stink, there was the pervasive chatter of soldiers engaged in gambling. Cards and dice were everywhere, depsite being illegal. Everytime Edwin dozed off, he was startled awake by a cheer as someone hit their point in craps.

Mostly, he had time to think. He wondered why God had sent him this decision to make. He wondered if God really had intended him to break His commandment and take another life. He wondered if he would have to do that. He'd been in the service five months already and hadn't fired a shot. Maybe it was a test, like God gave to Abraham. Could he take another man's life, if told to by God? Was it a test to see if he would join the Army, only to have God stay his hand at the critical moment?

He stared up at the ceiling of the cavernous ship, tried to shut out his surroundings and most nights he drifted off to sleep, dreaming of the waves lapping against the ship's hull.

CHAPTER TWENTY-TWO

England and France

The last thing Edwin expected his service to be was boring. But boring it was. And how. Once he arrived in Garouch, Scotland, he was shuttled down to Plymouth, where he observed other troops preparing for an invasion. There were plenty of rumors about when and where the invasion would take place. Edwin didn't much care. He just didn't want to be a part of it, and since he wasn't being trained for it, he assumed he wouldn't be included. He had originally been assigned to the 15th Cavalry Group, but a few days after arriving, these 1700 men were reorganized into the 15th and 17th Calvary Squadrons. Each squadron consisted of about 750 men, plus another hundred or so stationed at their headquarters. Each squadron was further subdivided into three reconnaissance squadrons (troops A, B, and C), one troop of assault gunnery (Troop E), and a Light Tank Company (Troop F). Each troop had about 150 men. Each troop consisted of about four platoons. Each platoon had about four squads of about ten men each.

Edwin was assigned to troop B, and felt thankful to see familiar faces. Although he really hadn't made any friends, he preferred to be with those he'd trained with. Somehow he felt he could count on them more. Over the next three months, his training became more specific. They were told that following the invasion they would enter France as a reconnaissance unit. A sergeant laid out traditional cavalry tactics for the men, much of it went right through the less attentive soldiers, but Edwin absorbed it all.

Initially the cavalry's missions were to provide surprise attacks into enemy territory, for recon and screening covering of larger forces. He was told that the elements of a recon squad could move as much as 180 miles in a single day in open country, though everyone was skeptical that they'd ever achieve that. It also gave some of the boys false hope that the Nazis would be sufficiently cleaned out prior to their arrival that such ground could truly be covered.

One fact about being recce cavalry was heartening to everyone. Troop B's captain, George Berlin, told them they were damn lucky not to be infantry. Those boys had to keep coming and coming, getting their asses shot. They might suffer seventeen percent casualties. But recce had it on them. Whereas an infantryman knew he was going to be fighting, a recce man had no idea what he'd be facing when he jumped off. If the recce did meet something, the cavalry would rarely take it on, unless it was small enough to brush aside. They might suffer eight or ten percent casualties because they go around the big obstacles, whereas the infantry is committed, and they know they're going to fight. In the cavalry, there are good days and bad days. The days of an infantryman are always bad.

Edwin actually had a little bit of fun during training here. It was almost like capture the flag, which he sometimes played back home. Captain Berlin trained them in diversionary maneuvers, how to guard the rear in the event of a retreat, and how to make wide flanking movements to cause confusion. They were told that, besides doing recon, they would have to move on foot, to help fill gaps between large units, as well as protect and execute lines of communication between troops. Edwin needed to understand how cavalry tactics worked in his head. He needed to see the forest for the trees, because if things got bad, he wanted basic concepts upon which he could fall back.

When it came right down to it, Edwin thought of recon cavalry tactics as being the glue on two blocks of wood. He thought of the two blocks of wood as the opposing armies. As the two blocks come together, the recons are the first to meet. As the two blocks press together, the glue pushes out to the sides. The cavalry would always be found out on the flanks when the two blocks came together. When one side is defeated and pulls back, and the blocks are pulled apart, the glue sticks. The defeated recon cavalry earns its pay by covering the retreat of their block. The winning recon keeps in contact. They don't lose contact when the other side retreats.

With that sorted out, Edwin could concentrate on the finer points of his maneuvers. He later learned that the Indians used these same tactics to do in the unfortunate General Custer, and was used by the Union to defeat General Lee at Appomattox. He liked the precedent.

There wasn't much free time, but he spent what he had by writing home to Ma, going to chapel, and doing a little sightseeing. Gasoline was being conserved, and since he couldn't drive anyway, he would grab a bicycle and ride into one of the little English towns. He felt out of place among the British. Although they were very polite folk who showed great appreciation to the Americans, their accent and manners intimidated him. He found a little teahouse in one small village, where some people were enjoying their afternoon tea. Even out here in the country, the men and ladies were well attired, with perfectly folded napkins resting in their laps, and nary a crumb to be seen on the table from the various cookies they nibbled at ever-so-properly. He took a seat at a table, was greeted warmly, and served an Earl Grey with milk. If only Ma could see him now. He felt like a prince, sitting upright in his chair, napkin across his lap, being certain to sip, and not gulp, his tea.

This lifestyle moved him. He liked it. He wanted to somehow incorporate it into his own. He knew it would not be possible now, but perhaps someday, he could feel like royalty.

It was a welcome respite from the food the Army provided. Most of the men were eating "K" rations, which came in a tin the size of a Crackerjack box. There was usually some potted ham in there, and maybe some scrambled eggs with it. There'd be powdered coffee, which Edwin only drank because he grew bored of water. The coffee also helped perk him up when he faced some of the longer days. An article in <u>Stars and Stripes</u> diplomatically stated that, "The Army's emergency rations may not stack up with a filet mignon upon a field of french fries, but they have their points all right. . .our field rations are the highest octane stuff ever devised to fit under a soldier's belt." There was widespread agreement about this statement for a week or so, but after eating the same thing for six weeks straight, everyone started spending their money on the local pubs and cafes. Edwin would only occasionally allow himself that luxury, instead sending most of his pay home.

When June rolled around, incessant chatter and rumor swept through Edwin's unit. Word was that the expected invasion of France would soon begin. Everything was still top secret, but the 17th was moved to Portsmouth. Security was tight. Edwin was given guard duty the night of June 3rd, watching over soldiers from the 1st Infantry Division, to make sure they didn't leave camp. The soldiers were all in their bunkhouses, the entire camp surrounded by a high wire fence. He thought it odd that he should be in this position. What if someone decided they wanted to leave camp and head into town? What if he had to confront them? His orders were to shoot anyone that failed to respond to warnings. Could he shoot another American? He pushed the thought out of his mind. The night was quiet. Nobody would run. Still, he could feel a tension. He smelled both fear and apprehension in the camp. His throat had tightened a little bit, as if expecting some terrible cloud to pass overhead and rain fire and brimstone down upon them all.

"Hey, buddy"

The voice startled Edwin. He'd been so deep in thought he didn't hear the soldier walk up to the fence behind him.

"Got any smokes?"

Edwin never smoked, but always carried a few because he knew others did, and would appreciate a freebie. He fished in his shirt pocket.

"So whaddaya think?"

Edwin found the cigarette and handed it to the soldier. He could barely make him out in the darkness. When the soldier fired up a match for his cigarette, the momentary flash of light illuminated him. He was maybe 22, with movie-star features, blue eyes, a lick of black hair swooping across his forehead. The match fizzled out and his face vanished.

Edwin asked, "What do I think about what?"

"The invasion. Got a bet with the guys. I say Norway. They say Yugoslavia."

He let out a long breath of smoke, and it swirled upwards, catching a hint of a distant worklight.

"Can't say. France is closer, though."

"Yeah, but the Krauts are expecting that." His voice was confident and assured.

"Maybe that's why we'll go there."

"The old double-cross. Yeah, I get ya. Hey, what's your name?"

"Barlow. From Massachusetts". That's how everyone answered that question. The first question after your name was where you were from, so everybody provided both. It was always comforting to hear that someone was from your state. They all wanted company. They all wanted the comfort of knowing someone from home was with them.

"Evans. North Carolina. Big Red One." He pointed to his arm patch. Sure enough, the familiar grey patch with a big red number "1" was there. Edwin knew this, of course.

A flash of distant lightning lit both faces for a moment. That's when Edwin saw Evans' blue eyes more clearly. There was fear in them, betraying the complacency of his voice. Thunder rolled across the countryside.

"Everyone thinks it's tomorrow but I gotta tell ya, smells like rain. No way do we go in the rain. Hey, what are you? Infantry?"

"Cav. 17th Recce".

"Lucky. I almost volunteered, you know, but just as I was about to, the draft notice came. I wanted to fly a Spitfire, now I'm down here."

A cold wind picked up. Another burst of lightning. Edwin really didn't know what to say.

"Not that I'm scared, right? I'm ready for anything. It's just that if they put us in those boats, the assault boats? Don't put me in the front. Door drops open on the beach and..." His voice trailed off as he blew out another puff of smoke. "Anyways, it'll be Norway. You watch."

He stubbed out the butt.

"Thanks again, Barlow."

"You're welcome."

Evans turned and sauntered back towards his barracks. He jammed his hands in his pockets, pressing his arms against his body to fight off the cold.

The thunder roared as Evans merged with the night.

On the 5th, Edwin and his troop were moved to Portland Island, where they helped the 1st Amphibious Brigade load their assault craft. Despite all the activity, an eerie calm had settled over the men. These men had seen battle, he'd been told, but that didn't make them any less afraid.

He thanked God his unit hadn't been chosen for the invasion. The word was that the French beaches were heavily fortified. He thought about Evans and where he might be placed.

The word came down as the sun began to set. The 17th got onto a train headed for Trowbridge, well inland and far from any kind of channel crossing. Edwin breathed a sigh of relief. They ate their rations and turned in. Nobody spoke much.

Tomorrow there would be news.

*   *   *

Edwin had always had a singular image of France that he carried with him in his memory. It was from a painting by an artist whose name always escaped him, and it depicted the Eiffel Tower and the Seine on a sunny day, with people walking in the streets, in suits and long dresses.

The France he saw on July 15th of 1944 bore no resemblance to that image. The town of St. Mére-Eglisse, about eight miles from Utah Beach, was a shell. Most of the buildings still stood, but a lot of them had been chipped away by machine gun fire, some had gaping holes, and rubble of every conceivable variety was strewn in the streets. The few trees that had lined the perimeter of the town square had been smashed to pieces. The town smelled of dust and smoke. Everything was dirty. Edwin found himself lost in the midst of several hundred soldiers who had congregated in the square, awaiting orders. A tank rumbled past him, followed by a convoy of jeeps. To his left, a group of ten French civilians carried wood towards a house. Three other men were trying to piece a house back together. A squadron of Americans filed past, many of them laughing, while on the other side of the square, a Frenchman offered Edwin's sergeant a cigarette. One café had managed to open and some waiters doted on the Americans, offering what few glasses of wine they had, and feeding them tiny plates of bread and cheese. Whenever he saw someone from the 1st Infantry, he asked about Evans. Nobody knew him.

So far, nothing was what he had expected. He'd been in the Service nine-and-a-half months, and hadn't seen a single second of combat. If this was representative of the state France was in, then he doubted the Eiffel Tower would look as majestic as it had in the painting. Most importantly, he hadn't seen anybody wounded or dead.

Troop B rode over to Les Peux the next day, assigned to protect the peninsula from airborne or sea attack. Most of the soldiers breathed a sigh of relief at the assignment, as word had spread that a German attack via the Channel was highly unlikely. Nevertheless, Edwin kept up his guard. He felt that some of his comrades were getting sloppy in their vigilance. Too many of them walked out in the open for too long. Snipers were rare, but the danger always existed. He worried about these men, about how they'd do in combat. These boys were always the most reckless in everyday life. They were the womanizers, the loudmouths, and the boozers. He hoped they'd live up to their boastfulness, but he knew from experience and the Bible, that this kind never fared well. He preferred to keep a low profile, both among his comrades, and when on duty. He always made sure to find cover when he had to be outside. The Army had given them helmets for a reason. You stick your head out too far and it gets shot off. Whenever he could, he stayed in the jeep he was assigned, because it afforded both cover and the ability to hightail it out of there.

There was a lot of discussion about chain of command. They joked about a boxing match between General Patton and the commander of the 15th Cavalry Group, Colonel John "Eyeball" Reybold. He had been so named because every time he'd go over a hill, he'd puff his eye up, shouting "Faster! Faster!" They made merciless sport of him, and one fellow did an excellent impression of the man. "I want no weaklings in combat," he'd say. When something positive happened, the result of man or machine or fate, Eyeball would blurt out, "WON-derful."

Edwin watched the proceedings with a little bit of amusement. A smile was hard to find for him, but he had come to enjoy some of the men. They were mostly good kids at heart, and before reaching France a few would pull the occasional prank that even Edwin would laugh at. Nobody seemed to talk about much of substance, save how much they missed their girl back home, but they all called themselves friends. He realized for the first time that actions spoke louder than words. They didn't know each other all that well, yet they felt they'd known each other all their lives after these few short weeks, a world away from anything they'd known. They ate together, a ritual Edwin came to enjoy because it reminded him of communion. It may not have been the body of Christ, but it felt almost as holy to break bread with strangers. With what little free time they had, they would wash out their socks, T-shirts, and shorts, and dry them on a tank under the sun. They lived and breathed together, and that was enough for Edwin to think of them as his brothers.

Edwin even slept fairly well during the two weeks in Les Peux. There was the occasional sound of distant combat, but otherwise all was quiet. His heart leapt into his mouth one morning when he heard a loud explosion in close proximity to his position. Steeling himself for a firefight, he dove for cover with the rest of the men. Word soon came down that a Major and First Lieutenant had been killed by a booby trap. Edwin closed his eyes and let out a breath. There would be no fighting this day.

CHAPTER TWENTY-THREE

War

The jokes about Patton vs. Eyeball suddenly didn't seem too farfetched when, on August 1, the 17th was placed under the command of Patton himself! The entire 15th Cavalry Group was being put into action on an important mission expected to last several weeks.

Eyeball strode in to the church at St. Mére-Eglisse. Rumor had it the church was chosen for the briefing because God must've been watching over a paratrooper named John Steele of the 505th PIR. His parachute had gotten snagged on the church spire on D-Day. He feigned death and miraculously was not shot by German soldiers.

This was Edwin's first good look he'd had of Eyeball. The stories followed him everywhere. Special Service Officer at West Point, finished in two years, just like Patton. Supposedly related to the Dupont family, had lots of pull in D.C. In boot camp, he made certain the officers didn't get too big for their britches, sometimes giving leave to the enlisted boys while putting the officers on latrine duty.

"The 15th Cavalry Group, 705th Tank Destroyer Battalion, 159th Engineer Battalion, and 509th Engineer Company have been consolidated. You are now called Task Force A and we are jumping off at 0100 on 3, August!"

The men stayed quiet as Eyeball continued, straining their necks to see past each other to a map hung on a wall of France's northern coast.

"Objective: secure estuary bridges along all double-track railroad from Rennes to Brest." He stretched his pointer from their location west to the Crozon Peninsula. "It's all about the supply line, boys. Brest does us no good without it. We've been told to button up these routes toot-sweet."

He straightened up, lowered the pointer and puffed his eye out. "Time is of the essence! We cannot have the Germans blow up these bridges. All non-essential and personal items are to be <u>dis</u>-carded." This generated some grumblings, but Edwin didn't really care. He didn't have any personal belongings, and stripping everything else meant for a lighter pack.

"Furthermore, all surgeons, collecting companies, and ambulances have been called east. I repeat—we are on our own! Medics only. They'll only slow us down, and time <u>is</u> of the essence."

"One last thing," Eyeball announced. "This Task Force is now under the Command of General Patton. Every man—to a one—will wear their neck-down." Before Eyeball could hear the complaints, he had Sgt. Cottone dismiss the troops. The absurdity of wearing a necktie while marching into combat, without the necessary medical corps to back them up, really peeved the men. Nobody complained about the mission itself. In fact, a lot of the boys were anxious to see some real action. The older men, and Edwin, would have been just as happy to stay where they were, neckties or not.

So, at one o'clock in the morning on August 3rd, after catching a few hours of restless sleep, Edwin hitched up his pack, loaded his rifle and set out with the rest of TFA. He was able to sit in a jeep with three other men. Nobody spoke much, or socialized. There was a job to do now.

Just after sunrise, as TFA rumbled along a bumpy road between Avranches and Pontorson, Edwin snapped out of a light doze. His head had dropped onto his chest suddenly, straining his neck and jolting him back to life. The sun streamed into his face, and he raised his hand to block the rays. When his eyes adjusted, he thought for a moment he had been transported to Heaven. There was a nearly untouched meadow off to the right, the orange light of the early morning sun stinging each blade of glass a brilliant gold. It was heartening to see something so beautiful in a landscape so torn apart.

The jeep lurched to a stop, almost tossing him off. He turned around. Several men were holding binoculars, looking to the western sky. He squinted and could make out ten distant planes, their engines revving as they suddenly turned and swooped towards the convoy.

"Cover!" came the order. Everyone scrambled at once. Men dove under their vehicles. Edwin hit the dirt and scrabbled under the rear of the jeep, joining his three other riders. Several men mounted machine guns on the back of their vehicles as the planes roared in for their attack. Edwin heard the planes grow closer.

The guns opened up on them, and the planes returned fire. Bullets tore up the dirt around the convoy. Edwin heard ricochets, the bullets peppering the armor of the tanks and other vehicles.

The planes roared over his head, but rather than hear them rev louder as they came around for another pass, they continued into the distance until he could no longer hear them. He and the men around him stood. The planes must have been low on ammunition. He looked around and did not see any medics running. No casualties.

Everyone mounted his vehicle. Edwin climbed aboard the jeep. He looked to the meadow again, but the sun had climbed high enough so its rays no longer kissed the grass. Now, it was just a meadow.

The convoy pressed on.

* * *

Edwin knew the sound had to be eighty-eights, because they were louder than anything he'd heard before. And they scared the wits out of everyone.

205

Darn things had a range of ten miles, could blow a plane out of the sky and flatten a tank.

And they were pounding Edwin and his troop, along with the rest of TFA. The shells hit with a fierce explosion, loud enough to make a man stone deaf if he was too close when it landed. Then there was the mortar fire. It just kept coming. All he could do was stay behind the stone wall he'd found, listen for the incoming artillery, and get the heck out if he heard it.

He looked around. Some men were screaming. As an eighty-eight shell threw up the ground a hundred feet away, one of his troopmates cried for his mother. Behind him, he could see a medic frantically working on a Corporal. He didn't know the man's name, but he'd seen him back in England. He was screaming, too. As he looked again at the men, he realized these had all been the loudmouths, boozers and womanizers.

He stayed cool. He wasn't sure why. He was definitely frightened. His mouth had gone dry. His hands gripped his rifle so hard he thought it might snap.

Another eighty-eight slammed into the ground only thirty feet away, spewing rock and stone and dirt into the air, which showered him from head to foot. He heard a man yelling, and looked to his left. It was a radio operator. He couldn't hear anything and shouted back into the phone. All around him the bombs were landing. He saw a man get hit by mortar fire and crumple to the ground. He felt useless. He wanted to do something instead of just hiding. But there was nobody to shoot at. The enemy was all hidden away, taking potshots at them.

He'd been sent along with the rest of Task Force into Le Vx. Bourg, just east of St. Malo. They'd barely gotten within twenty yards of town, when the Germans opened up on them. Everyone scurried like ants for cover, just like they had done outside Dol de Bratagne, a few hours after the strafing.

They'd been surprised. Eyeball had been in a jeep, was wounded, and captured. TFA quickly withdrew, and left Dol for the infantry.

The fire just kept coming and nobody seemed to know what to do. He heard orders shouted far to the front, but Sgt. Cottone hadn't told them what to do yet. He'd planted himself in the grass about thirty yards away, then shimmied over to the radio operator, who made a hand motion to show it was on the fritz. Cottone cursed and vanished towards the front of the line. That was five minutes ago.

A mortar streaked just overhead. He planted his face in the dirt and prayed as it found its target. Three men were blown apart behind him. He saw blood and arms cascade into the air.

Then came the rumble. One of the tanks from the 705th. It glided down the road just behind him. Cottone ran alongside, waving the troop with him. "Fall back!" he shouted. Edwin gratefully rose and took up position alongside the tank for cover.

CHAPTER TWENTY-FOUR

And God Departed

Edwin and rest of troop B were called before Captain Berlin. They'd been assigned to be reconnaissance cavalry, and now they'd finally do some reconnoitering. Edwin listened as the situation was laid out. St. Malo was the current goal. It was a coastal town with canals that the Germans had flooded, so as to create a bottleneck into the town. The 17th had already tried to get in, but got hit with coastal guns and some artillery ships along the estuary. A major offensive to take St. Malo was being planned, but to get to St. Malo, they had to get through the neighboring village of Chateauneuf. Their mission was to see what kind of resistance was holed up there.

As Edwin hopped into his jeep, he heard Cottone shout, "Ten-hut!" Edwin leapt to attention as Brigadier General Earnest walked into the assembly area. He was a fine old general who strode confidently among the troops. He seemed to be on some kind of inspection. He passed by Edwin and looked at him. He didn't look him in the eye, but rather at his neck. He did this with just about every soldier. Then he stopped beside another private, fingered the man's necktie, and said, "Get those damn things off," and strode away. Everyone gratefully stripped off his necktie.

Three squads from Troop B moved through the brush and forest outside Chateauneuf, and came to a halt when they spied the roadblocks. They'd been constructed out of criss-crossing iron rails over the causeway, and east of there was a canal. All was quiet, save a mangy dog digging for scraps just outside the roadblocks, which appeared to be unmanned.

Edwin kept silent as he watched Sgt. Cottone throw out hand signals. He would take one squad and move in from the right flank, while the other two would take up a frontal attack position. Cottone took the squad and moved to the right, as Edwin and his comrades moved to find clear shots at the roadblock. They'd gone about a hundred feet when two dozen Germans popped up from hiding places among the wall, and opened fire on them.

As Cottone's men ducked for cover, Edwin and his squad returned fire. Edwin hunkered down just on the edge of a copse of trees, using a huge triangular rock as cover. He placed his gun on the rock and, for the first time, began to shoot in live combat. He didn't think, he just reacted like Sarge had taught. Everything became so chaotic so quickly that he responded the only way he knew.

The Germans were initially confused by the wide spread of the squad, which had formed a semicircle around the roadblocks and had good cover. One German dashed out from behind a wall to get a better firing position on Cottone's flanking squad.

Edwin squeezed the trigger. There was the signature loud "CRACK" of his rifle. The German was cut down in his tracks as the bullet smashed into his chest.

And something shattered inside Edwin Barlow. He heard a noise that he thought must have been a bullet breaking a window. But the noise was so much more violent. It was more like a shriek, and it seemed to come from inside him. He realized later it was the sound of his spirit shattering or, possibly, the sound of God leaving him forever.

He didn't stop shooting. His body seemed to react by itself, while his mind went dormant. Two other Germans fell to his rifle. Bullets zinged around him but never came close. Tree branches snapped and splintered from errant gunfire. He had no idea how much time had gone by, or how many of the enemy had been killed when squad comrade Stephen Brown appeared beside him. A platoon of Germans had been spotted in the village, and Troop B would retreat so the infantry could handle it. Edwin slung his rifle. He cast a glance at the first young man he had shot. He had blonde hair and blue eyes, with an almost angelic face. He gazed at the dead boy for a moment, and then darted into the woods.

That night seemed to last forever, and yet not even exist to Edwin. He kept apart from everyone. He did not eat. He only stared to the south, at the distant stars. Behind him, to the north, Allied air strikes pummeled the German gunboats. The sky was choked with planes, a full thousand of them, buzzing in swarms, dropping bomb after bomb. BOOM BOOM BOOM. The deep, heavy explosions resonated in Edwin's chest. The sky lit up a bright orange and the flames climbed high. Then the 83rd Artillery Division started hammering the bottleneck into St. Malo. The THUMPS and BOOMS went on all night. Edwin did not sleep.

He tried to pray, but felt that God was not listening, that somehow he wasn't even there. He asked for forgiveness for killing those men, but didn't feel God heard him. Finally, he wept. Tears rolled down his face as he thought of his Ma, all alone in that empty house, the mothers of those dead German soldiers, his Pa laying in some cold gutter in a strange city, and the apple pie he wished he could eat right now. And he sobbed into his hands, for he could feel the shards of his damned soul coursing through him, jabbing and sticking every organ, every artery, torturing him with their pricks and stabs. His own doing was tearing him apart, from the inside out.

He cursed himself that night, but would not curse God. The tears dried up, and he asked the Lord for guidance, even as the artillery shells found their targets, destroying everything in their purview, reducing men and stone to dust.

*　*　*

Time no longer had meaning for Edwin. Very little had meaning. The days became indistinguishable. So did the little French towns. Avranches. Guingamp. St. Michel-en-Greve. Landivisiau. Loperhet. Chateaulin. Sizun. They swept over miles at a time, sometimes with no sleep, and little to eat. They accomplished what they set out to do, securing railroad tracks and bridges, spilling blood and dropping men in exchange for real estate. They captured Germans. Thousands of them. Patton had ordered that no prisoners be taken. TFA was moving too fast. They had no provision for them. So they just stuck them in a pen under guard. Many of them were Polish POW's anyway, so they were just as happy to be captured. As for the German POW's, Edwin heard that French Resistance Fighters were heeding Patton's order.

Edwin had become numb to it all anyway. When they fought for long stretches, he left himself and became a soldier. The fear went away. But when they pulled back and had a break, knowing they'd soon go back into action, that's when everyone got scared. They could only do that so many times without getting hit. And every time they left combat, it gave Edwin time to reflect. He would imagine the faces of the men he shot, as their bodies first taste the steel that collides with them.

He would think of Ma and he would offer up Mass for his fallen comrades. He prayed that Eyeball was still alive, despite the rumors that he wasn't. Beyond that, he tried not to think, because all thinking did was deepen the guilt. He knew what he did was for some greater good. He knew it might even be God's Will. But he struggled with why God would send him to break his Commandment. The paradox troubled him.

So he tried to drink the alcohol. He took his first drink the day after the assault on Chateauneuf. A corporal saw him stewing, and in some distress. Edwin felt the need to escape what he'd done, so he took the drink. Later, after St. Malo was left to the infantry, and the 17th began to drive west, he drank some more. It made him feel better, if for no other reason, that it made the hurt go away for just a little while.

On September 6th, Edwin found himself at the northwestern corner of France, by the Crozon Peninsula. VIII Corps transferred to the command of the Ninth Army. Insufficient infantry were available because all other resources had been committed to the attack on Brest, which Hitler demanded be defended to the death. Bombers and tank destroyers took on the heavy fortifications at Crozon. 350 Cavalry, including Edwin, were forced to dismount from their vehicles and serve as infantry.

They attacked the line on this day, and Edwin crumpled when the German bullet sliced into his right thigh. He hit the ground, pain shooting through him. He did not scream, despite the agonizing pain. He shouted for a medic, who ran to his side. As gunfire and artillery began to rain down on them, the medic and another soldier carried him to safety behind a hill. The medic pinched him with morphine and very soon after that, Edwin found God again.

The Lord drifted above the battle, with Edwin by his side. Edwin cried, and said he felt Him leave when he shot that first German. God told him that He never leaves any of his children. Never. Edwin begged forgiveness for questioning God's plan, and he heard God say to him, "My plan is your will."

Meanwhile, back home on September 20th, Ma Barlow received a letter in the mail. It was one of those callous Army form letters, with the stenciled words, "Casualty Message" splayed across the entire page. It read, "Deeply regret to inform you that your son, private Edwin D. Barlow was slightly wounded in action in France on Six September. Period progress reports will be forwarded as received. Signed, Adjutant General."

Ma Barlow went to church that night, and had Father Don pray for Edwin's recovery, and that all her boys would soon come to her side.

CHAPTER TWENTY-FIVE

The Pros and Cons of Being Wounded

Edwin was sidelined for almost two months, and was grateful for it. The netherworld of blood and bullets he'd slogged through was worse than even his childhood visions of Hell. At least here, in Avranches, there rarely was the sound of gunfire. Life had even returned to the village. He saw the French regularly, and even picked up some of their language, here and there.

After he was able to get out of bed and limp, he sat in a café from time to time, ate some bread and cheese, and indulged in some red wine, for which he'd developed a fondness. Wine had carried him through his convalescence. For four weeks, he'd been struggling with his healing thigh muscle. The pain was always there, but the morphine was not. The wine, in healthy doses, eased it. It also kept his mind away from the battlefield. He'd also written Ma several times, hoping in vain his letters had reached her before the casualty notice. He'd even received two letters back from her, and kept them in his shirt pocket, re-reading them any time he felt low. Her words were loving and kind, telling him that everything was fine, that she had plenty to eat and to pay the mortgage. She wrote of how she missed all her boys, that his brothers were well, and had not been wounded. She wrote how she waited for the day he would come home and be safe again, how his room waited for him with fresh sheets, and how much she prayed for all the soldiers. When he read those letters, Edwin always felt a little better.

He'd visited the chaplain often and spoke of his confusion over doing a work of Evil when it contributed to a Greater Good. The chaplain tried to defend God's way. He said that man had free will, that the war had been caused by evil men who had made a choice, that God did not guide their hands, nor did he guide ours. He told Edwin that by making a choice to fight, God was proud of him, for he was fighting to protect all that was good and true in God's eyes.

The words felt empty to Edwin. He felt he'd irrevocably corrupted himself, that what God would view as good and true was a man standing by His Commandments, even when presented with a great evil. So he prayed often and fervently, asking for guidance, for how can the acts he'd committed qualify him to become a priest?

When Edwin rejoined his outfit, the 17th Cav had been assigned to protect the Ninth Army headquarters. Nobody knew how long the assignment would last, but it would keep them out of action. As each day went by, Edwin felt his heart surge a little bit. Every day, every hour mattered. The 17th barely budged until early March of 1945. By then, Edwin could see a light at the end of the tunnel. Five months to go, the Allies were making decisive gains and combat had begun to drop off.

His spirits lifted a bit, and as he spent more time with the men, he got to know and appreciate them. They stood together through some tough scrapes, they fought for each other's lives, and they did what they could for the people they liberated. It struck him that perhaps God was present among them, after all. Perhaps the deeds they accomplished somehow might obscure the other acts they'd done. It was enough to think about, anyway.

Edwin didn't feel right the morning of April 6th. He knew things had been too easy for too long. The 17th was ordered to cut off enemy escapes near the Lippe River on this day. A big Allied offensive to choke off the Ruhr pocket was underway. Some Germans might try and flee in their direction.

Some did. When the 17th opened fire on the retreats, many Germans surrendered. Others, with no other way out of their predicament, tried to mount weak offensives at the 17th. They all failed.

The real nuisances were the snipers. They made Edwin nervous. Days would go by without hearing a thing, and then suddenly the loud crack of a rifle would sound out and men would scatter. Edwin always kept his helmet on and tried to stay out of sight. The problem was he was sometimes posted on guard duty, and that made him a sitting duck.

On the 6th, he actually was nestled in a ditch, eating his lunch when he heard the sound of a bullet slicing the air beside his head. He felt like he'd been stung by a wasp. He fell to the ground, holding a hand to his left ear. He felt a warm fluid on his fingers, withdrew his hand and saw trickles of blood running down his fingertips.

In that moment, fearful he'd been shot in the head, one thought entered his mind: "I am ready to go if You will it."

He put his hand back to his ear. The top of it had been sliced almost clean through, and was hanging on by a thin piece of cartilage.

The soldiers next to him quickly returned fire. A moment later a German soldier tumbled from a tree a hundred yards away.

Edwin's hand quivered uncontrollably. He let out a shaky breath. Another soldier knelt beside him and asked if he was okay. Edwin nodded silently, too frightened to speak. The soldier called for a medic, then looked at Edwin's ear.

The man smiled. "You're okay, Eddie. You're okay."

Edwin just nodded back silently, eyes wide.

"It just clipped off your ear. Man, you're one lucky sonofabitch."

The soldier ran off.

Edwin swallowed. He tried to calm himself. He looked to the sky, where a few puffy clouds hung. The sun passed behind one of them. A shadow was thrown over Edwin and he knew right then that God had sent him a message.

216

He knew because he understood the physics of it all. If the German who shot him had aimed even 1/32nd of an inch to the left, if the wind had blown the tiniest bit stronger, if he'd shifted even an ounce of his weight to his left, that bullet would hit him right between the eyes.

"Your will is to serve Me," God said.

Edwin blinked as the sun slid out from behind the cloud. The sunlight streamed onto the battlefield. It warmed his face.

"I don't know how anymore. I don't know how," Edwin replied.

"Don't know what?"

Edwin blinked. A medic hovered over him, a boy no older than twenty-four. Edwin just shook his head.

"Don't panic. You're alright. Don't know about this ear, though." He whispered into Edwin's damaged ear.

"Can you hear me?"

Edwin nodded.

"Does it hurt?"

"Not much."

The boy pulled out some gauze.

Edwin looked to the sunshine. God did not speak to him anymore, but at least Edwin knew He was there.

* * *

The stitches used by the medics to sew his ear back on had become useless. Within a week of the incident, the flap of his ear had turned black and fallen off. Although upset at the prospect of permanent disfigurement, Edwin thought it far preferable to being dead. There was some good to come from it all, because he'd been sent back to Paris on an extended pass.

For nearly a month, Edwin did not participate in any of his troop's activities. Seven of those days he wandered the City of Light endlessly, drinking in this exotic world of high culture and sophistication. He rarely had any particular destination in mind when he set out on his strolls. For the first time in his life, he had the freedom to go where he pleased, and not have to report to anyone what he observed or what he did.

Every single thing he saw generated awe and wonder in his youthful eyes. The buildings themselves were works of art. The language sounded like honey rolling off the tongues of the French. And the food! For a country under siege for so long, the people managed to recover quickly enough to serve delicacies the likes of which Edwin had never dreamed. Even the simplest of baguettes tasted far superior to Springfield's finest bakeries.

Had it not been for the enormous numbers of French and American soldiers milling about in their uniforms, Edwin would have felt self-conscious at his attire. Men and women strolled along the Champs-Elysses with such refinement, with perfectly tailored clothes, and properly coiffed hair. Edwin spent an entire day just staring at everyone's shoes. Even the footwear reeked of class.

Although initially elated at this wondrous new world, he settled into a funk thinking back on the poverty-stricken neighborhood from whence he came. As much as he missed Ma and his home, how could he return to such a life after seeing a city so beautiful, even though it was a war zone until recently.

He decided to experience Paris in all its glory for the short amount of time he'd been given there. Not knowing what day he would be required to return to the front, he hurried about the city, hoping to see all he could, and become as Parisian as possible.

The Pros and Cons of Being Wounded

He enjoyed two things the most. The first was sitting in a café, any one would do, and drink wine while sampling an assortment of cheeses. Although unable to compete with the French citizenry's fine garments, he could still mimic their sophisticated manners. He would sit at his table, quite properly, with a stiffened back. He would sip his wine with the greatest refinement. He would dab at the corners of his mouth with his napkin after each bite of cheese, and thereafter replace it in his lap. He would partake in the occasional cigarette, but rather than wave it about with the kind of gusto his G.I. comrades would do, he would grasp it with a rarefied air, tapping it twice every minute or so to keep the ashes to an acceptable length.

So grateful had the French been for their liberation that Edwin experienced great kindness from the café owners. He was quick with language, and picked up enough in just a few short days that he was able to converse in rudimentary French, which impressed them no end. He was often charged very little for what he consumed, and upon finishing an entire bottle of wine, another would frequently appear in its place, at no charge.

He knew every sip of wine was sinful, but found himself oddly compelled to partake of it whenever the chance afforded itself. For starters, it made him feel high-class to consume a beverage many considered too expensive to enjoy with any frequency back home. He liked the taste, particularly of the reds. And it made him forget, if only for a little while, the multitude of greater sins he had committed on the battlefield. It was much easier to look upon the world, and himself, when the alcohol distorted the images entering his eyes.

Notre Dame, of course, became a second home to him during his sojourn in Paris. Several priests carried on their services in French, but a few did so in Latin. Although he found the Latin far easier to understand, it didn't really matter what language was spoken. God's word was universal, as was the rituals surrounding His glorification. He went to Mass each and every day at the grand cathedral, endlessly fascinated by its structure and beauty.

When he got to Heaven, assuming God would have him, he hoped it would look and feel like Paris.

On May 6th, he was returned to his unit, the war, and a strongest sensation of fear he'd yet experienced. All this time away from the front lines had carried his mind to a safe place. Now he was dreading a return to the daily tensions associated with facing death. Now, more than before, he worried that he might never see Ma. He wanted so badly to tell her about his days on the streets of Paris.

The following day he knew he would see her again. It was the day when, instead of Germans shooting at them, their tanks would roll into the 17th's encampment and be filled up with gasoline. The tanks and their drivers would be sent to the rear, along with the thousands of other Germans behind them. It was V-E Day. The war, as far as most people were concerned, was over.

Edwin looked over the faces of the young Germans who filed past. Sure, they all looked tired. But more than that, their faces carried a look of shock and defeat on them. They all looked so young to Edwin. He'd heard the Nazis had gotten so desperate they started throwing children into uniforms to fight. He heard that translators were calling the Germans pathetic, that they were a sorrowful people, who could not understand how they had lost the war.

He found it hard to look at the Germans. They all looked the same to him, just like the first one he'd shot. Every so often, a passing soldier would catch Edwin's eye, and he would look away. He felt ashamed on the one hand, being unable to stare down in the triumph the very people who only a day earlier would have killed him where he stood. The real wounding, however, was the feeling that any one of these boys might be the brother of a man he had shot dead in combat. "Lord", he wondered, "how is it that one day these boys can be my enemy, and the next, be harmless?"

Anytime the Germans surrendered, Edwin would try and find some other kind of duty, or shield himself behind a group of comrades. Several times he almost burst into tears, as he drowned in tsunamis of guilt for wasting the lives of young boys from another land, pressed into service no different that he had been, ordered to obliterate God's greatest commandment with every pull of a trigger.

He would finger his severed ear, reflecting on the microdistances that had stood between life and death for him. Why had God chosen him to live over so many other good men in his unit? Surely the other men who breathed the same air, ate the same food, and slept on the same ground were just as worthy.

He needed to have a long talk with Father Don. Now, provided a sniper did not pick him off in the next five months, that seemed like a possibility. Each passing day brought him closer to that goal. The days were boring, but Edwin could not have been happier to be so bored. The 17th was shifted from one security detail to another in Holland and Germany. There were various pockets of resistance, but they were never involved with crushing them. Still, he kept his helmet on while others got sloppy and removed them, even in vulnerable open spaces. Every night he prayed, and struggled as he thought about his days in Europe.

The most wonderful piece of paper he ever received was the one handed him on August 11th. It was an order that he be sent back to the United States on the 18th. He put the paper in his pocket and looked around him. He felt a stiff pain in his shoulders. He rubbed them. He realized they hurt because his muscles there had been held taut for months at a time. This was the first time he let himself relax.

He sat down and wrote to Ma, to tell her he was coming home.

CHAPTER TWENTY-SIX

Home

Edwin took great care as he pinned his medals to his dress uniform. He wanted to look perfect for his reunion with Ma. He had spent the morning polishing the medals, the buttons on his uniform, and his shoes. Sarge would've beamed with pride at his meticulousness. He realized it was the first time he'd thought about Sarge in over a year. He wondered if the man had even seen combat and what became of him. Word had filtered back that Eyeball survived a POW camp on the Channel Islands, and consistently demanded on Geneva Convention treatment for the men under him. The Germans apparently had fits about it, but knew the war was not going their way and would be held accountable. Good for Eyeball.

None of it mattered now, anyway. Eyeball should be a distant memory. There was to be nothing involving the army in his life after today. He scanned his medals with a fine eye. There was the EAMET medal, signifying his participation in the European, African, Mediterranean Theatre of Operations, a medal granted to him for his service with the army during Germany's occupation, a medal for the overall victory in WWII, and a good conduct medal. There was the rifle badge indicating his classification as an "expert" with the weapon, a bronze star for meritorious conduct and, finally, there was the Purple Heart with one oak leaf cluster, indicating that he was wounded twice.

He looked in the mirror. Standing before him was a man he would no longer know after today. It would be the last time he would allow anyone to see him in this uniform. He wanted to forget the man he'd become overseas.

He shuddered at the memory of being shelled by those eighty-eights. His face in the dirt, his hand clutched tight around his rifle, the sounds of men being torn apart by the explosions.

He turned away from the mirror, grabbed his bag, and left the barracks at Fort Bragg in North Carolina. A bus waited for him. He got on board and decided to sleep as much as he could. He wanted to be rested.

Ma threw herself at Edwin as soon as she opened the door. He caught her in the embrace and there they stood, arms locked around each other in an iron grip.

The sun set behind them, dropping a curtain of orange down the front of the Barlow house, cascading over the mother and her son, as she began to sob quietly with joy.

* * *

"How can I best serve God?" Edwin asked Father Don. The priest thought for a moment as he looked into Edwin's desperate eyes. The boy had ruled out any attempt to enter the clergy. Despite every urging on his part, Father Don could not get Edwin to forgive himself for what he'd done in the war. He took the boy's confession, talked for hours about how God had directed Edwin into the service, and that every killing had been justified.

But the boy would have none of it. Between the teachings of the church and his family, Edwin held fast to his belief that a priest had to be perfect. He reminded Edwin repeatedly that man was born sinful, and was by nature imperfect.

Edwin just shook his head. "How could I stand behind the pulpit and deliver a sermon about not killing my fellow man when I've done exactly that, war or not?"

"The congregation needs to see you as human. They need to know that, even as a spokesman for the Lord, you too have sinned, and been forgiven."

Edwin sat in silence. Father Don had feared this might happen. Edwin had always adhered closely to the church's doctrines, and took every word to heart. The fact that he could not forgive himself even after receiving God's absolution was not merely an obstacle to entering the clergy, but would haunt the boy for years. He did not want to consign Edwin to that fate. Yet nothing he said about the topic resonated.

After days of discussion, and Edwin's sessions of marathon prayer, both resigned themselves to the truth. Edwin would not allow himself to enter the priesthood. Father Don tried a different route.

"You may wish to consider the Congregation of Christian Brothers," he suggested. Edwin asked for details, and Father Don told him that the organization was founded in 1802 by Venerable Brother Edmund Ignatius Rice, ostensibly to educate Irish Catholics who were otherwise prevented from receiving education by the Protestant English government.

"A Christian Brother is a layman who takes vows of Poverty, Celibacy, and Obedience, but does not serve in a parish or receive the sacrament of Holy Orders. They may serve the mission of the Church in a variety of ways, including teaching."

Edwin investigated this angle. Father Don sent him to Boston, on his own dime, to meet with the local chapter. The Brother who spoke to Edwin reported back that the boy fit the criteria for the group, and possessed the kind of altruistic spirit they craved. But after a week or so, Edwin rejected even this possibility. He told Father Don that becoming a Brother was only committing halfway to God. For all of their good deeds, they seemed like second-class priests, men who could not, or would not, give themselves over completely. For Edwin, life was all about commitment. All or nothing.

Eventually, Father Don realized that there was something else working at Edwin. The young man had been intrigued that many teachers were in the Brotherhood. Knowing Edwin's penchant for helping his fellow high school students, and Agnes' service to her neighbors, he suspected that Edwin may partially have rejected the clergy so that he could teach. As far as serving a community, the closest thing to being a clergy member was being a teacher. The two occupations had much in common. Edwin could also avoid feeling like a hypocrite, because God was not involved in teaching secular studies. This seemed like a more reasonable path.

Father Don was tremendously disappointed that Edwin had chosen against the priesthood. But his heart was lightened knowing that Edwin had decided on a way to serve God, his people, and do so in a noble manner.

For all Father Don knew, this might turn out to be Edwin's true calling instead.

CHAPTER TWENTY-SEVEN

College

For his matriculation at college, Edwin chose Holy Cross almost by default. Cost was not an issue since the G.I. Bill covered most of the expense. The school had the right balance of both secular and theological studies. Should he have second thoughts, and still desire to enter the clergy, this would be one way to straddle the line and keep open the possibility. The school was also in Boston, allowing him to make frequent trips home to see Ma.

He was placed on the fifth floor of Wheeler Hall dormitory, along with a significant number of other veterans. He didn't really like being around these people, because he didn't want to talk about the war. He'd kept silent about it around Ma, and even around all of his brothers, even though they'd all served.

He quickly discovered, though, that nobody at Holy Cross wanted to discuss the war much, either. Everyone had returned from the service feeling they'd put enough years of their lives into it that couldn't be recaptured. So rather than spend much time talking about the past, everyone was pretty darn serious about getting on with a productive life.

Creating a productive life was Edwin's primary goal now. He had made a firm decision in his mind that, beginning with college, he would begin anew. That meant severing all ties with who he used to be, with the exception of Ma and Father Don. He felt that, like Jesus, he'd been granted a kind of resurrection after spiritually dying in the war. As proud as he slowly became of his service, he still regarded his tour in Europe as akin to a visit to Hell.

227

If he were to be truly reborn, it meant he had to leave everything else behind. In some ways, he felt pained by it. But he was so eager to wash himself of all prior sin, of all prior unpleasant memory, that he followed his plan to the extreme. This meant slowly having to withdraw from his family. They probably wouldn't understand why he chose to cut them off, so he didn't bother to tell him he was doing it. Plus, life was about expanding horizons beyond what he'd already known. Family offered little in the way of intellectual benefit, so their utility had become limited.

He also wanted to break the alcohol's increasing hold. He found it difficult to break the habit he'd picked up in France. It was another reason why he wanted to defer his decision about the church.

He knew Al would be hurt the most when he withdrew from the family. You can't share a small home with a brother all your life, and not feel some bond. Al was always hard on himself, so he probably would feel that he didn't measure up in some way to Edwin's expectations. Al would have to deal with it. If he tried to make some kind of formal farewell, things would become emotional, and that was something Edwin definitely wanted to avoid. So even when he hitched a ride with Al and his girlfriend back to Boston, all he did was climb into the car, greet them, and then bury his nose in his textbooks until they arrived. It left Al feeling bewildered, but no words were ever exchanged about it.

He'd visit Ma whenever he could, though. It would break her heart if he didn't, and he couldn't bear to be away from her anyway.

Edwin focused all his energies on his studies, and to helping his fellow students. Math and physics held the most interest for him—they always had. He liked the intellectual challenge of it all. He liked understanding how the world worked. Perhaps most of all, he appreciated the fact that in mathematics and physics, every problem had only one right answer. Everything other than that answer was wrong. There were no issues of relativism, no questions regarding God's intent, no equivocation of any kind. There was only a strict set of rules to be followed, and if they were followed, a pure and correct answer would result.

Besides loading up on these courses, Holy Cross required tremendous amounts of theological study. The students were given heavy doses of Scholastic Philosophy six days a week, for two hours each day. Edwin ate up these lessons, while many students were left in a cloud of confusion. He admired the blend of Aristotle and Aquinas. It made sense to him. It was all very mathematical, especially the <u>Summa Theologica</u>. He loved how St. Thomas stated a proposition, then all the arguments against it, and solved them using syllogistic, inductive or deductive reasoning.

Yes. One right answer for everything. It all made perfect sense to him. For those who didn't understand it, he was all too willing to sort them out, and that meant helping them in math and physics, too. And why shouldn't he? They were all there for the same reason, after all. Plus, so many of them were Vets, and he would never leave a comrade hung out to dry, nor would he ever accept payment. For Heaven's sake, if Ma never took a dime for all the mending she did for the neighbors, why should he accept anything for his help? He was glad to do it, always dropped whatever he was doing to help out, and did so with a smile. He liked to see his fellow students succeed.

While studying at Holy Cross, he also came across Immanuel Kant. After digesting this philosopher's works, Edwin all but solidified his decision to become a teacher. Being a priest was a noble act to be sure, despite his reservations. But as far as serving society, as well as himself, he knew a teacher would have far more influence than a priest ever could. It was a simple mathematical analysis. A priest spoke to one congregation. A teacher's congregation turned over each and every year.

* * *

It took a lot to pry Edwin away from his studies. He was coaxed out from time to time by his floormates, usually at mealtimes. He might volunteer to go to a football game with Ted Keane, a Boston native who had seen action in the Navy. Going anywhere with Ted, though, was merely a front to carry out some prank on the poor fellow. Edwin would profess complete ignorance as to the game of football. Over the next hour, he would have Ted pulling his hair out trying to explain the game to an apparently uncomprehending Edwin. Eventually Ted would bellow, "How can you be so brilliant at math and be such a nincompoop about a very easy game?" He'd storm off in anger, and Edwin would laugh uproariously.

Ted was an easy target for Edwin's prankish sense of humor. There was the time Ted returned from the shower to find his roommate had locked him out. He asked Edwin if he could climb out on his ledge and see if the window had been left open. Edwin agreed, Ted clambered out, then promptly shut his window, turned out the lights and left—leaving Ted stranded outside in a towel in the freezing weather.

Ted and the others would always get after him about not socializing or having dates. There was the occasional dance, which he would go to if pushed enough, and he was always one of the boys to go stag. Frustrated by Edwin's lack of attention to the attractive girls on campus, one floormate pressed him that there must be a girl that Edwin was attracted to. Edwin admitted there was, which only got the floormate to press him harder.

"Wouldn't you feel terrible if she married someone else and you had never asked for a date?"

Edwin thought about it and replied that he would be disappointed.

"So, what would you do?"

Edwin knew his answer would drive the poor guy nuts, but at least it would push him off asking such intrusive questions.

"Well, some fellow would drown their sorrow in drink, but I guess I'd just do a lot of math problems."

Sure enough, the floormate threw up his hands in despair, to Edwin's considerable hidden amusement. The truth of the matter, as far as he knew, was that he was utterly terrified of girls. He always had been. Here were these beautiful creatures against which he could never measure up. They walked the earth with the finest grace and elegance. Why would one of them want to be with him, especially now that he was missing half an ear and sported an occasional limp? He was just plain afraid to even get close to them, or to speak with them.

This didn't even mention the fact that women personified the very temptations that might lead him down a sinful path. Were he a monk or a priest, and that had always been his intention, women would be strictly off-limits anyway. The path he had chosen now, while not officially a position in either the clergy or the Christian Brotherhood, still required he keep his personal vows to God concerning poverty, celibacy, and obedience.

He beat himself up, though, over his drinking. He tried so hard to turn away from the Imp. He had even succeeded for much of his first two years. But the flesh is weak, and sometimes when he was alone in his room and the rest of the school was at a football game, he would drink to excess. Thank Goodness that Kant had shown him the light. As a teacher, he believed he could hide his drinking much easier than if he was a priest.

231

He struggled valiantly with the Imp. It showed up often. He didn't want it to be a part of his life. He knew it was the real reason he wanted to cut himself off from the family. He knew he would lose this battle with alcohol, and that meant having to answer prying questions from his brothers. Al would get on him about turning into Pa. They might try and interfere with his life. He didn't want any of that. He was beginning a new life, and that included a place for Speakeasy. No way would he expose Al and his brothers to such a thing.

Every time he succumbed to the bottle, he always sobered up and repeated to himself that enough time had been spent doing other things. Now, time had to be devoted to study, and study is what Edwin did day-in and day-out, even over the summers. Every day was about learning, about establishing a foundation of knowledge to draw upon and serve to others some day. This is what Edwin did every day for almost three years. He continued to do it for a fourth, but that year it became far more difficult to concentrate.

CHAPTER TWENTY-EIGHT

His Last Earthly Love

The only other time Edwin had seen Ma so pale was when Pa died. In that instance, it was because she'd been shaken to her very core. This time her pasty complexion resulted from a medical condition. She had kept all the boys blissfully unaware about the cancer for some time. She would take the bus to see the doctor, and come home without telling them where she had been, or that she'd been suffering in utter silence for months.

Edwin sat beside her, paralyzed. She told him that it started with her losing weight, and not feeling hungry. Then her stomach started to hurt on-and-off for a few weeks. She thought it might have been an ulcer, but when she vomited blood one Sunday night a few months back, she decided to see the doctor. There had been lots of tests, and the doctor told her the bad news.

"But I'll be fine. I will. I promise. I just wanted to let you know."

Edwin nodded. He believed Ma implicitly. He asked if she was in pain. She said she was from time to time. The worst part was the doctor had been giving her all kinds of drugs, and they made her terribly sick. She was taking a break from all that now, though. She told Edwin to wipe off that long face and smile. She'd made his favorite apple pie, which Edwin ate with her that night.

After dinner, he ran out the door when Ma was in the back room. *O Father of Mercies and God of All Comfort, my only help in time of need.* He ran across the street to the church. *I humbly beseech thee to behold, visit, and relieve thy sick servant, Agnes, for whom my prayers are desired.* He scanned the sanctuary, and found nobody present. *Look upon her with the eyes of Thy*

233

mercy; comfort her with a sense of Thy goodness. He dashed to the altar and lay himself down before it, prostrate before the gleaming crucifix. *Preserve her from the temptations of the enemy; and give her patience under her affliction.* There he lay throughout the entire night, never moving, never stopping for breath, never rising, and never opening his eyes, even as a flood of tears ran down his face. *In Thy good time, restore her to health, and enable her to lead the residue of her life in Thy fear, and to Thy glory; and grant that he may dwell with Thee in life everlasting; through Jesus Christ our Lord.*

Dear Lord, do not take her from me. . .

From then on, any moment that Edwin could slip away from Holy Cross to see Ma, he did. He was with her constantly. Despite her every assurance, he saw that she was not getting better. Each day, she moved a little slower. Each day, she ate less and less. Each day, she would excuse herself and go in the back room, where Edwin could hear her vomit. But she'd shoo away any assistance he ever tried to give her, as well as any comfort.

That was Ma. She suffered in utter silence, just as she had when Pa was around. She never complained once. On the few occasions that one or more of the boys were home at the same time as Edwin, they'd all agreed that she was one step removed from a saint to have coped with this agony as she had.

He got the call from Al on a Thursday night. Ma had gone to the hospital and the doctors said she would die soon. Edwin was thunderstruck at the news. He knew she wouldn't get better any time soon, but. . .die? Even after he called upon the Lord? Even after he begged His forgiveness for his every sin? Why hadn't the doctors done anything to forestall this?

"The doctors said they couldn't operate. That was two months ago. She wanted to live at home as long as she could, to be with us," Al told him.

He was at her bedside within hours. The other boys were, too. She was smiling now, woozy but no longer in pain. The morphine helped a lot. She told her boys not to be afraid, that she'd be better soon. The sons all exchanged glances. But they didn't want her to worry about them, so they all acknowledged that her affliction was temporary. It would pass, as all things do.

Al cried when she passed. Dave and Billy put a hand on each other's shoulder. Each of them kissed Ma one last time. "Least she went quietly," Al said. The others nodded, except Edwin. All he did was hold her hand. He hadn't let go once since he got there. He held it for the next twenty-six hours before her death, he held it the moment she stopped breathing, and he held it for another hour after that. He asked his brothers to leave him alone for a bit, with Ma, and only after they left the room did he release her.

Never in his life had Edwin spilled so many tears at once. Nor would he ever again, for his one and only earthly love had departed, leaving him utterly alone.

CHAPTER TWENTY-NINE

Death

November 14, 1990. Greeley Vice-Principal Larry Breen sat in his office on the second floor of L-building, deeply troubled. Ed Barlow had to go to the hospital. He simply had to. On Monday morning, Ed's whole forehead was bruised black and blue. In typical Barlow fashion, he said somebody had opened the door to a car while he was in Boston over the weekend and hit him in the forehead. Larry couldn't believe Ed expected anybody to buy that story. He hadn't been in Boston. He probably hadn't even left the Greeley campus. He had fallen and hit his head, which caused this large hematoma.

The problem was how to get an ox to move when he doesn't want to move. He refined that thought further. How do I get an ox to move, if the ox can't move?

Principal Hart entered the office. The only solution, he announced, was to put it to Ed straight and not take "no" for an answer. They'd do it after school to avoid any embarrassment. Larry Breen nodded. Ed was literally falling apart. They had to do something.

Larry felt badly for Ed, who had made no concessions to age, and did not take care of himself. He really needed to have heart bypass surgery, and refused that back in June. It was such a foolish move by Ed, and all because had heard that it was dangerous, and that a certain number of people had died on the table. How ridiculous that a man who prized the intellect so highly could not understand how badly he needed medical care. Everyone else could see it, but nobody would confront him.

At that point, Ed wasn't even actively learning anything new. All of his life he had projects. "Let me learn Portuguese, let me learn differential equations." But now he was just turning into a walking corpse.

Larry had noticed that Ed had been short of breath for much of the spring semester. He had difficulty climbing stairs, and when he reached the top, he had to rest. He rebounded a little bit over the summer, but he wasn't back at school in the fall very long, before it was obvious he was declining further.

His world got smaller and smaller. For a while he couldn't drive and was using the microwave in the staff dining room. He was sleeping in the nurse's office, and showering in the locker room. Soon, even those activities became too strenuous. He couldn't even leave J-building or walk up the steps. He was a prisoner of one floor, four classrooms. He only ate the stuff that people brought him or crap that wasn't cooked.

What a shame. This was not the Ed Barlow he'd gotten drunk with, back in the seventies. There was that night he went out with Ed, Charlie Pollack, and a few other guys, and gotten plastered. He remembered how sick he'd been the next day, and how Ed showed up fresh as a daisy. The guy had that unbelievable constitution. Never came to school drunk or hungover, never chiseled on the kids. Amazing. Now look at him. What a goddamned shame.

Larry and Principal Hart had been in agreement about Ed for some time. Like all of us, he probably should have quit five years ago. He just hasn't been following the curriculum. It wasn't that he wasn't capable of it, Larry knew, but that he just wasn't doing it. Other teachers were inheriting kids who were supposed to have learned things that they hadn't. Kids who took the AP course with him were not covering the syllabus, and therefore couldn't get a good grade on the test. Those were big negatives, for the kids, and for everybody. But there was just no way he could be convinced to retire, because teaching was all he had left. The only thing that's kept him going is that mind, that willpower, just blasting away in the back of the room.

Larry and Principal Hart waited until five o'clock and made a cursory sweep through campus to make sure nobody was around. Then, they went over to J-2 and told Ed that he absolutely had to go to the hospital. They steeled themselves for a Barlow explosion, but he didn't battle them, at all. He knew. He couldn't really resist. Larry realized they should've tried this weeks ago.

An ambulance arrived and scooped up the venerable teacher. Larry figured he might not have many more opportunities to find out a few of Ed's secrets. So, as they were loading Ed into the vehicle, Larry spontaneously got up the courage to ask about how Ed had gotten wounded in the war.

"Forgot to duck," he growled back. And that was the end of that conversation.

The ambulance doors closed, and Larry watched it pull away. He cleared his throat, primarily to stifle the sudden and unexpected surge of emotion.

He'll never set foot at Greeley again. He may as well die.

*   *   *

The flesh is transitory. Only the soul is eternal. These concepts had been taught to Mister Barlow as a child, and he'd carried them with him, all his life. He hung on to them while crouching in foxholes, or convalescing with John Willard in the hospital. Intellectually, he knew he should take better care of himself, in order to prolong his ability to teach. He'd been diagnosed with hypertension ages ago, way back in the 50's. He never stuck to his medicine, and he knew he'd always been overweight. His doctor had warned that this would all catch up to him, and it did. Spiritually, however, he knew that God would carry him through any crisis, because of the work he did in the classroom.

Still, he feared that he'd just seen his last glimpse of his beloved high school campus. He pushed the thought away. "I've been shot, for Heaven's sake. If I lived through that, I'll live through this." He recalled his other ailments throughout the years and how they all amounted to nothing. He'd always had migraines, but those never got in the way, except when he saw the circles in front of his eyes. He had a fine tremor in his hands for some time, but that never impeded his ability to write. The occasional chest pains had been around since '74. Even the broken bones from the various car accidents hadn't slowed him down.

The doctor had also pushed him to have heart surgery, but there was no way he was going to have somebody cut him open and kill him, not after surviving the war. Besides, the prostatecomy he'd had three years ago left him feeling too weak to even think. Heart surgery would have sidelined him from teaching. He couldn't bear to be out of the classroom that long.

Now, though, things felt different. He thought that as long as he could speak, he could teach. But there was more to it than that. He had sores all over his body. It hurt to go to the bathroom. He could barely walk. Maybe he'd let things get out of hand this time. No matter. He'd be out soon. He hated leaving the students in the hands of someone else, though. They wouldn't learn enough.

Mister Barlow didn't like people seeing him in a hospital bed. Propped up on all those pillows, with that silly gown covering him—it was all so undignified. He considered prohibiting visitors, but then he'd have nobody to talk to. Besides, Eddie Dearborn was likely to show up and if there were one person he'd like to see, it was he.

Eddie did show up, of course, and Mister Barlow was prepared for any prank the miscreant might pull. But Eddie conducted himself with decorum and they spent many hours discussing students, the value of a rent-controlled apartment, and hamburgers at the White Horse. At times, though, Eddie didn't seem himself. Mister Barlow thought about Eddie's face when he first came by to visit. It was like he'd seen a ghost. Perhaps Eddie got a look at him and saw that he was in bad shape. Even though Mister Barlow told Eddie that he felt fine, Eddie never seemed to buy it.

A few students came by, and a few faculty. The computer teacher, Likeu Lee, showed up every single day with flowers. She would stay for quite awhile and talk. He mostly told his visitors the truth, that he wanted to get better quickly, so he could get back to teaching. Everyone nodded, agreeing that he wouldn't be in the hospital too long. Some students assured him that the substitute teachers were doing just fine with his classes but, of course, nobody could compare.

Doctors would shuffle in and out. Nurses would change his bedding and help him to the bathroom. He ate and he slept. He read some books. One, The White Spider by Heimlich Harrer, was one of his recent favorites. He'd taken an armchair interest in mountaineering, thanks to Steve Frauenthal, who'd loaned him the book. Steve was a great outdoorsman who'd scaled a few peaks himself.

Mister Barlow found the book intriguing not just for its drama, but for its author. He felt a kinship with Harrer. He wasn't sure why, until his third reading of the book. A man with a pack, pushing past every obstacle nature threw. The bitter cold. Snowstorms. Falling boulders that might crush him without notice. The possibility of being buried alive in a real avalanche. Astonishing. Simply astonishing. The more he read the book, the more he saw how closely the sport reflected his own philosophies. He was entranced by the compulsion many mountaineers had to conquer the various peaks that beckoned them. It felt consonant with his own calling to the clergy and, ultimately, to academia.

Mister Barlow had always appreciated a person's physical accomplishments. After slogging through Hell himself, anyone who could strap on a pack and brave a mountain earned his respect. So, too, the students who strapped on shoulder pads or helmets or jerseys, and plowed their way through other men or women, to reach a goal line, a basket, or a net. It took fierce determination and faith. They all had to find that place in themselves that forced them, absolutely required them, to succeed.

He also admired Harrer's devotion to the code of mountaineers. There were rules of conduct. There were ethics. It was no different, really, from the code that governed the clergy, or even the soldier. Much of it focused on being part of a team, aiding each other as necessary, not lying about how far one had ascended, and behaving in a way that reflected well on mountaineering. Most of all, the code emphasized that a fellow mountaineer should never be left behind. One must risk his own life to rescue that of another. The battlefield analogy was not lost on Mister Barlow. Indeed, Harrer showed particular contempt for the crowds who gathered to watch the deadly climbing feats from the ground below. To Mister Barlow, these were the same boys who chickened out of enlisting, or the bigmouths on the front line, who turned yellow when the action started.

But there would be no mountain climbing for him. Stair climbing, at this point, even seemed unlikely. Larry Breen had been gentle, but firm, about hiring a lawyer to make out a will. He acquiesced only because his substantial assets would be taken by the State if he didn't leave them to somebody. It was logical that he would die some day. He honestly didn't want to believe it would be soon, but either way he decided it prudent to disburse his funds properly.

His directions were easy to follow. He left the bulk of his estate to a charity he'd been giving to for many years, namely the Horace Greeley Educational Fund. Too many kids over the years who should have gone to college simply couldn't afford to do so. He'd helped out a number of them personally, and discreetly. This way, he would be able to formalize the arrangement. He threw $20,000 to his other annual charity, the Chappaqua Summer Scholarship program. This organization brought under-privileged kids to Chappaqua for summer school. He gave them ten thousand a year, never asked any questions about how the money was spent, never wanted to meet any of the students, and never wanted to visit the program during the summer weeks that the students were living in Chappaqua. Such was the nature of charitable giving, according to the Church. One must never become prideful.

There was one last asset he wanted to give away. English teacher Joan Tucci had always been kind to him, the way she brought a homemade lunch for him, every day, for the past few years. He had sampled some of her pasta, and loved it so much that she just kept bringing it, out of the kindness of her heart. It had been especially appreciated lately, when he couldn't even leave campus. So he left his car to her. She would probably sell it, which was fine by him. She deserved to have something, and this was the best he could do.

The attorney departed, along with Larry Breen. Mister Barlow looked out the window, onto one of Mount Kisco's three main streets. Dark clouds had rolled in, and a light drizzle began to fall. He thought about his classroom. He'd left an equation up on the board, for the algebra kids, as their daily quiz. There was a freshman in that class, Ella Knightly, who had just started to turn the corner. He could see her beginning to understand how to convert problems into equations. She had left class without solving the day's problems, and he wanted desperately to know if she'd succeeded. He'd have to call Larry and ask him to check up on that.

He looked at his hand. It was shaking, as it always did when he hadn't recently imbibed alcohol. No way would they let him have any here. Not a chance. Probably for the best. Keep the Imp corked up for awhile. It might do them both some good.

They called the incident that evening a "respiratory arrest." Mister Barlow heard the words, but did not register them. He had slipped into a coma shortly after it began. They put him on a ventilator.

Just before he slipped into blackness, he thought he heard singing. Yes, it was definitely a chorus of students...his students...from the '61 Senior Assembly....

To the tables in our classroom,

To the place where Blackie dwells,

To the dear old hard-wood seats we love so well,

Sing the blockheads assembled

With their pencils raised on high,

And the magic of their theorems casts its spell.

Oh, the magic of the homework,

That we didn't learn too well,

And the Russian that we've had along the way.

We will serenade our Blackie while life and voice shall last,

Then we'll pass (we hope) and leave here for a rest.

We're poor little blockheads who have lost our way,

Sob, sob, sob!

We're little square blockheads who have gone astray,

Sob, sob, sob!

Haunted by postulates, theorems and rules,

And all other things learned in schools.

Here we are just like little fools,

Sob, sob, sob!

He remembered the title. They called it, "The Poof Song". He never did figure out why they called it that.

CHAPTER THIRTY

The Executor's Mess

"This whole thing is a goddamned mess," thought Larry Breen. He'd only agreed to be Ed's executor because nobody else was in the room with him when he made out his will. Larry didn't even know that he was entitled to five percent of the estate. He wished all of Ed's money hadn't been wrapped up in the New York State Retirement system, where the percentage didn't apply, because he should've gotten something for all this trouble.

The federal people had been very easy to satisfy. The state people were impossible. They kept saying, "Well, where's Barlow's silverware? Where's the condo? Where is the stereo? Where is the TV? Where are his clothes? You can't tell us he left nothing." They just didn't get it. They didn't get Ed. Not that anybody did. He tried to explain that the man had been a secular monk, that money meant nothing. He told them how he gave away so much to charity each year, that the IRS always audited him and always left satisfied. That didn't sway them. He tried to tell them that nothing was found in Ed's apartment. Nothing, save a bed without sheets, a few raggedy outfits, a scarf, a hot plate, some dirty pots and silverware, and a single book of nursery rhymes entitled, Lavender's Blue. That didn't sway them, either.

They're convinced I stole Ed's stuff. Idiots!

Finally Larry just told them, "Look, let me give you the names of some people who work here. Walk around, talk to them. I'm telling you, there is nothing. He really was pure, in terms of his having no materialistic interests, in clothes or fashion. He died with a lot of money, but he could have had a lot more money. He just put his money in the New York State Teacher's Retirement System, which earned bank interest."

The state people went about their business. Larry reflected on Ed's passing, wondering how a man who had maintained such privacy, could elicit such an outpouring of emotion. His death made the front page of the local Gannett newspaper, The Reporter Dispatch, as well as a column in The New York Times. There was a standing-room-only funeral at St. Francis of Assisi church in Mt. Kisco.

Larry couldn't make the interment at Arlington, but Likeu Lee graciously videotaped it. He viewed it at home late one night. The tape revealed that Ed's burial took place on a cold, drizzly, overcast day. The endless rows of white headstones marched off into the distance. An honor guard solemnly carried his casket to its final resting place. As the Marines held taut an American flag over the coffin, the lead Marine spoke a few prayers. Only Likeu and her husband attended the interment, aside from the Arlington officials.

Another shame. That cemetery should be full of his kids. For all the people Ed touched in his life, for all the intellects he fostered, and students he tutored, only two people came to see him buried. Perhaps he preferred it this way. When the Marine's prayer concluded, the camera zoomed closer on seven Marines standing at attention in the distance. A command was given, and in perfect unison, they each fired three shots. The CRACK CRACK CRACK of the rifles overwhelmed the sound of the planes landing at nearby Dulles airport. A solitary trumpet delicately played Taps. The marines folded the flag and offered it to Likeu Lee. Nice that she could have it. But where on earth was Al?

Not seeing Ed's only surviving brother at the funeral disturbed Larry, who'd gone through a lot of trouble to contact him. Larry knew that after Ed died, a rent bill for his true lodgings would eventually arrive in his school mailbox. Sure enough, it came. Ed's apartment was in North White Plains, down one of the side streets, behind a garage. It was literally one room with a bathroom and very, very disconcerting. He'd expected to find hundreds of books, but instead found a paucity of material belongings. The guy really did live like a monk. Amazing.

Larry did a lot of digging, and turned up Al, who was living with his wife in North Carolina. Al didn't sound surprised by the call. He just said, "I always knew Edwin would turn up somewhere." Larry invited him up and showed him around Greeley, filling him in on his brother's legacy. Al was astonished that a Barlow had become so famous, and even seemed proud of the brother who had cut him off almost forty years ago. Larry didn't want to pry, but felt deserving of a few answers about Ed's life. Al filled him in on as much as he could.

"As for why Edwin cut us all off, all I can guess is that after Ma died, he wanted to start a new life. Or maybe that he was really religious, and we somehow didn't measure up to his expectations. It seems a little farfetched that we would, all four of us, feel this way, Yet, we were really convinced of it, that we didn't stack up to his religious way of life. He was as devout a Catholic as one could be. To him, there were never any gray areas. It was all black and white. My brothers and I didn't take Church seriously. I hadn't really gone since I was sixteen. So here Edwin comes out of the service and sees immediately that I don't take it seriously. And he expected more from me. And my younger brother Dave was even worse with respect to Church and confession and girls and carousing. In the meantime, I'm marrying outside the Catholic church. My oldest brother Billy was non-practicing.

"The last time we saw him was when Billy bought us out of our share of Ma's house. Never heard from him again. We tried to contact him over the years, even got so far as to speak to the attorney who handled Ma's affairs. But all he would say is that he'd pass on a message to Edwin, but it was entirely up to him if he wanted to respond. He never did."

Al delivered the information nonchalantly. He'd come to peace with the issue long ago. Larry liked Al for this, and for a lot of other things. Larry didn't think Albert had a lot of money. During his visit, Larry just waited and waited for him to ask about Ed's assets. Finally, Al asked about them, and Larry told him.

Instead of flipping out, or threatening to sue, Al just smiled and said, "Gee, that's just like Edwin. That's just like Edwin." Months later, Larry kept waiting for a claim on the money because, heck, this guy was his brother. Ed also had a niece and a nephew. They never once made the slightest comment about it, never contested the Will, and it soared through probate with nary a problem. Larry knew they were just quality people, and for some people, money wasn't the measure of everything.

After meeting Al and seeing the man's kind nature, he found himself actually wishing he'd known Ed better. If only Ed had let him.

PART IV

Understanding Mister Barlow. . .

CHAPTER THIRTY-ONE

Through Philosophy & Literature

My investigation into Mister Barlow's life reminded me of tracking footprints on a beach at high tide. Cutting through the veil of mystery he had surrounded himself with seemed like it would be impossible. Despite his best efforts to remain a secluded individual, however, he had contact with other people. That created a large enough doorway for me through which to pass. The simple truth is that he did reveal personal details to a select few. The facts about Mister Barlow had been available all along. They were just scattered to the four winds and needed someone to pull them all together.

So who was Mister Barlow? The question can be answered any number of ways, so I think it best to approach the question the way he would have urged me to: "Use your mind, Mister Meyers, and all the resources available to you to solve the problem".

I believe there is one major aspect to Mister Barlow's life that encompasses almost all his actions. It overrides all the other details about him. It was his guiding principle. His life was about the same thing that most people's lives are about, whether they are aware of it or not.

His life was about finding God.

Finding God consumed him, because he felt himself lose God when he took his first life in the war. He had to find Him again, or he would feel forever lost. Now, it's important to understand that I think Mister Barlow defined God according to the dogma of the Church at the time, and continued to do so until he entered college. That's where a new set of influences altered his defintion of God.

"Finding God" no longer meant "being saved" or "finding Jesus." It meant something based more in what we call reason-based faith. Finding God in this context means "self-transcendence." To paraphrase, life is about finding one's purpose, and we accomplish that by providing ourselves with ever-widening circles of experience. We should seek to continually improve, or transcend, ourselves through the vehicle of education. As our circles of experience widen, we hope them to fill the universe—in other words, approach the infinite, or God.

In this sense, religion might be thought of as "devotional self-transcendence." Since we cannot interpret God in any way other than symbolism, we devote ourselves to approaching God as best we can. So although Mister Barlow was raised a Catholic, I believe he likely clung to that dogma more out of respect for his mother, than for any particular teachings of the Church itself.

This is heady stuff, to be sure, but it's essential to delve into it, because it is the core of what Mister Barlow was all about. I've tried to simplify the concepts, so we don't lose sight of how they apply to his life.

Where did he pick up the concept of self-transcendence? It started when he was a boy, as so many of the Church's teachings urged Mister Barlow to emulate God as best he could. Viewed in this context, it is also no surprise why he was so fascinated by math and physics. Aquinas, Aristotle, and especially mathematics, were about finding the one right answer.

Given this theological background, finding God had a specific set of criteria, laid out in the <u>Summa Theologica</u>, which was an integral part of Holy Cross' cirricula. The <u>Summa</u>, as well as anything written by Aquinas or Aristotle, governed Mister Barlow's daily life. It is difficult to summarize the entire tome in these pages, but some of the most significant aspects of the <u>Summa</u> reflect deeply on Mister Barlow's life.

Understanding something's essence is, according to the text, the natural desire of the soul and the mind. This tenet drove Mister Barlow's unending curiosity about all things, his desire to learn languages, and to understand how the universe worked through math and physics.

Stemming from this concept is the idea that the existence of God and His power can be proven by using human reasoning alone. The mind has a natural hunger to understand something's essence, so why not God's essence? The Summa goes on to explain that God's essence is Divine Simplicity, or that the characteristics of God (goodness, truth, eternity) are identical to God's being, not qualities that compose His being. Thus, by emulating God's characteristics, one can hope to approach God. This drove Mister Barlow's lifestyle. His unending generosity, his desire to help kids use their minds so that they may also begin to see God's essence, are just two examples.

The Summa also tells us that a life of contemplation has greater value than the active life, but actually calling someone else to the contemplative life is of even greater value. This explains his interest in Narcissus and Goldmund, which dramatically explicated this tenet. This also fits right into his decision to live the esthetic lifestyle—no material possessions, attending daily Mass (he was often seen in a nearby Pleasantville church at the early service), the pure study of mathematics and physics, the lack of a television in his home, the gradual retreat from social functions, and his joy in discovering that Bob Gluck was to become a rabbi.

Mister Barlow also placed a high priority on perfection. The reason is that, again, it places one in close proximity to God. Perfection is defined as, "that which is complete, containing all the requisite parts," and most importantly, "that which has attained its purpose." Mister Barlow sought to attain his purpose in life, and this is closely akin to Kant's categorical imperative.

Student John Willard once challenged Mister Barlow's apparent contradictory beliefs in logic and faith, but to Mister Barlow there was no contradiction. Mister Barlow bridged the gap between logic and faith, much as Narcissus did:

> To realize oneself. . .for us disciples of Aristotle and Aquinas, it is the highest of all concepts: perfect being. God is perfect being. Everything else that exists is only half, is a part, is becoming, is mixed, is made up of potentialities. But God is not mixed. He is One, he has no potentialities but is the total, the complete reality. Whereas we are transitory, we are becoming, we are potentials, there is no perfection for us, no complete being. But wherever we go, from potential to deed, we become by a degree more similar to the perfect and the divine. That is what it means to realize oneself.

Mister Barlow believed that only by realizing our own potential could we come that much closer to perfect being, to God. In his interview with the Greeley Tribune, he even compared himself to Faust, who understood that man is a fallen creature, but that salvation is his as long as he continues to strive and grow—i.e. to self-transcend.

The Summa states that monks and bishops are in a state of perfection, that priests are pretty darn close, but all of them are much closer to perfection than being married. That helps explain his lack of interest in finding a mate. Interestingly, however, Mister Barlow deliberately chose not to become either a priest or a monk. He may have sensed a lack of perfection in those professions during his exposure to them. We also cannot discount his own feelings of unworthiness, by killing men in the war, despite the fact that the Summa expressly defines a "just war" and that World War II fit that criteria. He apparently held himself to an even greater standard. Another theory is that he may have decided that the Church was merely a dogmatic structure imposed by man upon man, and not truly arising from the Divine. He may have experienced enough authoritarianism in the army, and didn't want another structure imposed upon him. His anti-authoritarian streak demonstrated towards Greeley administration supports this theory.

Still, he admired other aspects of the clergy's lifestyle, so he chose the next closest thing: to live a monastic life, to give away large amounts of money to charity, to help others, and self-transcend by becoming a teacher. After all, how can one widen the circles of experience of others, without first doing so oneself?

He also decided he would become the best teacher possible. Thus, he encouraged students to achieve the highest possible goals, to use 110% of their minds, and to achieve perfection. It was why he also admired those students who were also athletes. He probably appreciated them excelling with their bodies as well as their minds, as well as seeing in them a reflection of his own physical challenges during the war. This also applied to his female students. He was equally respectful and impressed by the female athletes in his classes, as asserted by several of my interviewees.

So, being an idealist, he therefore chose a field where there was no moral ambiguity, where there would be only one single correct answer to any problem: mathematics! Physics, of course, was a close second because it also had concrete rules of how the universe worked.

Mister Barlow, however, had one other thing going for him. So determined was he to be close to God, that he recognized the significance of being wholly devoted to one thing, of being in the moment of intellectual thought. In that moment of action, of teaching, of contemplation, everything else fell away. It is like the painter when he is painting, the athlete who reacts instinctively in the game, or the ocean wave that hits the shore—it just does what it does naturally. It is those moments the Self is not conceiving of itself, in relation to itself. It is those moments that we are in touch with the Divine. The Danish philosopher Kierkegaard described this moment as, "The self resting transparently in the spirit which gives it rise," and notes that it is also "the absence of despair."

So when Mister Barlow was asked in the Tribune interview what he liked most about teaching, he naturally responded, "that it exists." For in the moment of teaching, he is touching God.

To Mister Barlow, there was only one right answer, one form of purity, and that was God. To devote oneself to God, to try and achieve the virtues of God, was paramount. So anything that allowed a person to approach God, or to approach perfection, was of the highest priority to him. The ultimate happiness actually comes in the afterlife, to a precious few, the Saints, those who revel in the beatific vision. In short, this means God eternally and directly perceiving someone. In life, we can only understand God indirectly, by means such as prayer or living the contemplative life. The beatific vision was what Mister Barlow was striving for—finding God once again, and God eternally finding him.

In a way, then, Mister Barlow was a missionary, but proselytized without ever once mentioning God, or Allah, or Yahweh, or Ra, or the Buddha— as these were all just dogmatic structures. Mister Barlow wanted each of us to realize ourselves and to rest transparently in the spirit which gave us rise. One did not need a religious institution to accomplish this. So, he felt that guiding me to become a writer and realizing myself, and my potential, was a greater deed than nudging me to stick with the more intellectual pursuits of chemistry. He recognized this as being my purpose. He and I were, indeed, Narcissus and Goldmund. And the final irony is that my chosen craft in fact employs both elements of intellectualism and artistry. I only wish I could have shown him that.

It is also worth touching on other of Aquinas' insights, in explaining Mister Barlow's life. Aquinas identified faith, hope, and charity as the three theological virtues. These seem self-explanatory, with regard to how Mister Barlow incorporated them into his life.

Aquinas also identified the four cardinal virtues as Prudence (judging between virtuous and vicious actions), Temperence (the practice of moderation), Justice (the proper allocation of things), and Fortitude (courage). Certainly two of these virtues played a daily role for Mister Barlow. He was under enormous temptation to give in to alcohol, yet was able to strike a deal with himself, to never permit it to affect his teaching.

As for Fortitude, he instilled that every day in his students. His love for them was endless. It was tough love, to be sure. However, based on the hardships of his early life, he knew the kids would be facing a dangerous world and they absolutely needed to be prepared. Unlike kids who grew up in the inner-city (where one might have expected him to teach), Chappaqua's kids were growing up in the soft underbelly of upper-class, white America. They needed toughening up, because they would likely be the ones to lead the nation into the next millenium, and for all he knew they might end up as soldiers.

To that end, it was essential his students have courage. The object of courage, after all, is to prepare a person to face death. He wanted them to be prepared for battle, whether in a foreign country, or an Ivy League school. However, while some teachers leave teaching behind when they exit the classroom, Mister Barlow's lessons could be delivered at any random moment.

Martha Holmes encountered Mister Barlow her freshman year. She was walking down a hallway and Mister Barlow was walking towards her. She happened to notice him wearing a pair of bright red socks and thus, her eye lingered on them. Mister Barlow marched right up to her, stuck his nose in her face and said, "What are you staring at?" At first petrified, Martha spat out, "Your red socks." He asked her name, she told him, he recognized her as the younger sister of another of his students, and in reply said, "Hmph. Another one." He then continued on his way. Weeks later, Martha heard that Mister Barlow had brought up her name in another context and called her, "A woman of high character who can be counted on."

Despite all these intellectual groundings, however, Mister Barlow also encountered someone who crystallized it all into a course of pragmatic action he could pursue. While at Harvard in 1951 obtaining his A.B. in Education, he took a class in *The Philosophy of Education* from Professor Robert Ulich. I believe Prof. Ulich was the single, biggest influence on Mister Barlow's teaching style, one that was consonant with his altered view of life after returning home from the war.

Ulich was a legend, an "educator of educators." He was born in Bavaria in 1890 to a family with deep roots as religious thinkers. He excelled in his studies, eventually graduating with a Ph.D. at age 25, and devoted himself to a new concept of education—that it must help direct students to find progress and happiness in life. He was instrumental in helping Germany rebuild itself educationally after World War I and taught philosophy at Dresden from 1923 to 1934. He resigned when a group of colleagues were fired for being, "racially and politically undesirable." His prescience allowed him to escape from the rising tide of Nazism to the United

States, where he was subsequently appointed a Professor of the History and Philosophy of Education, at Harvard. That is where Mister Barlow encountered him, and it was during the time, that Ulich was probably preparing to write his seminal book <u>The Human Career,</u> released in 1955. Thus, Ulich's concepts were delivered to an all-too-eager student, ready to absorb his wisdom.

Some essential quotations from Ulich's book will clarify how his theories impacted Mister Barlow, and took the teaching of Aquinas to a new level.

"Having a purpose helps the Ego overcome its own inner contradiction. A person gains true freedom to the degree to which he is able to sacrifice his smaller self (Ego) to his greater self (Purpose)."

The Ego is that which defines who/what we are in any given moment. Its nature is to be in stasis. If we give ourselves a purpose, then we are constantly moving towards something. This defeats the Ego, which wants us to remain in stasis. Thus, we sacrifice it (and its false comforts) in order to grow, or transcend.

"The sense of purpose will create in [man] criteria of the important and unimportant, and the increasing clarity of viewpoint can mould the variety of actions in a coherent life scheme. This is learning in its most profound and essential meaning."

So, with a sense of purpose, we'll start to understand the things that are going to help us achieve that purpose, and those that don't. That helps us *learn* how to make the proper choices at any given moment.

"Only out of the many purposes which may occur in life, and through an organic development of various capacities, can a person develop a meaningful and single purpose. And only when their development is inspired by an awareness of lasting commitment to the world to which he belongs, can he achieve the highest level of devotion and at the same time the highest level of existential self-realization."

Indeed, Mister Barlow had many perceived purposes in life: become a priest, be a good soldier, and be a devoted son. The war tore away the first purpose, its conclusion rendered the second temporary, and the death of his mother removed the third.

So there he was, purposeless. Once he realized that his ultimate purpose was to instruct, he devoted himself entirely to it, aiming to realize himself to the maximum possible extent. This was also entirely in line with Kant's Categorical Imperative, which he studied at Holy Cross.

Ulich specifically describes the importance of finding the proper vocation, which Mister Barlow himself echoed in his <u>Tribune</u> interview and to me directly: "It is through finding a vocation that man discovers his purpose. Is it not through his desire to be useful, which can be fulfilled only in some chosen work, that man finds his self-respect?"

Prof. Ulich solidified Mister Barlow's desire to become a teacher, and gave him specific tools on what to impart to his students, and how to do it. This is where he concocted his customized teaching cocktail—part drill sergeant, part Ulich, part taskmaster. It answers why Mister Barlow chose the teaching style he did. Instilling courage and fortitude in his students is part of it, but it goes deeper. No student or person can jump into a new experience, without first having a grounding and confidence (faith) is his foundation. Barlow was trying to give us that foundation, from a place of comfort and relative ease—a classroom in a privileged community. Ulich himself said a teacher's methods are irrelevant. What matters is they achieve a sense of purpose and that a lack of challenge in a young person's life may make them fearful of risk.

Self-transcendence is a continual process of ever-widening circles of experience, and those voyages are not without peril or failure. Ulich says that unadmitted, or unaccepted, failure is literally a tool of Satan. He doesn't refer to the red fellow with horns and pitchfork, but rather to man's own ability to delude himself. Accepting failure is how we <u>learn</u>, how we self-transcend. Thus, when Mister Barlow was yelling at us for making a mistake, or for disrespecting him, or for disrespecting our minds, he felt he was literally protecting us from Satan. And one thing is certain: whatever transgression caused him to explode was never repeated. We <u>learned</u>.

This applies right down to the seemingly little things, like not writing "Mister" on an exam booklet in front of his name. One little slip like that in the real world could cause you to lose out on a job—your chosen vocation, your purpose in life!

But most of all, Ulich believed that being an individual was, in fact, an illusion. We literally are at unity with one another and with God. Never is this more true than in war. There is a reason why soldiers are broken down as individuals, only to be built back up again, to perceive themselves as members of a team. They cannot survive on their own. Mister Barlow had first-hand experience with this. And another reason he was so hard on us was because we very well might find ourselves in combat one day, and one instant of slackened focus could be deadly to ourselves and to our compatriots.

*   *   *

Fortunately, there are some fictional pieces of literature that offer more concise views of Mister Barlow's life. By identifying his interest in various tomes to students and faculty, he revealed himself. If one assumes that a person's taste for a particular book stems from an identification with the subject matter or main character, then Mister Barlow tried to show people his soul in an indirect way.

So what of <u>Alice in Wonderland</u>? Certainly, the frequent sightings of him reading this book was part of his affectation, another prop of the Barlow persona, another attempt to tantalize the curious. Beyond that, Lewis Carroll was a mathematician, and there are numerous mathematical puns, puzzles and assorted references for the astute reader. Mister Barlow also enjoyed languages, and besides dabbling in many of them, his love of crossword puzzles and nursery rhymes suggests that any clever use of words caught his interest. Why? I suspect that he felt knowledge of clever wordplay was a signature of the intellectual royalty he tried to attain.

The book may also have generated a bit of curiosity from Mister Barlow. As much as he dismissed the arts, he ascribed quasi-Biblical importance to Carroll's text. Perhaps he was mystified how a mathematician could also have the ability to create an artistic work.

But most importantly, Mister Barlow said the book contains his complete "philosophy of education." How interesting that this was the name of the course he took from Ulich! So is this book is about self-transcendence? Yes, in a way.

As near as I can figure it, Mister Barlow wanted to turn out students who applied logic and rationality to a world that was unpredictable, chaotic and frequently made very little sense. They needed to learn from it the best they could. In fact, one might even see a moral in the story that Alice was not paying attention to her studies, and fell into a world with which she was unprepared to deal.

This may play into another mystery—specifically, why he spent summers in Portugal. He was fascinated with languages and had mentioned his interest in Portuguese in our class more than once. I believe he went there to learn and practice this language. It falls into the category of expanding his circles of experience. It's also notable that if one wishes to experience Wonderland first-hand, just drop into a foreign country where you don't know the language!

There may also have been some interest with Fatima, the village best known for multiple appearances of the Virgin Mary and her delivery of prophecies to three young children. Still, that seems a stretch. He wouldn't go every year just to hang out there. It also seems highly unlikely that he had an annual rendezvous there with someone he met in Europe during the war, so I discount that possibility.

Finally, there is a commonality that stretches from Alice, to his affection for Lovecraft's work, to The Catcher in the Rye. Each of these works brings up a longing for Mister Barlow's innocent childhood days. Can one blame him for wanting to return to his earlier days, before the War, before the bottle, before the responsibilities of adult life?

Alice in Wonderland has plenty of elements to delight adults. But at its core, it is a story written for a child, by a man who adored children, and unfolds in the way that very young children tell stories. They are fanciful, without structured narrative rules or transitions, and without a moral. Ask a three-year-old to tell a story and the result will be very much structured like Alice in Wonderland. In the final paragraph of Carroll's book, we see this theme of longing for childhood emerge as Alice's older sister reflects on her sister's dream:

> Lastly, she pictured to herself how this same little
> sister of hers would, in the after-time, be herself a
> grown woman; and how she would keep, through all her

riper years, the simple and loving heart of her childhood, and how she would gather about her other little children, and make their eyes bright and eager with many a strange tale, perhaps even with the dream of Wonderland of long ago; and how she would feel with all their simple sorrows, and find a pleasure in their simple joys, remembering her own child-life, and the happy summer days.

Mister Barlow gathered about himself plenty of children, and made their eyes bright and eager with many a strange tale—of himself. He told the Greeley Tribune that if he could be any person from history, it would be Lewis Carroll. Perhaps, like that mathematician, he yearned to tell silly tales of a world that existed halfway between reality and fantasy. Perhaps he yearned to tell the story of his own world.

Other stories cut to the very core of what Mister Barlow lacked in his life. Of all the gifts he could have given to Bob Gluck, why The Catcher in the Rye? The basis for Mister Barlow and Bob's association had been the Lovecraft stories that reminded Mister Barlow of his youth. Holden Caulfield's desire to catch the children exiting the rye, to prevent them from falling off the cliff (from childhood into adulthood) resonated with Mister Barlow. His happiest memories were of his youth, despite the hard times, because his mother was alive. He experienced, in the most fiery of ways, this transition to adulthood.

Likewise, he identified with Holden's desperate and awkward attempts to forge emotional connections with other people. Up until I re-read the book myself, I had thought that Mister Barlow was ignorant of his inability to create intimate relationships with anyone. However, the subtle

265

nuances and themes of literature were not lost on Mister Barlow. I think he knew he was incapable, or unwilling, to get close to people and that he also knew it was a tragedy.

This revelation was driven home when I read the final haunting paragraph of <u>Narcissus and Goldmund</u>. Goldmund had been dropped at the monastery as a youth by his father, who disapproved on his mother's sins of the flesh. Goldmund never remembered what his mother's face looked like, and when he left the monastery at Narcissus' urging, he began to seek out his path in life, and hoped to recall his mother's image. The story is ultimately about Goldmund's realization of the Self, and after discovering it, he finally recalls the image of his mother. Goldmund dies in the presence of his friend Narcissus, invoking the mother-image as the key to love and life.

> And now the sick man opened his eyes again and looked for a long while into his friend's face. He said farewell with his eyes. And with a sudden movement, as if he were trying to shake his head, he whispered, "But how will you die when your time comes, Narcissus, since you have no mother? Without a mother, one cannot love. Without a mother, one cannot die." What he murmured after that could not be understood. Those last two days Narcissus sat by his bed day and night, watching his life ebb away. Goldmund's last words burned like a fire in his heart.

Mister Barlow knew about a life without love. In the end, I think he regretted closing himself off to it. It made it difficult for people to approach him, then, because they read his vibe. They knew instinctively not to press him on anything personal.

Perhaps this tragic denial of love is best expressed in one final, mythological story. The fable of <u>The Fisher King</u> has many different versions, but at its core, it went like this: A young and innocent knight named Parcifal came across a castle during his travels. The lands of this particular kingdom had been laid to waste, and life was generally crappy. So Parcifal entered the castle and found an infirm old man sitting on a throne. The old man, known as The Fisher King, was very ill. He had, like Mister Barlow, suffered a terrible wound in his thigh. He hovered in a place that was not quite life and not quite death. The only time he felt better was when he went fishing (i.e. being quiet and reflective, in mythological terms).

Parcifal observed as a procession entered the hall, carrying a spear and some kind of chalice, and its participants looked to him expectantly. Rather than ask what the heck was going on and why the poor king had fallen ill, he stays politely silent, as he had been taught as a youngster. He was then kicked out of the castle and called a simpleton!

Well, Parcifal was mystified by all this and wandered off, only to later be told that the chalice in the Fisher King's castle was the Holy Grail itself. If only he'd done the right thing, he would have had the Grail and brought healing to the King and the land!

Poor Parcifal was upset by all this and struck out on his own to find the castle again. He searched for five years, and in the process, learned enough about life to more fully realize himself. As luck would have it, the castle appeared to him again. This time he entered, he saw the infirm Fisher King and the procession, and asked "What is it that ails you?" Simply asking the question, offering compassion, instantly healed the Fisher King and his kingdom.

I believe Mister Barlow to be the Fisher King. An old man, who spent much of his life in intellectual reflection, devastated by a wound (in his case, the literal and psychological wounds of the war), waiting for someone to ask the question, waiting for some kind of connection to be made, a connection he probably subconsciously desired but was afraid to pursue. Some, like Bob Gluck and John Willard, came close.

In another way, I think he may also have been waiting for the word of God, in the form of forgiveness. The idea that he turned away from the priesthood, and instead killed other men, must have haunted him all his life. This, coupled with a wound in the form of survival guilt, devastated him internally. Perhaps he was waiting for a Divine messenger to ease him of the burden that he could not release himself from. He became the Fisher King, waiting for a Parcifal who would never arrive.

CHAPTER THIRTY-TWO

Through His Secrets

The most intriguing aspect of Mister Barlow's desire for privacy was that he was not merely satisfied with keeping his secrets hidden. Instead, he relished in creating and nurturing multiple myths about himself. He could have been a master spy, given the sheer amount of disinformation he helped disseminate. This reminds me of Andy Kaufman, the brilliant comic who (some say) made life itself a kind of perpetual living theatre—life as theatre, theatre as life. Mister Barlow seemed to be cut from the same mold. Just as Kaufman devoted his life to guerrilla theater, or a bizarre style of performance art, I think Mister Barlow did, too. People would walk out of Kaufman acts wondering what the heck they'd just witnessed. Comedy? Entertainment? A mental breakdown?

The difference lies in intent. Kaufman seemed to want to destroy the boundary between performance and life, behaving like a Dadaist. Mister Barlow did the same, but it was directed towards keeping his True Self hidden. Ironically, this attempt to throw people off course seems to have been the way he most connected with people—he piqued their curiosity and bonded with kids on a prankish level.

But it is exactly those secrets, of course, that hold keys to understanding him. Uncovering those secrets meant investigating the most painful parts of Mister Barlow's life. Reporting these items, though, felt like a betrayal of his memory. I had spent so much time finding such extraordinary things about Mister Barlow, that to report that the two strongest influences in his life were negative ones, troubled me. And yet, to be true to my search and to his memory, to provide others with all the lessons

269

of his life, I cannot omit the unfortunate facts of his life. On the other hand, it is precisely these negative influences that propelled him on his journey to seek a reconciliation with God.

There can be no denying the influence alcohol had on him. I even hate to mention it, as if it were the paramount force behind his character. In truth, it isn't. However, it did shape many of his life decisions. I think his decision to reject the priesthood was based on several factors. His personal sins, such as the taking of human lives and alcoholism, made him feel that he did not fit the mold of perfection he ascribed to the priesthood. I think he would also have endured more scrutiny as a priest, and that might make it more difficult to hide his alcoholism. I also suspect that he had a need to be involved in something utterly pure, and instinct told him that despite the favor he granted the Church, it had some very serious flaws, as well. I believe he rejected the Christian Brotherhood for the same reasons. If he couldn't be a priest, then being a monk paled in comparison.

The third choice was to teach. I think he felt he could better serve a coummunity as a teacher. His destiny was sealed once he began studying scholastic philosophy at Holy Cross, and discovered it was possible to be observant, be a servant to God, but also instruct. And, of course, Ulich's teachings brought it all together.

Mister Barlow's other shocking action was cutting himself off from his family. I think there were several reasons for this, but his drinking was likely a significant factor. Just as Agnes had hidden her bout with cancer, I think Mister Barlow wanted to hide his affliction. The Barlow family always projected stoicism in the face of difficulty. An acknowledgement of his disease might have made Mister Barlow feel that he would appear weak. Already, his brother Dave had battled alcohol troubles and landed in rehab more than once. As the Barlows were not ones to share feelings, and Mister

Barlow already displayed a desire for privacy and an avoidance of intimate relationships, the easiest course of action was to run away.

He did not want to be beholden to anybody, and the last thing he needed was for Al, or anyone else, to meddle in his affairs. I think he also just wanted to try and start over, without familial obligations, and without having to submit to invasive discussions about his lifestyle. Still, the stark and unforgiving nature of this choice is disturbing. It shows that Mister Barlow, while capable of showing great compassion, could also be coldly logical and unemotional.

This choice to live the life of a quasi-monk also stemmed from alcohol abuse. There were philosophical reasons for it, but this lifestyle may have been the only way he could control the chaos in his life. I believe it was only through faith, prayer, and strict mental discipline that he could tackle the Demon. Perhaps this was akin to a penitent's self-flagellation. By removing all materialistic possessions from his life, by denying himself pleasures of the flesh, he could focus his mind on his work and his battle against drinking. This may also be a reason why he so neglected his physical health. He may have compartmentalized his physical afflications and his intellectual powers. He could revel in the life of the mind, and let alcohol destroy his body, mistakenly believing that his mind could always outrun and outlive his body.

Unfortunately, he was never a particularly healthy man, and the mind has only so much power over the body. In examining his medical records, Mister Barlow suffered from obesity and hypertension, which went untreated from the first diagnosis in the 1957 through the mid-seventies. While arguably malpractice by today's standards, this sadly may not have been unusual in those days.

By 1979, he was developing early heart failure, his blood pressure was far too high and never properly controlled. By mid-1987, he was suffering from biventricular heart failure and generalized vascular disease, both of which resulted in fluid and pressure buildup. Indeed, the primary cause of death was congestive heart failure.

*   *   *

So, partially as a result of alcohol, Mister Barlow utterly imprisoned himself in a life without love. The Barlow family never spoke to each other about life, about feelings, or about much of anything. There was no true intimacy. To that end, Mister Barlow never developed the tools to allow himself to cope with life's greatest treasure. For all his attempts to instill us with fortitude, he lacked it himself, in this one area. He loved God and he loved his mother, to be sure. This, however, was where love stopped.

In many ways, I think this is because he believed there could be no greater loves than God and Mother. I am loathe to invite Freud into my analysis, but my instructor appears to have suffered from a lifelong Oedipal Complex. Agnes was Mister Barlow's first love object—a nonsexual, sacred love object—and because he never outgrew that, this fixation became entrenched in his psyche. Thus, no woman was capable of matching the love he received, and felt for, his mother. She was the Madonna, and when you've had the love of the Madonna, there is nowhere to go but down. So why bother? Toss in the Summa's assertion that being a monk and priest brought one closer to perfection, and physical love seemed a pointless exercise.

This naturally brings up the question of whether or not he hated women, other than his mother. Despite an apparent chivalry demonstrated to adult women, that is where his interest in them stopped. They were treated almost as royalty, with not a shred of sexual innuendo dropped either in their presence, or in front of his male colleagues. From where did this gentlemanly attitude come? It likely lay in his past. I suspected it had to do with the manners he was taught as a youth. I had ruled out the possibility that he'd been married, as not a shred of evidence even suggested the possibility. Marriage also contradicted his philosophical and theological principles.

His treatment of women in the classroom was a source of consternation. In one sense, I was viewing his comments and attacks through the prism of 21st century gender attitudes. His comments never would pass muster today, to be sure. We can look back on some of his inflammatory statements and feel shocked at his insensitivity. For me, the question boiled down to two difficult subjects: Did he hate women, and did the women receive treatment any different from the boys?

If he hated women, then it would fail to account for the deference shown to both adults and those brilliant women in his classes. Being as outspoken as he was, I think disparaging comments regarding women would have been heard outside his class. Yet nobody reported that he said or did anything of the sort. He certainly never did in my presence.

His attack on Elissa Grossman might have been sexist, but everything he did had a specific objective. He'd thrown down the gauntlet to other female students, telling them that going to any of the "Heavenly Seven" colleges was a waste of time because they'd only learn to "pour tea" at those institutions. Was this some type of affirmative action? Given that Mister Barlow prized education above all else, and his educational philosophy seemed to have a definitive grounding in the venerable Summa Theologica, I didn't believe he was consciously or intentionally sexist—which is hardly an excuse.

Elissa may have been targeted because she made Mister Barlow look foolish in front of his class. The greatest sin, short of being stupid during class, was to undermine his authority. Elissa was not the only person to discover this. Several students reported witnessing or being on the receiving end of a world-class verbal crucifixion for committing the same crime. In the early days, and even in his algebra classes throughout the 80's, he would frequently punish mutinous students by having them write some admonishing sentence 1000 times. Those who showed disrespect to the details of a class, such as leaving a piece of paper behind on the floor, might be required to write "Litter" 2000 times. . .and then recite it in front of the class. These punishments were actually meted out more on the males than the females.

He also spoke to this issue directly in his interview with the Greeley Tribune in 1984: "I am entitled to respect. When I was at Harvard...when the professor walked in there was absolute silence. The students didn't have to be silent, they just gave him that respect. If Greeley is supposed to be a preparation for Harvard, etc, then I should be accorded that same respect. I won't even debate the issue. I expect it from the beginning."

Let's examine Elissa's story through Ulich's prism. She could be accused of cheating in college for what she did, and thus cause her endless trouble. By announcing the answer in class when confronted by Mister Barlow, she made him look foolish. Making an authority figure look foolish is the surest way to lose a job—or again, one's purpose in life could hang in the balance by disrespecting an occupational hierarchy. She got reamed for it, and now we understand why—although we are free to disagree with the tactic.

Regrettably, he did call on the boys to perform more often in my class than the girls. Others reported the same. To that end, inequity existed. While his classroom method dictated that only the "Who's Who" was generally called to the board, it seems unlikely that only boys should hold those top seven spots, year after year. Yet Mister Barlow was filled with contradictions. One brilliant woman from the class of 1985, Margo Schlanger, told me, "His sexism was trivial compared to the degree to which he encouraged girls to excel in math." Whereas some males felt Mister Barlow did ignore women, Jane Beaman ('84) told me that she was the one most often called upon to explain correct answers to boys who had made a mistake.

From his perspective, he may not have believed that girls were as capable as boys. I was disappointed in this revelation, but before condemning him individually, I noted that his attitude was unfortunately very common. In a 1988 study commissioned by the American Association of University Women Education Foundation entitled, <u>Gender Gaps: Where Schools Still Fail Our Children</u>, I found this telling quotation: "Excellent education—education that meets high standards—requires equitable teaching. But teachers, because they receive little or no training in equity from schools of education, are unprepared."

And what of his other relationships? Neither the topic of love, nor marriage, ever came up in any conversation he ever had. Such matters of the heart weren't even on his radar. As much as I rely on philosophical and theological arguments for this behavior, the truth may simply stem from his inability to forge intimate relationships.

Thirty-five years in Chappaqua yielded only intellectual and prankish companions. His only close relationships were with men, and even those he kept at arm's length. The closest relationships he could muster were with John Willard, Robert Gluck, and an alcoholic Eddie Dearborn. In them, his behavior suggested a yearning for a kind of familial relationship, to forge a kind of father-son bond. The kind of affection Mister Barlow showed to John in particular, the warmth that accompanied John's recollections, the sharing of poetry and gifts, reminded me of the behavior of a mentor or a father, but which was not quite either.

The comparison of John's relationship with Mister Barlow to that of Narcissus and Goldmund seemed particularly apt. It was intellectually based. It was fatherly in tone. But it never was about love. In further examining Hesse's text, one thing struck me about Narcissus that deepened my understanding of Mister Barlow.

Narcissus, as self-aware as he was concerning his place in the intellectual world, was utterly oblivious about what role human love could actually have in his life. It was as if he never gave love a single thought, expunged the concept from his person, and therefore had no understanding of its value. Mister Barlow apparently shared Narcissus' ignorance, and never knew what he was missing. This seemed a tragedy, that a man should never know love, but simultaneously a blessing, for he never knew the pain of missing life's most exquisite gift.

It was this exact moment of realization, that Mister Barlow did not know everything about life, that he suddenly became more real to me. This man, the brilliant mathematician, physicist, linguist and literati, was ignorant about life's most important aspect!

Mister Barlow was either terrified of revealing himself, or simply did not know how. Whatever the reason, his lack of any kind of love relationship made him a very lonely man. He'd so insulated himself in the life of the mind, and so closed himself from human emotional contact, that he was forever destined to be alone.

CHAPTER THIRTY-THREE

Through His Own Words

The interview with Mister Barlow that appeared in the <u>Greeley Tribune</u> (Chapter 16) is unique. No other resource, save alumni notebooks and memories, contains Mister Barlow's own words. Some of his answers speak for themselves, others fill in a few missing details in my theories, others now allow us insight into what he was willing to share about his life, and others are outright lies. It is also instructive to see exactly how he answers specific questions, and which words and phrases he uses.

Q: How did your educational background influence you as a person and as a teacher?

A: "Neither experience did anything for me as a person. I was the same person when I went into college as when I came out."

It strikes me as odd that someone would claim they remained unchanged after four years of doing anything. The trick lies in Mister Barlow's definition of "person." While the reporters, Messrs. Feldberg and Robin, obviously meant the word "person" as a kind of gestalt impression of oneself, Mister Barlow chose a more narrow interpretation of the word. If the intellect was all that mattered, then his physical state did not change, nor did his aspirations. In his answer, he also omits the fact that his mother died while he was in college, and this irrevocably changed him in the gestalt. However, we have since learned that his educational background influenced

277

him a great deal! So he appears to have deliberately dodged that question, as it really does speak to the core of his personality.

"In my household, no one dared say anything during supper. We had to read books, or newspapers. It was all academics in my household. My mother was a teacher. My parents were interested only in academic excellence."

As we learned, Agnes was not a teacher—at least not one who worked in a classroom. She may have taught him many lessons about life, but that's stretching his statement pretty far. Nor were his parents only interested in academic excellence.

"Everyone who shows up in this world has a vocation. If you fight that feeling, you'll be unhappy. If you don't, you won't be unhappy."

We first must note that this is a direct application of Ulich's, and Kant's, philosophy. So as much as he dodged the college question, this statement reveals just as much as that question could have. But note how he says, "You won't be unhappy." Why not say, "You'll be happy"? The reason is Mister Barlow believed that more was required to achieve happiness than a satisfying vocation. To put it in logical terminology: A satisfying vocation guarantees that one will not be unhappy, but more is required to achieve true happiness. But what is true happiness? It is self-transcendence, but explained in another way. In Walter Farrell's <u>A Companion to the Summa</u>, Vol. II, Chapter 1, entitled The Essence of Happiness, we find this oversimplified explanation:

All men...want what they want...In the attainment of what they want we have the essential notion of happiness. It is the possession of the object of desire which constitutes happiness...The object of his pursuit of happiness is not outside man and in the universe; it is not within man, body or soul...it is above man and the universe...it is the absolutely universal good, outside and above man. The attainment of the final goal, not its mere existence, marks the close of the pursuit of happiness. And that means no less than our having reached out and taken possession of the final good, bringing it into ourselves, making it our own. In The Meaning of Right and Wrong, (New York: The Macmillan Co., p. 112 ff, 1936) Dr. Cabot of Harvard insists that man's business in life is to grow.

In short, Mister Barlow told us that finding one's true vocation puts one on the road to happiness because we will self-transcend as human beings in that vocation. Because we have at least begun to reach out for the final goal of happiness, we will therefore not be unhappy.

Thus, when asked what he likes most about teaching, he naturally replies, "that it exists." To him, the mere existence of his desired vocation put him on the road to happiness, and through inductive reasoning, proved that a Universal Good existed towards which he could strive.

"It would be obscene to offer something less than first class. Whatever is the categorical imperative for me, has to be done first class."

This again speaks to his level of devotion. He considered his vocation his duty, and for him to achieve happiness, it meant that he was required to pursue it to the best of all possible means. Hence, the reason why he never took a day off.

It's also worth mentioning his obsession with things being "first-class." It's a phrase he used often, and his gifts of Chivas Regal (the gift of kings), speak to his desire to achieve a kind of royalty in his life—not material royalty (since he expunged material wealth from his life), but an intellectual, attitudinal, and behavioral royalty. He'd spent much of his life among the lower class, and his taste of England and Paris during the war likely awakened him to the possibility of a better lifestyle. It's another reason he likely cut ties with his family, and also chose a wealthy suburb in which to teach—he wanted to leave his Depression days behind.

"Boston Latin School was a big school which was very impersonal. Oddly enough, I chose Greeley because it offered personal assocations on my terms...This is sort of an oddity because while I try to avoid close associations with students, I chose a school where they could happen."

This speaks to the paradox of Mister Barlow. He was a man at conflict within himself, about the extent to which personal relationships should exist in his life. He was aware of his limitations with intimacy, yet desperately desired it, just like Holden Caulfied in The Catcher in the Rye. Mister Barlow went on to say:

"[I chose high school over college because] in the lower grades, a teacher only deals with the personal aspects of education. In college, the emphasis is

purely intellectual. At high school, there is the perfect balance between the two."

He virtually states that he is in conflict between the personal and the intellectual, and that he chose a place where both existed. From an educational point of view, I believe high school also afforded him the opportunity to have a greater impact on students, a place where he could prepare them for the difficult world they would face, a place where he could directly teach fortitude, per the Summa Theologica. In college, the students have already passed the more vulnerable period of life where he could make a greater impression.

"[During the Vietnam War] I wasn't affected by all those riots, demonstrations, and flag burnings"

This is a curious statement coming from a Veteran. Clearly, his service played a formative role in his life. He must have had some opinion, if not actual feelings, about the Vietnam War. On one hand, I'm sure that as a Veteran he would have wanted to see more support for the troops. On the other hand, considering how violently the war affected him, I suspect he would have liked to see the U.S. pull out of Vietnam. So the truth is that he was certainly affected, but rather than reveal that he was a Vet himself, he dodged the question. Of one thing we can be sure: he would have vastly preferred that all those young men have gone to college and used their minds instead of going overseas with rifles in their hands.

Q: You are considered to be a very enigmatic person. Could you tell us a little about your interests to shed light on yourself as a person?

A: The one thing that I find most intriguing is that television program "Lost in Space." It is thoroughly delightful. I also like...Sesame Street. I like to imagine the way kids are reacting to that show and if they're getting what they're supposed to get. Everything I do relates back to education. I also like reading for pleasure. I enjoy good spy novels, and I think I've read every single book written on U.F.O.'s They're adult fairy tales and, of course, they're all nonsense."

First, take note of how everything he does relates back to education. That is 100% Ulich. As for <u>Lost in Space</u>, he had mentioned that to me, as well. What did he find interesting about that show, and the similar world of UFO's? The key lies in his description of these as adult fairy tales. Given his love for <u>Alice in Wonderland</u>, there is some significance to his interest in stories that thrust people into strange worlds. Some of the characters in <u>Lost in Space</u>, particularly during the later seasons when the show became more campy, are similar to the odd denizens of Wonderland. These characters required the protagonists to shift their perspective in order to survive. They are in their own Wonderlands. Also, he was fascinated by Lovecraft novels as a youth, because of their horror and science-fiction angles, so these interests seem to be an extension of that love.

"[My favorite character in literature] is Moby Dick. The whale, not Ahab." That whale personifies so much."

The whale in Melville's novel is generally considered symbolic of unattainable excellence, which is certainly consonant with Mister Barlow's fascination with perfection. Interestingly, Melville also compares whaling to

282

royal activity, as when he mentions Louis XVI's devotion to the whaling industry, and considers the whale as a delicacy fit only for royalty. Mister Barlow's consistent aspirations to royalty are also reflected in his admiration for the whale. Melville also maintains the whale as an ambiguous figure through much of the novel. There is no literal interpretation provided for it, its whiteness is representative of its absence of meaning, and the multiple detailing of its various aspects only serve to further shroud it in mystery. Sounds a lot like Mister Barlow himself.

"If I could be anybody in history, I would be Charles Lutwidge Dodgson, that is, Lewis Carroll."

As it has been difficult enough to research one man's life, I shall leave specific comparisons of Mister Barlow and Dodgson to intrepid readers who peruse the latter's biography. On the surface, however, there are striking parallels between the two men. Dodgson was a resident and alumnus of Oxford (Christ Church). He was a math teacher. He enjoyed logic and mathematics puzzles. His physical appearance was asymmetric (shoulders of unequal height, eye level not equivalent), and he was deaf in one ear (recalling Mister Barlow's wounded ear). He walked with a strange gait. He did not care for profanity, and according to Martin Gardner's <u>The Annotated Alice</u>, "was so shy that he could sit for hours at a social gathering and contribute nothing to the conversation and was...a confirmed bachelor whose life was sexless, uneventful, and happy."

Dodgson himself even once wrote, "My life is so strangely free from all trial and trouble that I cannot doubt my own happiness is one of the talents entrusted to me to occupy with, till the Master shall return, by doing something to make other lives happy." This pursuit of happiness is expounded on at great length in the <u>Summa Theologica</u>, and when I analyze it, it seems obvious that this was one of Mister Barlow's primary goals in life.

"I have become extremely liberal in my extra-curricular associations. I would never have allowed this interview in my first ten years. I would have had nothing to do with students outside of the classroom."

Of course, these are all falsehoods, save his comment about the interview. He frequently socialized with faculty in his early days, and also cultivated close relationships with John Willard, Bob Gluck, and Eddie Dearborn. What is interesting to note is whether or not Mister Barlow intended these statements as lies, or if he honestly believed himself to be more open in 1984 than when he first arrived. If so, I would argue that the image he had of himself was wrong, and that he was deluding himself. More provocative is the assertion that he wanted to become more liberal in his associations and thus projected that that is what he had done.

CHAPTER THIRTY-FOUR

Through Me

"When my children were small, I occassionally brought them with me to Greeley on a Saturday or Sunday. We would frequently find Ed Barlow sitting at a desk and exchange greetings. In their youthful innocence, my children honestly believed Ed was Horace Greeley himself. Maybe they were right"

- Larry Breen, in his eulogy for Mister Barlow.

* * *

The distinction between hero and mentor is usually very clear. Mentors provide teach and train a budding hero, and are a reflection of our wise and noble inner voice. They prepare students for their own hero's journey, the mythological path we all take to complete ourselves, to achieve our highest aspirations, to discover life's meaning. Mister Barlow devoted his life to being a mentor to many students, including myself.

Yet, Mister Barlow seemed a flawed mentor. He was not the perfect, wise old man so often seen in stories. He was lonely, irascible, alienating, rigid, uncompromising, judgmental, and socially dysfunctional. In many stories, some mentors are themselves still on their own hero's journey. They have become unable to complete the final steps of their transformation into complete human beings. Think of Walter Matthau's washed-up drunken ex-baseball player in The Bad News Bears. He had gone as far as he could on his own journey, and looked to his charges to help him complete himself by finding self-respect again. Hence, the hero-mentor relationship can be a symbiotic one.

Are Mister Barlow's flaws balanced by the good he did? I think that is the wrong question to ask. I don't think we can judge people by how their behavior measures out on a scale, but based on the standards they set for themselves.

It's been said that, in the Jewish afterlife, one is asked four questions. The most important one is, "Were you honest in business"? By dispensing with the literal interpretation of "business," and replacing it with Rabbi Ed Feinstein's phrase, "the business of life," we arrive at a much more intriguing question.

In his 1984 Greeley Tribune interview, Mister Barlow was asked how he would like to be remembered by students. He replied, "I would like them to be aware that I provided them with what they needed, whether or not they wanted it. If they want to continue in mathematics, they have the preparation for it. It is better to have it and not need it than to need it and not have it."

He constantly demonstrated the necessity of paying attention. This concept was a hallmark of his classroom, the one overarching goal beyond insisting that kids use their minds. Edward Chapman ('61) sums it up with this anecdote: "For lapses of whatever nature, he'd call us blockheads and/or vegetables, but always in the kindest possible way. One day, I had not heard my name called out. So Mister Barlow asked if perhaps I thought he was talking of Chapman's Homer. I had no idea what Chapman's Homer was. And so, for the next day Mister Barlow assigned me to memorize On First Looking Into Chapman's Homer by Keats. In my notebook, I was also required to write, 'I, Edward Weston Chapman, say that in order to be sure that the teacher is talking about Chapman's Homer and not to Edward Weston Chapman, all I have to do is, and perish the thought, Pay Attention.'"

So Mister Barlow was certainly honest is the business of life. But was he a great teacher? The question is not so easy to answer. On the one hand, the vast majority of interviewees believe he was a great teacher.

On the other hand, math teacher John Lee felt Mister Barlow had a net negative effect on his students. "I think the one positive thing he gave them was a source of lifetime stories about their school experiences. Except I'm not convinced that that's super valuable." Likewise, Russell Powers ('59) felt: "That he taught school at Greeley for 36 years suggests that he became a changed person after I graduated, or is testimony to the power of teachers' unions for job preservation. He will most likely be remembered for his eccentricities in the classroom, rather than as a teacher for the subject at hand."

The question itself may be where the problem lies. Even Elissa Grossman, in the "Statement of Teaching Philosophy" she wrote for her UCLA doctorate, demonstrates the dichotomy of trying to answer such a question:

> Students were so darn afraid of Mr. Barlow that they would work harder than they'd ever worked before. And in working that hard, the students began to realize they could achieve far more than they had previously thought possible. At the end of the year, they would reflect on all that they'd learned, and decide: "He really taught me something. He's the best teacher I've ever had." At the end of the year, I thought: "He really taught me nothing. He's the worst teacher I've ever

had." Today, I think: "He's the worst teacher I've ever had. And, boy, did I learn more from him than from any other teacher."

Larry Breen, however, provides some criteria for answering the question in a eulogy at Mister Barlow's memorial service:

> What was the mystery and magic of his success with students? Other faculty were gentler than he was, other faculty spent more time outside of class with students than he did, others were as brilliant as he was and almost every faculty member employed a greater variety of teaching strategies than Mister Barlow. At a time in their lives when young people feel body and image are all that matters, he demanded that they respect their minds. He made them pay attention to their intelligence. His teaching was not an invitation to learn, it was a command performance.

So what makes a great teacher? Some believe a great teacher inspires and motivates, or they make boring material interesting, or make obscure things clear. Larry Breen has a more philosophical approach: "I don't really believe in the great teacher. I believe in the right teacher at the right time, at the right place. Because if you took this faculty, which supposedly has a lot of great teachers in it, and you took them twenty minutes away to Ossining High School you'd find that a lot of the 'great teachers' are not great teachers."

So there does not seem to be any real consensus on Mister Barlow's talents. This brings us back to the initial question: Was Mister Barlow honest in the business of life? Only he can answer that question, and he did. In his final "Summary of Professional Growth Experience" for 1989-90, he was asked how he implemented his professional growth plan and how the experience benefited him professionally.

> I used the criterion of Dr. Haike, a former Superintendent of Schools at Greeley, for discovering the best teachers. On the occasion of my winning the first Teacher of the Year Award, he sent me a note of compliment (incidentally, the only member of the school community to congratulate me) saying, "As has always been so, students know who the great teachers are." So he has dictated that students would know truly great teachers. True to his directive, I have asked three of my students to evaluate me. The fourth person I've asked is Dr. Haike, by indirection and his comment, ex post facto, is attached. I did not ask non-A students to comment since if I did they'd tell their parents they couldn't get an "A" because they were always evaluating me. This experience has benefitted me professionally by continuing to ensure me that perfect knowledge of your subject and the ability to cause understanding of it in others is what makes teachers truly great. And as a truly great teacher, I find it difficult to be humble so I find it encouraging to know that I still reflect the

standards of a truly great teacher. What is there to
learn when you are the best there is?

Beyond the question of whether or not he was an effective teacher, I
think Mister Barlow would want to be remembered for his devotion to the
profession, and to his students. Here he succeeds without a doubt. His
ability to do so, even in the face of his alcohol troubles, makes him all the
more heroic, in my eyes. The extent of his devotion, however, was a secret to
many. Throughout his entire tenure at Greeley, he frequently tutored
students for no pay. He was so impressed with one student that he helped
prepare the young man for the Oxford entrance exam. Despite generally
refusing to allow Americans into their hallowed halls, the esteemed
institution permitted this student to matriculate because of his outstanding
score.

The money he left to the two Greeley educational charities went
beyond normal generosity. However, he also financially assisted some
students who could not afford to go to college. In another instance, a former
student found herself on welfare, and Mister Barlow helped keep her afloat
during her difficult period.

Language instructor Irene Berns summed up Mister Barlow
concisely, "He had a devotion that is hard to second. To give up yourself to
that degree, you had to have nothing else. This man gave it all. And then he
gave his money. Whatever he had, he gave."

* * *

Oddly, I think Mister Barlow would also want to be remembered for his war
service. Despite his enormous contributions as an educator, he still

considered Veterans to be his real community. Of all the places he wanted or could have been buried, he chose Arlington. I think it was the one thing he kept secret all his life that he was tremendously proud of, and I don't think when he joined the Army that he expected to have been proud of his service. Of course, leave it to Mister Barlow to add a dose of mystery to his feelings about the War. He had earned several medals along the way, but they were not found among his belongings. Logic dictates that there are a limited number of possibilities that would account for their fate. He gave them away, he lost them, or he threw them out.

To whom could he have given them? Nobody was close to him. Perhaps he gave them to his mother, but when she died they would have turned up again, and that leads us back to the same three possibilities. He might have given them to a museum of some kind. This seems out of character, though it would speak to his desire to have some kind of legacy.

Given his constant change of residence, it is possible he lost them in a move. That, however, doesn't seem likely because he had so few belongings. These medals would probably have been the one set of things he would have been certain to keep track of.

I think he threw them out. It may have been intentional, perhaps doing so after he returned home from the War, and realized how much his experience had damaged him. Likewise, they may have been disposed of in a drunken rage. Given that the war is what awakened his alcoholism, and how much the war devastated his psyche, they may have fallen victim to his emotions—emotions only expressed when he was under the influence of alcohol.

Given Mister Barlow's disdain for material objects, however, I suspect that he would not want us to focus on his medals anyway. It was his decision to serve that ultimately mattered, and he did so even though he had a legitimate right to be exempted from service, based on his own morals. Even more interesting, he would not permit himself this moral exemption. His sense of duty was too great—to his mother, and to his country. He thought of himself last.

This was a real sacrifice, not just because it eventually cancelled out the pursuit of his dream, but because it would also provide income for his mother. One might even argue that his mother would not have even needed that income, that she would have preferred her son to remain safe at home than go to war, and would have found work herself. If one buys this argument, his sacrifice becomes all the more profound.

Although he felt his actions might have disqualified him from joining the clergy, I believe he took solace in the fact that he helped defeat the twentieth century's greatest evil. He was fortunate to have lived long enough to see that his sacrifice was valued by the world.

Thus, his experiences on the battlefield are what ultimately shaped his life. It partially disqualified him from the priesthood, but it also forced him to examine another yearning: to teach. Mister Barlow went from being an apprentice priest, to an expert rifleman, to a quasi-monk who taught children how to survive with their minds. Whether it is priest or soldier or teacher, there is one consistency across all these professions. It is what elevates Mister Barlow, in my mind, to a level of admiration. All of these occupations serve the interests of others. That is the key to his life.

It was his war experience that also shaped his classroom methods. Without the war, would he have truly prepared as many young lives to face the world than if he'd been a priest? To me, that may be the single greatest lesson I learned from Mister Barlow's life. He demonstrated that it is possible to transcend the loss of a personal dream and great personal sacrifice.

Through Me

I am reminded of the soldier in J.D. Salinger's <u>For Esmé, with Love and Squalor</u>, another book mentioned by Mister Barlow. An American soldier meets a little girl in a suburban London café just prior to D-Day. She asks that he write stories and send them to her from France, and in exchange, gives him her late father's watch, which always kept perfect time. Months later we find the soldier in Germany, the war nearly over, the watch and his soul shattered by his battlefield experience, unable to write the young girl.

The difference is that Mister Barlow would have found a way to get that watch working again, returned to England, and taught the girl mathematics.

Mister Barlow's life can also be viewed through one final prism, that of the mythological hero's journey. Today, we tend to toss the word "hero" around rather casually, without really examining its definition in the mythological context. Certainly a person can demonstrate heroic characteristics, such as the fireman who rushes into a burning building to save a life. But what if that same fireman goes home and beats his wife? Is he still a hero?

"Know Thyself." This is what the hero's journey is all about. It is also in line with Ulich's teachings of self-transcendence. It is about each person struggling through life in order to understand who they truly are—not in the eyes of others, but by looking inward and seeing one's own honest image. The process of self-realization is, in reality, a never-ending prospect. I believe Mister Barlow achieved that state. I think he knew who he was, faults, and all. The one thing I hope I have assisted him with is opening up his life to those who loved him. I don't think he would have wanted that, but then again, I think it was because he was deathly afraid of it. It is one thing to be proud to be buried in Arlington, but what is the point if nobody knows he's there?

EPILOGUE

The final irony of Mister Barlow's life was that Al Barlow, his sole surviving brother, tried desperately to attend the interment at Arlington. But a fierce storm with thick fog waylaid him. Mister Barlow found a way to keep his family at arm's length, even at the end.

That didn't stop Al Barlow from sending a letter to the students of Horace Greeley, which was read at the memorial service. It says a great deal about Albert Barlow that he never held any bitterness in his heart over his brother's decision to sever ties with his family, nor anger over being excluded from receiving any of the estate.

The Westchester edition of the <u>New York Times</u> had a big article about Edwin when he died, and one of the reporters asked me for some kind of reaction to him and his allegiance to Horace Greeley. I probably at that point was as proud of Edwin as probably I ever could be if he had been in contact with me all those years. The thirty-eight missing years was wiped out in a flash by the woman on the phone asking me for my thoughts about him dying and leaving that big insurance policy to the Education Fund. And all I could say to her was, I am sitting here as proud as a peacock of him. And I still feel the same way today.

Edwin came to you as an only child, he said, and had no remaining family. But even only children grow up and have families; and so I think Edwin started his own family at Horace Greeley High School and the members of it were the thousands of students that passed through his classroom.

The original Barlows of Edwin's family are now almost a vanished breed, but the thousands who made up his new family while under his tutelage had to carry away something of the Edwin they learned from, and his influence is now operating in their lives around the world. Edwin wasn't a man without a family. He was a man with the biggest family you and I ever knew. I think the war made him formulate a philosophy that killing young people before their time is a sin, and decided that when he returned, to do all he could to help assure that any future young people who came his way would have every chance to become old people. He may have accomplished it.

Edwin isn't dead. He's just gone to start his next class. I hope his new Administrator can cope with this "administrator's nightmare." I leave it to your own thoughts as to what he did with the "entrance forms" and what ideas he had for the "Head Man" for improving the place.

Eighteen years later, Al Barlow lives in North Carolina. He now knows the full story of his brother's life. And after requesting copies from his congressman, Edwin's war medals are proudly displayed in a glass case above his mantle.

As for me, whenever I find myself staring at a blank screen needing to fill it with words, must finish a script in a day's time, but feel more inclined to procrastinate, whenever there is a job to be done, and it must be done well and I just feel a bit too lazy to tackle it, a voice gurgles up from the depths, a commanding and powerful voice that has no equal.

It is Mister Barlow's voice.

"Come on, Mister Meyers, you're dogging it!"

And I try harder.

*   *   *

As he expelled his final breath, Mister Barlow felt a curious sense of weightlessness. Strangely, he was also able to move. He'd been trapped in his own body for so long, that this sudden freedom surprised him.

Below, he could see his expired body, and the doctors hovering over him. He thought he might rise right through the very ceiling, but instead he hovered in place, and the images beneath him began to fade.

He felt himself rotate gently, as if being held aloft by a gentle hand. He began to feel motion. His body seemed to arc and glide along invisible curves. He looked around and found himself surrounded by stars. The curves he moved upon seemed endless, looping from one into the other, like some enormous child's slide.

Then he saw it. An enormous three-dimensional axis. A graph! What was it doing here? He realized that he glided upon a curve fixed within that axis, the living embodiment of an equation. As he swooped and curled, around and around, up and down, numbers and mathematical symbols appeared out of the void. They began as pinpoints of light, then lumbered towards him, ever growing, becoming enormous monuments—swooping past him, dwarfing him like skyscrapers passing over insects. He moved within and without the equation, passing through it, around it, whooshing along its slope.

And as he drifted through the living equation, he saw it was the One Equation which lead to the One Solution, the One that brought him closest to God, the One that was God.

He was basking in God's eternal and direct perception. The beatific vision. He was at one with Him again, and forevermore.

And he slid for what seemed forever, falling asleep in the cradle of God's Equation, and soon he left the stars and drifted as a feather through the roof of a house, a house he knew well, for it was his home in Springfield. And the window was open in the room, a cool breeze wafted the lace curtain, and the afternoon sun showered the room with its orange kiss.

And as Edwin awoke, he was not a man any longer. His decrepit body had been discarded and replaced by his youthful self, 6 years old. He alighted on his mother's lap, and curled up tight next to her, laying his head upon her shoulder, as she opened the book of nursery rhymes and read.

Lavender's Blue, dilly, dilly,
Lavender's green;
When I am king, dilly, dilly,
You shall be Queen.

Edwin had reached Heaven, as the Good Lord had promised.

THE END

298

APPENDIX A

17th Cavalry History

Much attention has been given to the Allied press towards Paris and Germany during World War II, but the Brittany campaign has been given short shrift. It remains a controversial aspect to the Allied assault on Europe, due to the commitment of valuable troops and supplies, following the Normandy invasion. Patton wanted to push into Germany immediately, but was prevented from doing so. Nonetheless, some historians postulate that, had the Germans been confronted with only minor forces in Brittany, they could have caused tremendous havoc against the Allies in this region.

As a result, the role that the 17th Cavalry Reconnaissance Squadron played in World War II has been regrettably passed over by most of the history books. I only know of one book that discusses the Brittany Campaign in any detail. As part of an effort to supplement that lost portion of military history, and to fill in all the blanks of Mister Barlow's wartime maneuvers, I've compiled this appendix that more completely explores this part of the Allied campaign. This is less about Mister Barlow, than it is tracing the 17th's path through Europe during the War.

Mister Barlow arrives in Scotland on March 7th. The regiment moves further inland to Trowbridge, England, where it was reorganized into the 15th and 17th Calvary Squadrons. Each squadron consisted of about 750 men, plus another hundred or so stationed at their headquarters. Each squadron is further subdivided into three reconnaissance squadrons (troops A, B, and C), one troop of assault gunnery (Troop E), and a troop occupying tanks (Troop F). Each troop has about 150 men. Each troop consists of about four platoons. Each platoon has about four squads, of about ten men each.

The recon squads carried everything from .30 and .50 machine guns, M-1 rifles, bazookas, 60mm and 81mm mortars, submachine guns, small hand guns and flares. The assault troop had six 75mm howitzers mounted in M-5 light tank chassis. The tank troop initially consisted of seventeen light tanks with .37mm cannons. More than one Vet I spoke to felt the .37 was far too small to be really effective, and they got their wish when .75mm cannons replaced the .37's in early 1945. Besides these tanks, there were forty six-wheeled armored cars, which could zip along at 55 mph. They were also armed with .37 cannons and were considered the best firepower of the group. In total, the 15th Cavalry group sported five hundred vehicles.

The 17th's first mission begins in England itself, serving as security for the D-Day invasion force. The squadron also guarded loading sites on Portland Island, where the 1st Infantry Division and 1st Amphibious Brigade were loading aboard assault craft for the invasion. On June 5, the 17th is sent back to Trowbridge, where they wait for a month before joining the rest of the Allied forces in France on July 15th aboard two English ships, the *Sir Francis Drake* and the *William King*. The ships arrive at Utah Beach and Mister Barlow joins his comrades in bivouac in the town of St. Mére-Eglisse, 3 1/2 miles away and utterly destroyed by fighting. The next day he arrives in Les Peux, near Cherbourg, where his troop is assigned to defend the Peninsula against airborne and sea attack. The mission lasts about two weeks, and the only casualties are a major and 1st lieutenant, who fall to an explosive booby trap.

From August 1 to September 6, Mister Barlow faces the most difficult part of his service. The 17th is placed under the command of General Patton's Third Army, as part of a larger group consisting of the 15th Cavalry Group, the 705th Tank Destroyer Battalion, the 159th Engineer Battalion, the 509th Engineer Company, and the headquarters for each of these units. This mass of men and machine is dubbed Task Force "A" (TFA), and is assigned to exploit a breakthrough in German defenses in Normandy.

Chain of Command

U.S. Third Army	Gen. George Patton
VIII Corps	Gen. Troy Middleton
Task Force A	Brig. Gen. Herbert Earnest
15th Cavalry Group	Col. Reybold
17th Cavalry Rcn Sqd.	?
Troop B Commander	Capt. George Berlin
Tr. B Staff Sergeant	Anthony Cottone

Ostensibly, the Task Force is to cut across the Brittany Peninsula and make what is to become known as, "The Dash to Brest," securing bridges for the double-track railroad running from Brest to Avranches. They would face upwards of twelve thousand enemy infantry, and anywhere between 20,000 and 50,000 marines and coastal defense troops. The XIX Tactical Air Command would provide air support for TFA, and would also be utilized to transport supplies because the purpose of the mission is to move as rapidly as possible towards Brest.

So rapid is this mission to be that the soldiers are told to discard all but the most essential personal equipment prior to departure. Additionally, and perhaps ominously, no provision is made for a surgeon, collecting company or ambulance to provide evacuation for the wounded. Despite this, 15th Cavalry Group Commander, Colonel "Eyeball" Reybold instructs the members of TFA to wear their "neck downs," or neckties, when they moved out on August 3. "That's how General Patton likes to operate," they are told.

Colonel Eyeball was so-named because, in the words of C-troop member Jeff Philips, "Every time he'd go over a hill, why he'd puff his eye up like, faster, faster!" Jeff also tells me that "after two or three days in combat old General Earnest, who was a fine old general, he come around and saw all the people in neckties and said, 'Get them damn things off.'"

TFA sets out at 0100 on August 3rd. A dozen enemy planes strafe the Task Force on the road from Avranches to Pontorson. There is no air support for TFA during this assault and miraculously, there are no casualties. Welcome to France.

Later that morning east of Dol de Bratagne, Troop C of the 17th encounters a well concealed, and heavily mined roadblock made of iron rails, and defended with small arms and automatic weapons. TFA suffers twenty-eight casualties in the battle, including the commander of the 15th Cavalry Group, Colonel "Eyeball" Reybold, who is wounded while riding in a jeep and captured. He spends the remainder of the war as a POW on the Channel Islands. The June 15, 1945 issue of Yank Magazine reported that Col. Reybold repeatedly made written demands upon their captors, consistently quoting the Geneva Convention, and signing those letters, "Eisenhower's Representative on the Channel Islands". Conditions improved as a result of this constant harassment.

Meanwhile, the 17th learns that Dol is strongly defended, so General Earnest shifts TFA to the south to bypass it. Col. Logan C. Berry is assigned command of the 15th Cavalry Group. After bypassing Dol, TFA is sent to reconnoiter the coastal town of St. Malo, but they encounter immediate resistance near the east side of the village of Le Vx. Bourg. 88mm guns, mortar and small arms fire hammer them, radios fail to work properly, causing commanders difficulty in organizing their troop. The action is called off and the 17th falls back to an assembly area.

TFA tries again to move towards St. Malo the following morning. Significant distance is gained, but at 1400 hours outside the village of Chateauneuf, TFA is again hit hard by artillery from gun ships and coastal guns along the estuary. To make matters worse, the Germans had flooded the canalized areas south and east of the town, creating a bottleneck to enter the town. It is here that Mister Barlow and B Troop are called upon to assist the advance, by reconnoitering the area towards Chateauneuf. He sets out with his troop and soon encounters three roadblocks. He fires his weapon in combat and kills his first man.

Troop B then reports a platoon of Germans in Chateauneuf. Air strikes against the gunboats commence at 1612, 1630, and 1930 hours, leaving them in flames. The 83rd Division Artillery shells the bottleneck through the night. The next day, Mister Barlow joins the rest of the 17th in a major offensive against Chateauneuf. Light tanks, tank destroyers, infantry and engineers plow their way through. The 17th storms a roadblock at 1400 hours and Mister Barlow enters the town. He and the 17th are recalled to the south, having captured 665 prisoners during the operation.

St. Malo proved to be heavily defended, so it was left to the 83rd. General Earnest made an exchange, leaving a platoon of tank destroyers to assist the 83rd, while securing a battery of 105mm Howitzers and a badly-desired medical collecting company for TFA. From now to the 8th of August, TFA sweeps 140 miles up the Brittany Peninsula from Avranches to Morlaix, and takes 899 prisoners. It also accomplishes its major objective of securing key railroad bridges at Morlaix. The 17th also engages the enemy at Guingamp.

TFA receives orders on the 11th of August to secure the beaches at St. Michel-en-Greve, which they did with no resistance. The 17th Cavalry helps conduct recon in the area and returns with information regarding enemy troops. Mister Barlow's troop got a chance to rest, while the remainder of TFA took on the enemy to great success, including the capture of 589 prisoners.

Mister Barlow and the rest of the 17th Cav is held at Morlaix and St. Michel to provide security until August 18th, where they bivouac three miles west of Landivisiau. Mister Barlow faces further combat over the next week, however. Frequent recon patrols are sent out to the south, and Mister Barlow encounters "moderate resistance" before securing the town of Loperhet and Le Faou, eventually reconnoitering as far as Chateaulin and Sizun. Heavy resistance is found on the Plougastel-Daoulas peninsula, including 88mm guns on most road intersections, and TFA is unable to make significant gains. The 17th attempts to move into the Crozon Peninsula, but even with an additional tank destroyer platoon and a battery form the 83rd Field Artillery Battalion, a strongly defended line running through St. Nic, Menez-Hom, and Brigneum stops them. Intelligence indicates a reinforced German battalion holds the line. It is now August 28th, and TFA is forced to reduce activity to patrols, with air support. Poor weather prohibits offensive activity by TFA until the 30th, when a significant hill with expansive views of the peninsula, is finally captured. Some of this success is attributed to the surrender of Russian POW's who had been forced to fight for the Germans, thus leaving gaps in the German line. The Germans are forced to retreat to close the gaps, leaving uninspired Russian, Polish, Caucasians, and Luftwaffe troops to guard the retreat. They are unable to stop the advancing cavalry. 324 prisoners are taken on this day.

The remainder of the Crozon Peninsula, however, proves to be highly fortified and difficult to dislodge. General Middleton of VIII Corps describes the resistance. "In all my military experience, I have never seen anything quite so good as the fortifications in the Crozon area. They are the most highly organized I have ever seen." The enemy line faces open ground on the north flank, and low swamp ground on the southern flank. The hilly terrain allows for accurate direction of mortar and artillery fire, which includes a 155mm, two 105mm, and two 75mm batteries on the northern end of the line. The central section is loaded with two batteries of 88mm guns, a 105mm, a 76.2mm, and a 75mm battery. Machine guns, mortars, and minefields round out the opposition. There were excellent fields of fire located in each direction. TFA sends out numerous patrols, which are constantly harassed by enemy fire.

On September 5th, VIII Corps is transferred to the command of the Ninth Army. Insufficient infantry is available, because all other resources have been committed to the attack on Brest. 350 Cavalry, including Mister Barlow, are forced to dismount from their vehicles and serve as infantry. They attack the line on this day, but back off to allow bombers to assault the stronger points of the Peninsula. On September 6th, after tank destroyers unleash a heavy barrage, the dismounted Cavalry attacks the enemy line. Mister Barlow is shot in the process, and the attack only serves to push the enemy back into their outposts.

Task Force "A" continues to battle in Western France until September 22nd when its objectives were achieved and they were disbanded. Mister Barlow is still recovering in October, and misses the opportunity to escort top brass at one point, including General Eisenhower. When Mister Barlow rejoined his outfit, the 17th Cav had been assigned to protect the Ninth Army headquarters, where it saw little action until March 1st of 1945. He does encounter some heavy fighting near the small village of Lohn, on November 21st, but Troop E provides excellent 75mm fire support, and allows for successful assaults on the nearby towns of Vierhoven, Shophovan and Pier.

For all of his seventeen months in the Army, Mister Barlow managed to only see six weeks of heavy fighting. The first five days of March sees him patrolling with his comrades along the Roer, and continuing their drive along the Rhine. They encounter heavy fighting at Geldern, defeat the enemy there and link up with Canadian forces driving southward, in the process closing a trap on several thousand Germans on the Rhine's west bank. By now the Germans are on their heels, morale is low, and the Allies are making decisive gains.

The 31st of March sees the 17th begin its mission to encircle the Ruhr, an industrialized pocket of Germany. They defeat some well-defended roadblocks at Bochum, and move into the vicinity of Hamm. Mister Barlow's last major assignment is a highly dangerous one. B-Troop must advance during the night of April 2nd through German-held terrain, to establish a security screen along the Lippe canal, which runs between Hamm and Bockum. The infiltration is successful, and they hit Bockum from all sides. They capture three 88mm guns and 300 prisoners. Not a single man nor vehicle is lost during this daring maneuver.

Five days later, Mister Barlow's ear is shot off. The 17th was maintaining security along the Lippe River and faced a large number of enemy units that were on the defensive. Colonel Dwan indicated that their mission had been to cut off enemy escape. The moment of Mister Barlow being wounded is not recalled in my interviews, but he is sidelined for a month. If we are to believe his account to Preston Trusler ('75), Army doctors supposedly attempted to sew the top of his ear back on, but it turned black and fell off a few days later. He also supposedly recuperated in Paris at this time, but I am unable to confirm this. He returned to duty the day before V-E Day, and spends the rest of his tour with the 17th on security details.

On August 18th of 1945, Mister Barlow is sent home. He arrives in the United States ten days later, and is officially discharged on October 30th. The 17th Cavalry Recon Squadron nears the end of its existence, as well. At the end of July of 1946, it is assigned to Heidelberg to become "Palace Guard" for the Ninth Army. While there, it is rated the best unit of its size among all of Patton's Third Army troops. It is deactivated and redesignated the 17th Security Squadron on January 20th of 1947.

Appendix B

Photographs

Leave it to Mister Barlow to create an impediment to obtaining photographs of him, even from beyond the grave. He permitted very few photographs for Greeley yearbooks during his tenure. When he received the 1983-4 Teacher of the Year award, the <u>Tribune</u> published three photographs of him along with an interview (See chapter 15).

These photos were part of a set of 24 taken by a Greeley student named Dick, and represent the most emotive images of Mister Barlow left on film. The images are unique, and even contain a pose that shows mock frustration, as if a student had just stumbled over a simple blackboard equation—helping to solidify the assertion of his self-awareness and appearance to the student body.

The book cover had originally been designed around one of these images, operating off a tentative verbal agreement I'd achieved with Dick in 2001. However, as publication approached, Dick decided that he was reluctant to have his photos included in the book because of the treatment he suffered in Mister Barlow's class—treatment no worse than anyone else had received. Somehow concerned that permitting his photos to appear in a book that might say anything laudatory about Mister Barlow, he began a lengthy and onerous negotiation process. The ensuing psychodrama included outrageous financial requests (when everyone else had contributed their stories and photos without charge) and an insistence that he be able to author an essay to appear in the book's introduction.

What puzzled me the most was that despite Dick's awful experience with Mister Barlow, he subsequently agreed to photograph his tormentor for an issue of the school newspaper. This wasn't just any edition, but the one extolling Mister Barlow for winning Teacher of the Year. While not having any problem having these photographs seen by an audience of several thousand Greeley students and Chappaqua residents, he conveniently and self-servingly decided he had been too damaged by Mister Barlow for them to appear in a book.

Those who knew Dick told me it was pointless trying to work with him, referring to him as a "twerp", and "inconsequential loser". John Willard reminded me that Dick's critical comments regarding Mister Barlow, "miss the point of Blackie's pursuit of excellence and intolerance for dishonesty and inhumanity (or perhaps Dick fell into that category, hence his disdain). Blackie had no tolerance for either stupidity or fools. Neither should you."

I didn't want history to lose sight of these wonderful photos. Yet, after enduring weeks of constantly shifting and increasingly irrational demands, I had to let them go. It's a real shame. They are wonderful.

Mister Barlow certainly made an impact on students, and even now, twenty-five years later, he continues to do so in strange and mysterious ways.

Teacher of the Year

College of Holy Cross Yearbook, 1954

Horace Greeley High School Yearbook, circa 1957

Coach Barlow receives League Trophy.

Horace Greeley High School
Yearbook, circa 1957

Horace Greeley High Yearbook, 1957
Photograph by Bill Miller

Horace Greeley Yearbook
1963

MATHEMATICS DEPARTMENT

John —
L'homme ivre Lune ombre qui passe
L'homme ivre Lune ombre qui passe
Porte toujours le châtiment
D'avoir voulu changer de place.
mr. Barlow

Horace Greeley Yearbook, 1964

Mr. Edwin Barlow
Fair creature of the hour.

Horace Greeley Yearbook, 1965

Mr. Edwin Barlow
You vegetable!

Horace Greeley Yearbook, 1966

Unknown, circa 1963

Horace Greeley High School Yearbook, 1968

Horace Greeley High School Yearbook, 1969

Horace Greeley High School Yearbook, 1970

As for the final photograph on the next page, every picture certainly tells a story—or vice-versa. Yearbook photographer David Highbloom was assigned to attempt a photo of Mister Barlow for the 1985 Yearbook. Following class one day, he trailed Mister Barlow into the Teacher's Lounge, camera in hand.

"Mister Barlow, could I take—"

Mister Barlow roared, "TAKE THE PHOTO!"

David quickly composed the shot, hit the **shutter** and skedaddled. After viewing the photo, which was slightly over**expo**sed and out-of-focus, the Yearbook teacher asked David to get another **one**. David refused, out of abject fear of being given a failing grade from Mister Barlow.

Horace Greeley High School Yearbook, 1985

APPENDIX C

Military Records

The following are various military documents from Mister Barlow's war service. These include his discharge notice and casualty reports. Note the singed edges on some of the pages, the result of the fire at the Army's St. Louis archive.

United States of America

Certification of
Military Service

This certifies that

Edwin D. Barlow
31 415 488

was a member of the

Army of the United States

from

October 7, 1943

to

October 30, 1945

Service was terminated by

Honorable Discharge

Last Grade, Rank, or Rating

Private

Active Service Dates

Same as Above

Given at St. Louis, Missouri, on   April 4, 1991

National Personnel Records Center
(Military Personnel Records)
National Archives and Records Administration

THE ARCHIVIST OF THE UNITED STATES IS THE PHYSICAL CUSTODIAN OF THIS PERSON'S MILITARY RECORD.

(This Certification of Military Service is issued in the absence of a copy of the actual Report of Separation, or its equivalent. This document serves as verification of military service and may be used for any official purpose. Not valid without official seal.)

Army of the United States

Honorable Discharge

This is to certify that

EDWIN D. BARLOW 31 415 488 PRIVATE
TROOP (B) 17TH CAVALRY RECONNAISSANCE SQUADRON

Army of the United States

is hereby Honorably Discharged from the military service of the United States of America.

This certificate is awarded as a testimonial of Honest and Faithful Service to this country.

Given at　　SEPARATION CENTER
　　　　　　　FORT BRAGG, NORTH CAROLINA

Date　　　　30 OCTOBER 1945

BEN B. MABSON JR.
LT　　COL　　CE.

ENLISTED RECORD AND REPORT OF SEPARATION
HONORABLE DISCHARGE

1. LAST NAME - FIRST NAME - MIDDLE INITIAL	2. ARMY SERIAL NO.	3. GRADE	4. ARM OR SERVICE	5. COMPONENT
BARLOW, EDWIN D.	31 415 488	PVT	CAV	AUS

6. ORGANIZATION	7. DATE OF SEPARATION	8. PLACE OF SEPARATION
TR B 17TH CAV RCN SQ	30 OCT 45	SEPARATION CENTER FT BRAGG, NC

9. PERMANENT ADDRESS FOR MAILING PURPOSES	10. DATE OF BIRTH	11. PLACE OF BIRTH
SPRINGFIELD, MASS. HAMPDEN CO.	11 DEC 22	AGAWAM, MASS.

12. ADDRESS FROM WHICH EMPLOYMENT WILL BE SOUGHT	13. COLOR EYES	14. COLOR HAIR	15. HEIGHT	16. WEIGHT	17. NO. DEPEND.
SEE 9	BROWN	BROWN	5'7½"	156 LBS.	0

18. RACE	19. MARITAL STATUS	20. U.S. CITIZEN	21. CIVILIAN OCCUPATION AND NO.
WHITE X	SINGLE X	YES X	FILER, HAND (6-93.520)

MILITARY HISTORY

22. DATE OF INDUCTION	23. DATE OF ENLISTMENT	24. DATE OF ENTRY INTO ACTIVE SERVICE	25. PLACE OF ENTRY INTO SERVICE
7 OCT 43		7 OCT 43	FT. DEVENS, MASS.

SELECTIVE SERVICE DATA	26. REGISTERED	27. LOCAL S.S. BOARD NO.	TR. COUNTY AND STATE	28. HOME ADDRESS AT TIME OF ENTRY INTO SERVICE
	YES X NO	141	SPRINGFIELD, MASS.	SEE 9

30. MILITARY OCCUPATIONAL SPECIALTY AND NO.	31. MILITARY QUALIFICATION AND DATE (i.e., infantry, aviation and marksmanship badges, etc.)
RIFLEMAN (745)	NONE

32. BATTLES AND CAMPAIGNS
NORMANDY, NORTHERN FRANCE, RHINELAND, CENTRAL EUROPE.

33. DECORATIONS AND CITATIONS
EAMET CAMPAIGN MEDAL WITH 4 BRONZE SERVICE STARS, GOOD CONDUCT MEDAL SO 23 17 CAV RCN SQ DRD 19 MAR 45, PURPLE HEART WITH 1 OAK LEAF CLUSTER GO 105 HQ 40 GEN HOSP APO 887 DTD 6 MAY 45.

34. WOUNDS RECEIVED IN ACTION
EAMET 6 SEPT 44, 7 APR 45.

35. LATEST IMMUNIZATION DATES				36. SERVICE OUTSIDE CONTINENTAL U.S. AND RETURN		
SMALLPOX	TYPHOID	TETANUS	OTHER (specify)	DATE OF DEPARTURE	DESTINATION	DATE OF ARRIVAL
4 JUL 43	5 AUG 45	20 APR 44	TYPH 2 JUL 45	2 JUN 44	EAMET	11 JUN 44
				18 AUG 45	USA	28 AUG 45

37. TOTAL LENGTH OF SERVICE				38. HIGHEST GRADE HELD
CONTINENTAL SERVICE		FOREIGN SERVICE		
YEARS	MONTHS	DAYS	YEARS	MONTHS	DAYS	
0	9	27	1	2	27	PRIVATE

39. PRIOR SERVICE
NONE

40. REASON AND AUTHORITY FOR SEPARATION
CONVENIENCE OF THE GOVERNMENT RR1-1 (DEMOBILIZATION) AR 615-365 15 DEC 44.

41. SERVICE SCHOOLS ATTENDED	42. EDUCATION (Years)
NONE	Grammar 8 / High School 4 / College 1½

PAY DATA

INSURANCE NOTICE						
IMPORTANT				YOU NO. 11 V55		
48. KIND OF INSURANCE	49. HOW PAID		50. Effective Date of Allotment Discontinuance	51. Date of Next Premium Due (One month after 50)	52. PREMIUM DUE EACH MONTH	53. INTENTION OF VETERAN TO
Nat. Serv. U.S. Govt. None	Allotment Direct to V.A.		31 OCT 45	30 NOV 45	.6.50	Continue Continue Only Discontinue
X	X	X				X

54.	55. REMARKS (This space for completion of above items or entry of other items specified in W. D. Directives)
RIGHT THUMB PRINT	NO TIME LOST UNDER AW 107 LAPEL BUTTON ISSUED ASR SCORE (2 SEPT 45) (63)

56. SIGNATURE OF PERSON BEING SEPARATED
Edwin D. Barlow

57. PERSONNEL OFFICER (Type name, grade and organization - signature)
L. V. MORAN, CAPT. AUS.

JAN 31 1946

WD AGO FORM 53-55
1 November 1944

This form supersedes all previous editions of WD AGO Forms 53 and 55 for enlisted persons entitled to an Honorable Discharge, which will not be used after receipt of this revision.

322

CASUALTY BRANCH
RECORD SECTION

Name: *Barlow, Edwin D*   Serial Number: *91415 4*

Grade: *Pvt -3*

Organization: *Cav.*

OFFICIAL REPORTS: (IMPORTANT - Unofficial reports or information will not be shown below. This information will be indicated -- "Code X.")

Type of Casualty	Date and Area	Classification & Message No.	Battle	Non-battle	Date E.A. notified
SWA	6 Sept 44	E 20 Ship # 191			20 Sept 44
RJD	4 Nov 44	" E 30 " #251			25 Nov 44
SWA	7 apr 45	E 30 " 108			25 apr 44
RJD	7 May 45	E 30 " 139			No act.

E. A. *Mrs. Agnes S. Barlow (mother)*
40 Ebenett Street, Springfield Mass.

REMARKS: _____

No Casualty Reported_____

Is there a Casualty Branch File?   No ___ Yes ✓

Form No. 43?   No ___ Yes ✓

Clerk furnishing report *Justice*

Date of Report *11 July* Room No. *2826* Group No. *Op*

Dispatch, Composite Section

24-32139 100000

VISI–CARD AND RECORD REPORT

WAR DEPARTMENT
THE ADJUTANT GENERAL'S OFFICE
WASHINGTON 25, D. C.

—BATTLE CASUALTY REPORT

AG 201	NAME BARLOW, EDWIN D ASN 31 415 488	GRADE PVT SON		DATE CAS REPORT RECE
				JBW
NAME AND AD- DRESS OF E. A.	MRS AGNES S BARLOW 40 EVERETT STREET SPRINGFIELD MASSACHUSETTS		25 APRIL 1945	DATE TELEGRAM SENT

THE INDIVIDUAL NAMED BELOW DESIGNATED THE ABOVE PERSON AS THE ONE TO BE NOTIFIED IN CASE OF EMERGENCY, AND THE OFFICIAL TELE-
GRAPHIC AND LETTER NOTIFICATIONS WILL BE SENT TO THIS PERSON. THE RELATIONSHIP, IF ANY, IS SHOWN BELOW. IT SHOULD BE NOTED THAT
THIS PERSON IS NOT NECESSARILY THE NEXT-OF-KIN OR RELATIVE DESIGNATED TO BE PAID SIX MONTHS' PAY GRATUITY IN CASE OF DEATH

THE SECRETARY OF WAR DESIRES ME TO EXPRESS HIS DEEP REGRET THAT YOUR SON

GRADE	NAME	SERIAL NUMBER	ARM OR SERVICE	REPORTING THEATRE	F OR J STATUS	SHIPMEN NUMBER
PVT	BARLOW EDWIN D	31415488	CAV	ETO		108
WAS	TYPE OF CASUALTY	PLACE OF CASUALTY	DATE OF CASUALTY DAY MONTH YEAR			CASUALTY CODE
	SLIGHTLY WOUNDED	IN GERMANY	07 APR 45	6		

CONTINUE TO ADDRESS MAIL TO HIM AS FORMERLY OR UNTIL NEW ADDRESS IS RECEIVED FROM HIM

OFFICIAL: ADJUTANT GENERAL

J. A. ULIO
THE ADJUTANT GENERAL

REMARKS:

☐ CORRECTED COPY

File in Enlisted Branch
Date 25 Apr 45
Initials

ACTION BY PROCESSING AND VERIFICATION SECTION. REPORT VERIFIED_____FORM 43_____AG 201 REQ.
CASUALTY BRANCH FILE ATTACHED_____OR CHANGED TO_____DATE_____
PREVIOUSLY REPORTED_____NO_____YES_____(AS INDICATED BELOW):
FILE NO._____MESSAGE NO._____TYPE_____DATE AND AREA_____R. A

FORWARDED
TO →   ☐ SPEC. IDEN. ☐ TELEGRAM ☐ WOUNDED ☐ LETTER ☐ CORRES. ☐ S. R. & D. ☐ CERTIF. ☐ M. & M.
REPORT NOT VERIFIED_____NO FORM 43_____NO CAS. BR. FILE_____CHECKED BY_____REVIEWED BY

WD AGO Form 0366-1 (This form supersedes
1 January 1945)

324

WAR DEPARTMENT
THE ADJUTANT GENERAL'S OFFICE
WASHINGTON 25, D. C.

—BATTLE CASUALTY REPORT

AG 201	NAME		GRADE		DATE CAS. REPORT RECE
NAME AND AD. DRESS OF E. A.					13
					54
					DATE TELEGRAM SENT

THE INDIVIDUAL NAMED BELOW DESIGNATED THE ABOVE PERSON AS THE ONE TO BE NOTIFIED IN CASE OF EMERGENCY, AND THE OFFICIAL TELEGRAPHIC AND LETTER NOTIFICATIONS WILL BE SENT TO THIS PERSON. THE RELATIONSHIP, IF ANY, IS SHOWN BELOW. IT SHOULD BE NOTED THAT THIS PERSON IS NOT NECESSARILY THE NEXT-OF-KIN OR RELATIVE DESIGNATED TO BE PAID SIX MONTHS' PAY GRATUITY IN CASE OF DEATH

THE SECRETARY OF WAR DESIRES ME TO EXPRESS HIS DEEP REGRET THAT YOUR

GRADE	NAME	SERIAL NUMBER	ARM OR SERVICE	REPORTING THEATRE	F OR J STATUS	SHIP NU
PVT	BARLOW EDWIN D	31415488	CAV	ETO		1

TYPE OF CASUALTY	PLACE OF CASUALTY	DATE OF CASUALTY			CASUALTY COD
		DAY	MONTH	YEAR	
RETURNED TO DUTY	IN	07	MAY	45	G6

OFFICIAL: ADJUTANT GENERAL

J. A. ULIO
THE ADJUTANT GENERAL

REMARKS:

☐ CORRECTED COPY

File in Enlisted Branch
Date
Initials MAY 25 1945

ACTION BY PROCESSING AND VERIFICATION SECTION: REPORT VERIFIED___FORM 43___ AG 201 REG___
CASUALTY BRANCH FILE ATTACHED___OR CHARGED TO___DATE___
PREVIOUSLY REPORTED___NO___YES___(AS INDICATED BELOW):
FILE NO. | MESSAGE NO. | TYPE | DATE AND AREA | S. A.

FORWARDED TO →

| SPEG. IDEN. | TELEGRAM | WOUNDED | LETTER | CORRES. | S. R. & D. | CERTIE. | M. & M. |

REPORT NOT VERIFIED___NO FORM 43___NO CAS. BR. FILE___CHECKED BY___REVIEWED BY___

WD AGO Form 0363-1

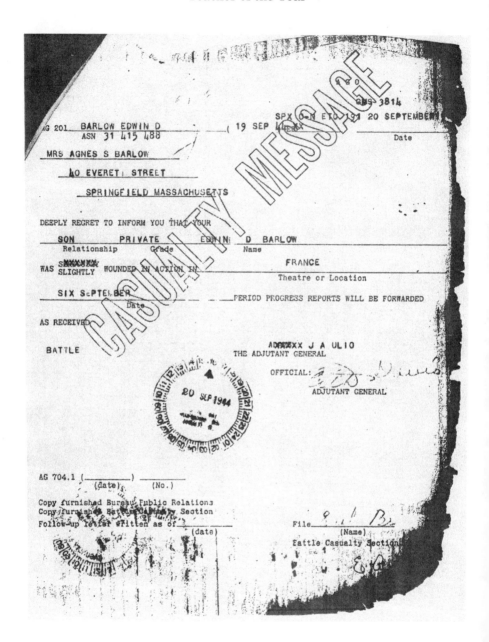

JUN 2 1 2000

1. IN REPLY, REFER TO	
BARLOW, EDWIN DAVID 31415488	NRPM ___A-M___ **AUTHORIZATION FOR ISSUANCE OF AWARDS** For use of this form, see AR 672-5-1; the proponent agency is ODCSPER

2. TO:	Commander U.S. Army Support Activity Philadelphia, PA 19101-3460	4. DATE 13 June, 2000

4. CODE NUMBERS FOR AWARDS

1		17	Joint Service Achievement Medal	33	Medal for Humane Action	49	Expert Field Medical Badge
2	Distinguished Service Cross	18	Army Achievement Medal	34	National Defense Service Medal	50	Letter "V" Device
3	Defense Distinguished Service Medal	19	POW Medal	35	Korean Service Medal	51	Bronze Oak Leaf Cluster
4	Distinguished Service Medal	20	Good Conduct Medal	36	Antarctica Service Medal	52	Bronze Service Star
5	Silver Star	21	Presidential Unit Emblem	37	Armed Forces Expeditionary Medal	53	Bronze Arrowhead
6	Defense Superior Service Medal	22	Meritorious Unit Emblem	38	Vietnam Service Medal	54	French Fourragere
7	Legion of Merit	23	Joint Meritorious Unit Emblem	39	Humanitarian Service Medal	55	Belgian Fourragere
8	Distinguished Flying Cross	24	Valorous Unit Emblem	40	Armed Forces Reserve Medal	56	Netherlands Orange Lanyard
9	Soldier's Medal	25	Army Superior Unit Emblem	41	Army Reserve Components Achievement Medal	57	Philippine Defense Ribbon
10	Bronze Star Medal	26	Women's Army Corps Service Medal	42	NCO Professional Development Ribbon	58	Philippine Liberation Ribbon
11	Purple Heart	27	American Defense Service Medal	43	Army Service Ribbon	59	Philippine Independence Ribbon
12	Defense Meritorious Service Medal	28	American Campaign Medal	44	Overseas Service Ribbon	60	United Nations Service Medal
13	Meritorious Service Medal	29	Asiatic-Pacific Campaign Medal	45	Army Reserve Components Overseas Training Ribbon	61	Republic of Vietnam Campaign Ribbon w/Device (1960)
14	Air Medal	30	European-African-Middle Eastern Campaign Medal	46	Combat Infantryman Badge	62	Honorable Service Lapel Button WWII
15	Joint Service Commendation Medal	31	WW II Victory Medal	47	Expert Infantryman Badge	63	
16	Army Commendation Medal	32	Army of Occupation Medal	48	Combat Medical Badge	64	

The Secretary of the Army directs that the following awards be engraved according to current regulations and issued to address shown below. *(Engraving to be as indicated in classification or below.)*

5. AWARD CODE	6. SERVICE STARS		7. OAK LEAF CLUSTER		8. ARROW HEAD	9. CLASP	10. "V" DEVICE	11. GOLD STAR LAPEL BUTTON					
	BRONZE	SILVER	BRONZE	SILVER				A. ENGRAVE	B. ISSUE			C. TYPE	
46									☐ COST			☐ CLUTCH	
62									☐ GRATUITOUSLY			☐ PIN	

EXPERT BADGE W/ RIFLE BAR

NOTHING FOLLOWS

--------- PAGE ~~ONE~~ OF TWO ----------
              Two

12. REMARKS

The awards and decorations indicated above will be forwarded from the U. S. Army Soldier and Biological Chemical Command, IMMC, Soldier Systems Directorate, 700 Robbins Avenue, P. O. Box 57997, Philadelphia, PA 19111-7997 within 120 days.

U.S. ARMY SUPPORT ACTIVITY
Philadelphia, PA 19101-3460

OFFICIAL BUSINESS

MR. ALBERT BARLOW
C/O HONORABLE HOWERD COBLE
330 S. GREENE ST, STE 100
GREENSBORO, NC 27401

For: Robert James O'Neill

VIRGINIA A. BARRETT
Chief, Army Reference Branch

NATIONAL PERSONNEL RECORDS CENTER
(Military Personnel Records)
9700 Page Avenue
St. Louis, MO 63132-5100

DA FORM 1577, AUG 90

EDITION OF 1 NOV 75 IS OBSOLETE

3

327

Also provided is a photograph of copies of Mister Barlow's medals. The originals could not be located, so the Army issued these copies to Albert.

1 – Upper left corner. EAMET medal, signifying participation in the European, African, Mediterranean Theatre of Operations.

2 – Lower left corner. A medal granted for service with the army during Germany's occupation.

3 – Upper right corner. A medal for the overall victory in WWI.

4 – Lower right corner. Good Conduct medal.

5 – Bottom center. Grey rifle badges, indicating classification as an "expert".

6 – Middle Center. Purple Heart with one oak leaf cluster, indicating that he was wounded twice.

7 – Middle, Off-Center (red). Bronze Star for Meritorious Conduct.

Fort Riley - Camp Maxey - Louisiana Maneuvers
Camp Coxcomb (DTC) - Camp Shanks (NY - P/E)
Greenock, Scotland - Trowbridge, England

17TH CAVALRY RECONNAISSANCE SQUADRON

Campaigns: ****
            NORMANDY
            BRITTANY
            RHINELAND
            CENTRAL EUROPE

The coat of arms for the 17th Cavalry Reconnaissance Squadron.

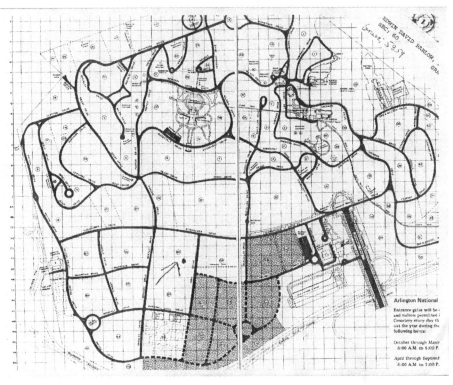

A map of Arlington National Cemetery, and the location of Mister
Barlow's grave (Sec.60; Grave 5959)

A photo of myself by his grave, which I visited in March of 2001.

The Commonwealth of Massachusetts

Town of Agawam

CERTIFICATE OF BIRTH

I, EDWARD A. CABA, hereby certify that I am clerk of the TOWN OF AGAWAM; that as such I have custody of the records of births required by law to be kept in my office.

Name of child	Edwin David Barlow
Date of birth	December 11, 1922
Place of birth	Agawam, Massachusetts
Sex Male	Color White
Father	William Frederick Barlow
Residence	Agawam, Massachusetts
Place of birth	Springfield, Massachusetts
Occupation	Janitor
Mother	Agnes Anna Smith
Residence	Agawam, Massachusetts
Place of birth	Suffield, Connecticut
Date of record	1/12/24
Volume	2
Page	135
Number	135

And I do certify that the foregoing is a true copy from said records. Witness my hand and seal of said TOWN OF AGAWAM on this ....13th.......... day of ..November,..1979

Edward A. Caba
Town Clerk
P.O.

A copy of Mister Barlow's birth certificate.

FURTHER READING

Aquinas, Saint Thomas. <u>Aquinas' Shorter Summa: Saint Thomas's Own Concise Version of His Summa Theologica</u> (Sophia Institute Press; New Ed edition, 2001)

Carroll, Lewis; Gardner, Martin; Tenniel, John. <u>The Annotated Alice: The Definitive Edition</u> (W. W. Norton & Company; Upd Sub edition, 1999)

Farrell, Walter. <u>A Companion to the Summa – Volumes 1-4</u> (Christian Classics, 1974)

Gawne, Jonathan. <u>Americans in Brittany 1944: The Battle for Brest</u> (Histoire and Collections; 1st edition, 2002)

Hesse, Herman. <u>Narcissus and Goldmund</u> (Bantam, 1984)

Lovecraft, H.P. <u>The Best of H.P. Lovecraft: Bloodcurdling Tales of Horror and the Macabre</u> (Del Rey, 1987)

Renick, Timothy Mark. <u>Aquinas for Armchair Theologians</u> (Westminster John Knox Press; 1st edition, 2002)

Salinger, J.D. <u>The Catcher in the Rye</u> (Back Bay Books, 2001)

Seung, T.K. <u>Kant: Guide for the Perplexed</u>. (London: Continuum, 2007)

Ulich, Robert. <u>The Human Career</u> (Harper, 1955)

Aronow, Ina. "The Unexpected Legacy of a Legendary Teacher." <u>The New York Times</u> 20 January 1991: unknown page

Feldberg, Greg and Robin, Cory. "Teacher of the Year Interview." <u>The Greeley Tribune</u> 17 February 1984: 6

Haney, Nancy. "Teacher Leaves $500,000 to Fund" <u>The Patent Trader</u> Unknown date and page

Stark, Steven J. "37-year teacher wills $500,000 to high school." <u>The Reporter Dispatch</u> 8 January 1991: A1

About the Author

Lawrence Meyers is a veteran writer-producer of dramatic television. He has written for *Picket Fences, The Pretender, The Outer Limits, Early Edition,* and *Crossing Jordan,* among others. He also devotes part of his time to entrepreneurial efforts in the fields of finance and entertainment. His next book *Inside the Writer's Studio* is due to be published in 2009.

Printed in the United States
132204LV00002B/1/P

9 780982 018316